The opening chapters of Genesis f[...] the human race. For too long they [...] debates. Michael Wittmer has reclaimed their mind-shaping mission in a sane and thoughtful treatment.

> —John Ortberg, author of *If You Want to Walk on Water,*
> *You've Got to Get Out of the Boat*

This deeply biblical book enriches the perspective promoted by such Christian leaders as Richard Mouw, Charles Colson, and Neal Plantinga. It combines evangelical piety, sound doctrine, and the world-engaging view of the Christian life developed in the Reformed tradition of Abraham Kuyper.

> —John Cooper, Ph.D., Professor, Calvin Theological Seminary

Abraham Kuyper was arguably the supreme pastoral theologian of modern times, and this racy study book on being human in God's world is a shrewd Kuyperian corrective of popular pietism. As such it is a work of real value, perhaps even a landmark

> —James I. Packer, Professor, Regent College

This book is a long overdue corrective for a century of conservative church teachings that have produced more guilt-ridden Christians than cultural impact. I wish that every Christian college and seminary in America would make it required reading. Read this and begin to enjoy your Christian life again.

> —Rex M. Rogers, President, Cornerstone University

Michael Wittmer deftly guides the church to the earthly implications of confessing Jesus and calls us to joyous, obedient service for God in this world. We do well to learn from him and teach others also.

> —Stephen R. Spencer, Professor, Wheaton College

HEAVEN
is a place on
EARTH

MICHAEL E. WITTMER

HEAVEN
is a place on
EARTH

WHY EVERYTHING YOU DO
MATTERS TO GOD

ZONDERVAN™

GRAND RAPIDS, MICHIGAN 49530 USA

ZONDERVAN.COM/
AUTHOR**TRACKER**

Heaven Is a Place on Earth
Copyright © 2004 by Michael Wittmer

Requests for information should be addressed to:
Zondervan, *Grand Rapids, Michigan 49530*

Library of Congress Cataloging-in-Publication Data

Wittmer, Michael Eugene.
    Heaven is a place on earth : why everything you do matters to God / Michael
E. Wittmer.—1st ed.
        p. cm.
    Includes bibliographical references and indexes.
    ISBN-10: 0-310-25307-1 (pbk.)
    ISBN-13: 978-0-310-25307-5 (pbk.)
    1. Christian life. 2. Life—Religious aspects—Christianity. I. Title.
    BV4501.3.W59 2004
    248.4—dc22   2003027623

All Scripture quotations, unless otherwise indicated, are taken from the *Holy Bible: New International Version®*. NIV®. Copyright © 1973, 1978, 1984 by International Bible Society. Used by permission of Zondervan. All rights reserved.

Italics in quotations of Scripture are the author's.

The website addresses recommended throughout this book are offered as a resource to you. These websites are not intended in any way to be or imply an endorsement on the part of Zondervan, nor do we vouch for their content for the life of this book.

All rights reserved. No part of this publication may be reproduced, stored in a retrieval system, or transmitted in any form or by any means—electronic, mechanical, photocopy, recording, or any other—except for brief quotations in printed reviews, without the prior permission of the publisher.

Interior design by Beth Shagene

Printed in the United States of America

---

06 07 08 09 10 11 12 • 20 19 18 17 16 15 14 13 12 11 10 9 8 7 6 5

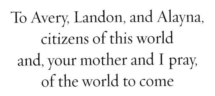

To Avery, Landon, and Alayna,
citizens of this world
and, your mother and I pray,
of the world to come

geadreved PS 168 169

Contents

List of Illustrations

Preface

This book is about the meaning *in* life. A slew of Christian books already address the meaning *of* life. Most of these rightly observe that we exist to love God through personal devotions and minister to others by sharing the gospel and making disciples of all nations. I wholeheartedly embrace these spiritual values. It is a privilege to ponder the Word of God, to pour out our heart to him in prayer, and to persuade other people to repent and follow our Savior. But this book is not about that.

Instead, I want to examine what these "meaning *of* life" books typically overlook. They are right to tell us that we were created for worship, ministry, evangelism, fellowship, and discipleship, but they are wrong to stop there. Look at that list again. While it more or less covers our responsibilities as Christians, it says little about what it means to be human. Does our purpose for life consist entirely in these spiritual activities, or is there also some value in showing up for work, waxing our car, playing with our children, or taking a trip to the beach—just a few of the many things we do, not because we are Christian, but primarily because we are human?

It is these distinctly human activities that this book seeks to address. Rather than encourage you to stretch forward to further pietistic pursuits (an important topic that has its place), I am more concerned here to renew our appreciation for the ordinary things we are already doing. In the process we will inevitably touch upon the meaning *of* life—that is, the purpose for our existence—but all the while our focus will be on the meaning *in* life—that is, the value within the normal, everyday activities that mark our human experience.

If I do my job well, you will come away from this book convinced of two important truths. First, God wants us to enjoy our earthly existence. We need not feel guilty for feeling at home in this world, for this planet is precisely where God wants us to be. As we learn from the opening pages of Genesis, it's good to be human and it's good to be here, on planet earth. Second, because this life matters to God, you will also be challenged to redirect every aspect of this existence to his honor and glory. No longer free to brush aside this earthly life as mere batting practice for our future, heavenly existence, we now recognize that whatever we do, regardless how seemingly small and insignificant, should be done with excellence "in the name of the Lord Jesus, giving thanks to God the Father through him" (Colossians 3:17).

Both truths only make sense within a full-orbed Christian worldview, which is why I spend some time in chapter 1 explaining what a worldview is, how it works, and what might comprise its foundational beliefs. Finally, I have concluded the book with discussion questions and case studies for each chapter in a section entitled "Expanding Your Worldview." Those who use this material to facilitate small-group discussions will be able to contact me and download a free leader's guide and two bonus chapters (on the foundational beliefs of the Christian worldwiew) at www.heavenisaplaceonearth.com.

Acknowledgments

It is sometimes difficult to know how far back to extend one's thank-yous (witness the long and tiresome acceptance speeches at the Oscars), but I must begin with Joe Crawford and James Grier. I had attended twelve years of Christian school, four years of Christian college, one year of seminary, plus church services three times a week during that span and yet had never heard the life-changing truths of this book until I sat under their ministry at Grand Rapids Theological Seminary. I would also like to thank Doug Felch, who kindly permitted me to use his informative chart on the image of God, and Neal Plantinga, whose inspiring lectures and writings have further enlarged my understanding of the Christian worldview.

Besides these mentors, I am indebted to the editorial contributions of the gracious staff at Zondervan—Paul Engle, Jim Ruark, Tim Beals, Katya Covrett, and Greg Stielstra—and the many friends, such as Wendy Widder, Sharon Ross, Scott Morter, Jeff Lindell, Phil Wittmer, and Gary and Julie Childers, who gladly volunteered to read and comment on major portions of my manuscript. Their encouragement and insights have made this a better book.

Finally, I offer my most profound gratitude to my dear wife, Julie, who not only carefully (and critically!) read every page but, more important, daily implements its truth in our home, enabling me and our three children to enjoy firsthand the privilege of living within the liberty of the Christian worldview.

1

What You See Is What You Get

Give me but one firm spot on which to stand,
and I will move the earth.

ARCHIMEDES (3RD CENTURY B.C.)

I don't want to go to heaven. Not that I'm lobbying for the other place—I want no part of everlasting fire and unbearable, unquench-able torment. The reason why I first repented and asked Christ to for-give my sin was to avoid going to hell. I became a Christian to get out of hell, not because I wanted to get into heaven. Before you judge me, remember why *you* said the Sinner's Prayer.

The delights of heaven may be to die for, but isn't that precisely the problem? Everyone who makes it into heaven has to leave this life to get there. Granted, death is not the worst thing that can hap-pen to a person, but it's pretty close. All things being equal, I'd rather continue the earthly existence that I currently enjoy.

I'd love to go to heaven—for a visit. It will be unspeakably exhil-arating to stand in the presence of God and sing his praises—but to do nothing except this forever and ever? That's a lot of rounds of "Shine, Jesus, Shine." Perhaps you think I'm being unfair. Well, what else do people do in heaven but worship God? As one preacher put it, "I don't know what we're going to do there, but I promise you it won't be boring." Thanks for the help. I want to believe you, but in the absence of any hard facts, I'm siding with Huckleberry Finn.

In a futile attempt to persuade a fidgety Huckleberry to behave, the stern Miss Watson warned her young charge about the hellish destiny of restless boys and the heavenly reward awaiting those who sit up straight and study their spelling books. According to Huckleberry, "Now she had got a start, and she went on and told me all about the good place. She said all a body would have to do there was to go around all day long with a harp and sing, forever and ever. So I didn't think much of it. But I never said so. I asked her if she reckoned Tom Sawyer would go there, and she said, not by a considerable sight. I was glad about that, because I wanted him and me to be together."[1]

Huckleberry Finn is right: Heaven does sound boring. Who wants to go there? We are not cut out for the clouds. We don't make very good angels. Humans weren't made for heaven. As wonderful as it will be to praise God in his celestial glory, there is still one thing better—to kneel in the presence of God with the bodies he created us to have in the place he created us to live.

Heaven Is Not My Home, I'll Just Be Passin' Through

And this is precisely what God promises. Contrary to popular opinion, the Christian hope is not that someday all believers get to die and go to heaven. Indeed, the only reason anyone ever goes to heaven is sin. If Adam and Eve had never sinned, they would have continued to live on this planet, enjoying the beauty of creation as they walked in close fellowship with their Creator. However, as we will see in chapter 9, Adam's sin brought death into the world. Now all people must die—an event that separates their souls from their bodies. Their bodies immediately begin to decay, but their souls continue to live, either in hell with the damned or in heaven with Jesus Christ.

But even those of us who make it to heaven have not yet achieved our perfect state. It must be extremely satisfying to join the other saints in heaven who continually stand in the presence of God. Yet even the saints who are there still long for something more. They long to be whole again, not merely to bow before God as a disembodied soul but to praise him as a fully restored person, possessing both a renewed spirit and body.

This is why our temporary stay in heaven—what theologians call the intermediate state—is not the primary focus of Scripture. There are only a few verses that even allude to it.[2] Scripture is relatively silent on our intermediate state in heaven because it is not the Christian hope. The Christian hope is not merely that our departed souls will rejoice in heaven, but that, as 1 Corinthians 15 explains, they will reunite with our resurrected bodies.

And where do bodies live? Not in heaven: That's more suitable for spiritual beings like angels and human souls. Bodies are meant to live on earth, on this planet.[3] So the Christian hope is not merely that someday we and our loved ones will die and go to be with Jesus. Instead, the Christian hope is that our departure from this world is just the first leg of a journey that is round-trip. We will not remain forever with God in heaven, for God will bring heaven down to us. As John explains his vision in Revelation 21:1–4, he "saw the Holy City, the new Jerusalem, coming down out of heaven from God" to earth, accompanied by the thrilling words, "Now the dwelling of God is with men, and he will live with them." In short, Christians long for the fulfillment of Emmanuel, the divine name that means "God with us." We don't hope merely for the day when we go to live with God, but ultimately for that final day when God comes to live with us.

Diamonds Are Forever

In their effort to focus attention on what matters most, well-meaning pastors and teachers often remind us that only two things last forever:

the Word of God and souls. Since nothing else is permanent, people who wish to make their lives count for eternity will concentrate their energies on evangelism. These leaders suggest that bringing people to Jesus is more than urgent—ultimately it is the only thing that really counts.

I am not convinced that permanence alone guarantees importance. (After all, the lake of fire seems to last forever, yet no one argues that we should live for that.) But even if it did, I think we should expand our list of things that last forever (that is, items that will exist in our final, everlasting state). Certainly the Word of God and souls head the list, but what about physical things, such as our bodies and even this planet? While our resurrection bodies and the new earth will be somewhat different from those we currently enjoy,[4] they apparently will also be quite similar.

For example, consider the post-resurrection body of Jesus. Although his spiritual body could pass through solid walls, he went out of his way to prove to his disciples that he was not a ghost but the actual, physical fellow they had known for three years. He invited them to touch his hands and feet, and when they still would not believe, he ate fish and perhaps some honey in front of them.[5] Jesus wanted his friends to know that the resurrection did not obliterate his humanity but rather restored it from the ravages of sin and death that he had suffered on their behalf.

Because Jesus is "the firstfruits of those who have fallen asleep,"[6] we may surmise that, like the resurrected Christ, our future life on the new earth will repair rather than remove our humanity. Isaiah says as much when, in words echoed by John in Revelation 21:24–26, he describes the new earth as a place of commerce, wealth, and flourishing human culture.[7] Speaking of the New Jerusalem, Isaiah 60:11 declares that "your gates will always stand open, they will never be shut, day or night, so that men may bring you the wealth of the nations—their kings led in triumphal procession." We will examine this further in chapter 11, but for now note that rather than transforming us into quasi-angelic beings who have no use for gold, houses, and vineyards,[8] our final salvation redeems these human products from the corroding cancer of sin.[9]

The point is that not only our souls but also our bodies and the earth itself, together with our cultural contributions, appear to survive the transition from this world to the next. Thus, if we grant that permanence is at least one indicator of a thing's importance, it seems evangelical Christians should stretch beyond their usual (and justified) concern for "spiritual things" and develop a well-rounded view of the world. We need to become, in the best sense of the word, "worldly Christians."

Worldly Christianity

Besides this issue of permanence, the sheer breadth of life compels us to develop a Christian worldview. Evangelical Christians have rightly emphasized spiritual activities, encouraging one another to "have their devotions," attend church, and witness to their unsaved family and friends. Personal acts of piety like these are the heart of the Christian life. They are extremely important activities, and all of us Christians, if we are honest, know that we can do better.

Still, it seems that many evangelicals have oversimplified the Christian life, reducing it to nothing more than these personal acts of piety. When someone asks how we are doing spiritually, we immediately examine our prayer lives, perhaps answering the question according to whether or not we had our "quiet time" this morning. When a preacher exhorts us to "return to our first love" or to "stop being lukewarm Christians," we immediately know what he means. We need to beef up our devotions, expand our prayer list, and extend ourselves to more unsaved friends. These things may be the heart of the Christian life, but I wonder whether they aren't overemphasized in some evangelical circles.

Think about your typical day. You wake up early so you can have a quick breakfast with your *Daily Bread* or other favorite devotional.

After a hot shower, you're off to work, alternately praying and listening to the news as your car inches its way through the morning commute. Depending on your line of work, your day consists of meetings, phone calls, consultations with colleagues and clients, and tending to various other emergencies. Or it may consist of hammering wall studs and mounting drywall. On a good day you finish early enough to get a head start on the afternoon rush hour. As you breeze home, you savor the day's successes and fret about tomorrow's challenges while keeping one ear open for the traffic report. When you finally make it home, your evening may consist of reading the paper, a hasty meal, routine maintenance around the house, an hour or two of television or perhaps a trip to soccer practice. Somewhere during the late evening news you concede that you've had enough, and you head for bed, wondering how another promising day so quickly slipped away.

In this more or less typical day, look at how much time you spent on activities other than Bible reading, prayer, and evangelism. If Christianity speaks only to these personal acts of piety, then it does not address most of our lives at all. If *life* includes more than Bible reading, prayer, and evangelism, then the *Christian life* must include more as well.

It's a lot like sex. I propose that personal acts of piety are to the Christian life what sexual intimacy is to marriage. Sexual intimacy is one of the high points of marriage. For some, it's the main reason for getting married. But in the back of our minds we know that marriage involves much more than sex. After all, if a good marriage needs nothing more than sexual intimacy, why do the world's most beautiful people have so much trouble staying in love? Hollywood couples quickly discover that they need more from each other than just good lovin'. To survive, their marriage requires the more foundational glue of commitment, companionship, patience, encouragement, shared values, and sacrifice.

Just as intimacy is the climax but not the entirety of married life, so the Christian life culminates in—but is not exhausted by—personal acts of piety. Marriages succeed when both partners learn to live together and support each other in every area: physically, emotionally, vocationally, and spiritually. In the same way, Christians succeed when they learn to honor God in every area of life.

This is why Christians need to develop a well-rounded worldview. It is not enough to have a "soul-view" or a "piety-view." We must learn to think Christianly about every aspect of our world. For instance, what should we think about brushing our teeth, making the bed, mowing the lawn, going to movies, buying a CD, playing softball, driving an SUV, watching the Simpsons, getting a job, starting a hobby, playing the stock market, weeding a garden, or taking music lessons? Or the Arab-Israeli conflict, global warming, abortion, genetic engineering, human cloning, the terrorism of September 11, drilling for oil in the Arctic wilderness, and mercy killing? In short, what should we think about all of the many big and small things we do or consider every day, choices that comprise our lives not so much because we are Christian but because we are human? Such questions only receive answers within a full-orbed Christian worldview.

What Is a Worldview?

Not everyone possesses a Christian worldview, but every person, whether or not they have ever heard of the term, has *a* worldview. The English term "worldview," a translation of the German word *Weltanschauung*, has been variously described as "perceptual frameworks," "ways of seeing," the "set of presuppositions . . . which we hold . . . about the basic make-up of the world," and "the conceptual framework of one's basic belief about things."[10]

The common theme running through these definitions suggests that a worldview is a framework of fundamental concepts or beliefs about the world. In short, a worldview comprises the lens through which we see the world. This lens is more like contact lenses than eyeglasses, for like the former, we so take it for granted that we often aren't consciously aware that we are wearing it.

While hassle-free living may be a key selling point for contacts, being hassle-free can be dangerous when it comes to worldviews. People who take their worldview for granted, never questioning its basic assumptions or wondering if a particular perspective is accurate, risk staking their lives on an unstable foundation. In time, when a major crisis thunders their way, they may discover, too late, that their worldview could not bear their weight.

To avoid such catastrophes, one goal of this book is to help us think more deeply about the worldview we currently own. Certainly we want to learn the content of the Christian worldview, but just as important, we must decipher the beliefs of our current perspective. Only by knowing both the truth and our present situation can we make the necessary adjustments to protect ourselves from the onslaughts of life.

The Structure of a Worldview

As a framework of basic beliefs about the world, it may help to picture our worldview as a series of concentric circles. Although every belief is related, at least indirectly, to every other belief in the web, the beliefs near the center form the core of our worldview while those on the fringes are more easily given up. Which beliefs are near the middle and which are on the margins depends largely on the ordering criteria we have in mind. Much as computer files may be sorted by date, size, or alphabetical order, so the beliefs in our worldview may be variously arranged according to their relative importance or level of certainty.

For example, a worldview arranged by importance may include on its margins such trivial notions as the widespread opinion that the New York Yankees will win the World Series (Fig. 1.1). This is a reasonable belief to hold, given the Yankees' recent track record and their ability to outbid any other team for the players they want. However, every now and then another team has a really good year and, with a few lucky bounces, rises up to defeat the mighty sluggers from the Bronx.

I suspect that apart from a couple of million die-hard (and some might add, spoiled) Yankee fans, New York's losses are not a crushing blow. Most Americans, even most New Yorkers, manage to get out of bed the next morning and go to work. The Yankees' defeats make for interesting conversation, but they do not dramatically alter anyone's life, including even the players themselves.

The Yankees' prowess is such a marginal belief that some may question whether it even deserves to be considered part of our worldview. But that's true of all beliefs on the fringes. They are so inconsequential that they can come and go and barely be missed.

Not so as we travel deeper into the center of our worldview. Related to our opinion of the Yankees, in increasing order of impor-

**Figure 1.1: The Structure of a Worldview
—Sorted by Importance**

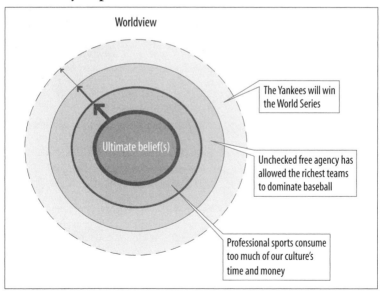

tance, is our belief about free agency, the role of money in sports, and the role of sports in culture. Each topic drives us deeper into the heart of our worldview until we finally confront the more ultimate questions of life such as "what is the meaning of human culture?" and "how do I contribute?" Thus, even unimportant topics like the New York Yankees are connected to deeper pylons buried in the foundations of our worldview. If we follow the circles toward the center, we will eventually arrive at our most fundamental beliefs.

These most fundamental beliefs include the answers to life's perennial questions: Who am I? Where am I? What's wrong with me and with my world? and What's the solution to this problem?[11] How we answer these questions will chart our course for life, for they describe our basic understanding of the world and our place in it. If we are wrong here, then we will ultimately fail at every other point. Regardless how successful we become in the eyes of others, we will live and die as failures, never having understood the meaning of life.

But these four questions, as important as they are, do not yet take us to the very heart of the Christian worldview. There are beliefs even more central, more definitive, than these. We will discuss them below, but first let's consider how a worldview also can be arranged by level of certainty.

Our beliefs are more or less certain according to how we come to know them. In brief, the beliefs that are inferred from prior beliefs tend to be less certain than those that are accepted on their own merit. For instance, let's say that as I'm writing this, I hear strange voices downstairs that lead me to believe that unexpected callers have dropped by to visit. The idea that visitors are present in my home is a marginal belief, for it may easily be wrong. When I head downstairs to greet our guests, I may find that the voices are coming from the television or radio, or perhaps my wife is practicing her celebrity impressions. In that case I would grin at my mistake and, with a plea to turn down the offending voices, return to my study to finish my work.

The situation would be more disturbing should I find the television and radio off and no human in sight. "That's odd," I might think. "I was sure I heard voices. What's wrong with me?" This is particularly upsetting because I have learned to rely on my sense of hearing to deliver accurate information about the world. I may be able to shrug off this isolated instance, but if it happens too frequently, I will probably check myself into a mental health facility. My belief that my mind and sensory equipment are functioning properly lies near the center of my worldview, and I can scarcely imagine living in a world in which I cannot trust them (Fig. 1.2).

But this belief, as certain as it is, does not yet take us to the core of the Christian worldview. There are beliefs even more fixed, more foundational, than this. We call these beliefs our ultimate commitments or presuppositions, for they lie at the very center of both

Figure 1.2: The Structure of a Worldview
—Sorted by Certainty

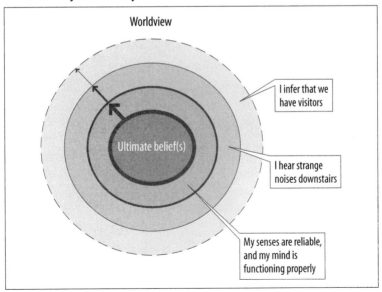

worldview diagrams. They are both the most important and most certain beliefs we hold. Can you guess what they are?[12]

I suggest that you pause for a moment, put this book aside, and think hard about what you believe. Start with any belief you are fairly sure about, and ask yourself why you believe that. Why do you believe that the sun will rise tomorrow, that your spouse loves you, or that you ate blueberry pancakes for breakfast? Whatever reason or belief comes to mind, ask yourself why you believe that. If the answer surfaces another belief, ask yourself why you believe that, and so on. Continue asking yourself these hard questions until you have pursued the chain all the way back to the beginning.

For instance, perhaps you believe the sun will rise tomorrow because you've seen it rise every day of your life. But what makes this event so predictable? One likely answer is natural law. Fine, but why do you believe that there are laws of nature? Where do they come from? And what causes whatever it is that generates these laws?

When you cannot go any further back, when you throw up your hands in exasperation and say, "I don't know why I believe this, I just do," you will have reached the very center of your worldview. This belief, whatever it is, is your ultimate faith commitment. It is the foundation of who you are and everything you believe. It is the one (or more) thing that you have staked your life on. It is your most basic presupposition, or starting point.

I don't mean to imply that your presupposition(s) comes without reasons. You may well have reasons for your ultimate belief, but unlike all other beliefs, these reasons are not why you believe it. You may be able to produce a good argument for this belief, but the fact is, you would continue to believe it even if you did not have the argument. To summarize: As your starting point, your presupposition is a belief that you argue *from*, not *to*. It is not a destination but a place to begin. What is your foundational belief(s)?

The Interpreter of Experience

It is important to discover our ultimate beliefs, for these give rise to our worldview, which in turn serves as the lens through which we see the world (Fig. 1.3). Thus our presuppositions ultimately determine how we interpret reality. Where we start determines where we end up.[13]

The events of our lives do not convey obvious, objective messages that mean the same to everyone. Our experience does not come self-interpreted. Instead, the meaning of any event depends on the worldview that interprets it. And since worldviews vary from person to person, there may be any number of interpretations for the same event.

For instance, let's go back to the New York Yankees' recent domination in the world of baseball. How we interpret their success depends largely on our worldview, or where we are coming from. Yankee fans point with pride to a rich tradition of championship clubs and a well-stocked farm system, while disgruntled Red Sox partisans moan that the Yankees merely buy championships through free agency. Both sides have a point that resonates so loudly within their own worldviews that it squelches the other perspective.

Or consider the 2000 presidential election. How we interpret that debacle depends largely on whether we are a Democrat or a Republican. Democrats are apt to suggest that the Republicans stole the election. For their part, Republicans would concede that the election was

Figure1.3: How a Worldview Mediates Experience

a mess, but would just as confidently assert that in the end, cooler heads prevailed and justice was served. Same event, two interpretations.

These partisan roles were reversed during President Clinton's impeachment trial. Republicans adamantly declared that the president disgraced his office and deserved to be impeached. The Democrats conceded that the situation was a mess, and they certainly did not condone his behavior, yet they maintained that the country must distinguish between a person's private and public life. Same facts, two widely different interpretations.

This interpretive importance of worldviews holds for matters of religion, and perhaps especially there. True believers of every stripe support their faith with stories of miraculous intervention and answered prayer. For instance, many Christian churches designate entire portions of their worship services for "testimony time." Here the faithful encourage one another with recent accounts of healing, strength, and other successes that they perceive have come directly from the Almighty.

While these reports are often true, we should not forget that other religions have similar stories. Just south of Toledo, in an open field off Interstate 75, stands North America's largest mosque. Several years ago a tornado swept across the cornfields of western Ohio in its direction. For a long moment it looked as if God might register his displeasure with Islam by taking out the mosque. However, he apparently had second thoughts, for though the tornado destroyed several homes in the vicinity, it did not touch the mosque. Toledo's Muslims praised Allah for hearing their prayers and sparing their house of worship, while area Christians offered a decidedly different interpretation.

One religion's miracle is explained away by another. The difference is not the event itself, for its objective reality is the one thing both sides accept. The difference lies in our competing worldviews. Because Muslims and Christians possess markedly divergent worldviews, they are bound to produce different interpretations for the same event, especially when that event touches upon a crucial difference between them.

Because the events of life are open to such various interpretations, what matters most is not what happens to us but the worldview that interprets what happens to us. To rephrase a popular Christian aphorism, life is 10 percent what happens to you and 90 percent how you read what happens to you. Say you have an automobile accident on your way home from work. What does it mean? Is it fate? Did random chance draw your unlucky number? Is a stern God getting back at you for skipping last night's prayer meeting? Or is it merely an event allowed by a provident God who lovingly protected you from serious harm? In each case the facts are the same: Your car is totaled, your insurance premiums will undoubtedly rise, and you must go through the hassle of finding a way to get to work tomorrow. But though the facts are the same, different worldviews produce entirely different outlooks on the situation. Depending on your worldview, you are left cursing your karma, haunted by the unpredictable lottery of life, cowering in fear before a vindictive deity, or praising God for his fatherly care.

The secret to a satisfying life is not to avoid all unpleasant experiences—we can't—but rather to have a worldview that knows how to correctly read such experiences. A proper worldview can empower sturdy believers to endure any number of daunting challenges. Waves of disappointment and disaster that would certainly have swamped lesser vessels only make them more determined to hang on. It seems that their robust faith can endure almost anything.

Challenged by Experience

Almost anything. Worldviews are elastic structures that can bend and stretch to accommodate almost any experience. But they can bend only so far. An unexpected, entirely foreign experience may directly challenge the foundations of a worldview (Fig. 1.3). Straining to make sense of this new experience, the worldview contorts itself into a pretzel, stretching credulity before supplying a satisfying explanation. An experience may be so undeniably powerful that we would rather exchange important pieces of our worldview than live in a universe that cannot account for what happened to us.

So a wife's broken cheekbones penetrate her excuses and self-loathing, forcing her to admit that her beast of a husband is not the loving provider she has defended to others. An earthquake turns a subdivision into toothpicks, prompting its survivors—many of them secularists—to thank God for their safety. A devout mother comforts her dying newborn, wondering why, if God does exist, he could be so cruel. A first grader learns that his parents are splitting up, and he vows that he will never trust an adult again.

It is not just bad experiences that can shatter a worldview. Sometimes good experiences change a worldview for the better. A black soldier risks his life to rescue his racist comrades, who in turn gratefully view the entire black population with new eyes of appreciation. A resplendent sunset viewed from a bluff overlooking the ocean causes an involuntary lump of gratitude to catch in the throat of a hardened skeptic. Its sheer beauty melts away his intellectual problems, and he realizes that he can't help but believe in God. A lifelong Muslim, confronted by the love she received from her missionary friend, forsakes her family's tradition and becomes a follower of the Christian God.

In each case, people recognized that their worldview could not adequately explain their new experience. At first they might tell themselves that their husband just had one too many drinks, the earthquake and sunset can be entirely explained by natural causes, God must want to bring something better from their baby's death, their parents will one day get back together, the black soldier is a rare "credit" to his race, or the missionary has some hidden agenda that her selfless spirit seeks to conceal. This stretching and contorting allows people to retain their worldview, but at great cost. In time, each person must decide which is more likely—that their experience is a fluke, an aberration from the normal way things are, or that in important ways their worldview is mistaken.

If they choose the former, they risk living in denial. Then view remains intact, but important pieces of it increasingly appear to be sheer fantasy. Their worldview no longer explains the world as it is, but only as they want it to be. Despite its obvious danger, this option is always available. How else to explain the Egyptian and Saudi parents who refuse to concede that their sons were the hijackers who crashed two planes into the World Trade Center on the morning of September 11, 2001? In the face of overwhelming evidence to the contrary, they doggedly insist that their kind and gentle children would never commit such a heinous act. While any parent can commiserate with the emotional pain that would produce these denials, we also cannot help but pity those who through sheer force of will are able to pull the wool over their own eyes.

If these people select the latter option, then they are in for a rough ride. There is nothing more unsettling than having one's worldview shaken to the core. However, if they hang on through the sifting process, they should come out on the other side with a powerful worldview that can more plausibly account for their experience. For example, the events of September 11 shattered our fundamental belief that Americans were safe between our shores. Though it was painful to lose our security, America is a stronger country for facing up to and working through this problem. Our increased concern for world affairs, upgrade in our military and homeland security, and reflection upon the brevity and meaning of life have better prepared us to live in this new, dangerous world. No one would choose to endure the events of September 11, but neither can anyone deny that we are better for it.

The Patience of Job

A good example of the pain of worldview transformation is the biblical story of Job. Job's worldview informed him that a just God always blesses the righteous, and for most of his life, this worldview correctly interpreted his experience. Job walked with God and received in return numerous children and great wealth. Then on one very bad day—one that he had every reason to expect would be similar to his previous days—Job lost his oxen, donkeys, sheep, camels, most of his servants, and all of his children. Very soon he also lost his health. Afflicted with festering sores across his entire body, Job retired to an ash heap to scrape away the pus. The only thing he kept was his nagging wife, and she was the one thing he wouldn't mind losing. In his agony and confusion Job cursed the day of his birth and pleaded with God to take his life.

Job's friends attempted to say the right words to make things better, but they were operating from within his old worldview, the one that assumed that God always rewards the righteous and punishes evildoers. Job's rash of new experiences easily discredited this assumption, so his friends could not help him. Job had moved, and they could not reach him from where they stood. Their counsel, so appropriate within their own worldviews, meant nothing to Job now. He responded in exasperation, "So how can you console me with your nonsense? Nothing is left of your answers but falsehood!"[14]

Poor Job didn't know what to believe. He knew he could never go back to the simple faith of his friends, but neither did he know where he would eventually land. His crisis of faith appeared headed for despair when God graciously responded to Job's request and granted him an interview. However, rather than allow Job to air his grievances, God did most of the talking. And when God spoke, notice what he said—or more important, what he did not say. God never mentioned what was on Job's mind—his dead children and his painful disease. He completely ignored Job's felt needs. Instead, he simply reminded Job that he is the Creator, that everything is under his control. And Job was satisfied.

Perhaps even more important than what God said is the simple fact that he showed up. The presence of God overwhelmed Job's cries for justice. It significantly expanded Job's worldview. No longer did he worship a small, predictable God who on cue delivers rainbows to the righteous and storms to the wicked. Instead, Job experienced first-hand what he had suspected all along—that the true God is large enough to tolerate loose ends in this life. Job never received an answer to his complaints or a reason for his trial, but his face-to-face encounter with the living God convinced him that his life was still in good hands. He may not have understood what God was doing, but he now knew that he could trust him. In Job's words, "My ears had heard of you but now my eyes have seen you. Therefore I despise myself and repent in dust and ashes."[15]

Like the story of Job, the purpose of this book is to expand our worldview by entering the presence of God. While most of us will not experience the divine storm that swept into Job's world, we still have access to the same powerful words he heard. By studying this divine revelation we intend to answer the fundamental questions of life: Where am I? Who am I? Why am I here? What is wrong with me and this world? And what is the solution for this mess? We will sketch the contours of the Christian worldview, which will enable us to read our culture and interpret any fact or experience through the eyes of God.

Part One

What Is This Place?

CREATION IN GENESIS 1–2

Where Lies the Great Divide?

In the beginning God created the heavens and the earth.

GENESIS 1:1

F ind a blank space and arrange the following items according to their level of being: a rock, a rose, an angel, God, a human, and a donkey. Draw a picture, create a diagram—do whatever you need to do to satisfactorily express the relationship between these things. While you're working on that, let me tell you a story.

And They Call This the Dark Ages?

Late in the eleventh century a group of monks in northern France challenged their abbot to construct a proof for the existence of God. They already believed in the God of Scripture, but wondered what their up-and-coming abbot could prove on the strength of his mind alone. The abbot, named Anselm, accepted their challenge and produced a sizable book, called the *Monologion*, that did appear to demonstrate not only that God exists, but also that he must be the Father, Son, and Holy Spirit of the Christian Trinity.

The monks were duly impressed, but pushed their abbot to go one better. Could he reduce his lengthy, convoluted argument to a single sentence? That would be pretty neat—to have one simple, handy argument that indubitably proved to all rational people that God exists. Anselm didn't know if he could simplify his complex argument to a single line, but he promised to try.

Then one evening during Mass, it came to him. With "joy and jubilation" Anselm hit upon the single line that hereafter would demonstrate the existence of God to all thinking people. The sentence, startling in its simplicity, is this: "God is that than which nothing greater can be conceived."[1]

How does this sentence prove God's existence? Easily. If God is "that than which nothing greater can be conceived," then he must be the greatest possible being. And what must the greatest possible being be like? For starters, he must possess all of the best possible attributes—he must be the most powerful, most loving, most righteous, most just, most kind, and most beautiful being we could ever imagine. Any and all desirable qualities must be found in the greatest possible being—and to the fullest measure.

What about existence? Must our greatest possible being necessarily exist? Anselm thought this was obviously true, for a most powerful and most loving being who was only the product of our imagination would not yet be the greatest possible being, but would come in second to a being who was most powerful and most loving and who also did exist. Thus, to qualify as the greatest possible being, any candidate not only must possess the best possible attributes but must also exist (Fig. 2.1).

Here is the brilliance of Anselm's argument: he demonstrated that by definition God must exist. Whether or not they believe in God, everyone, including professed atheists, concede that the idea of God represents "that than which nothing greater can be conceived." But

Figure 2.1: Anselm's Proof for God's Existence

List of Perfections		Existence?		
All-righteous All-powerful All-loving Etc.	✚	No		Second greatest possible being
All-righteous All-powerful All-loving Etc.	✚	Yes		Greatest possible being (God)

once they concede that the idea of God means the greatest possible being, all rational people, including atheists, must immediately admit that this God is more than an idea and must actually exist. If they deny that God exists, all this means is that they are not yet talking about God, for they are not yet speaking about the greatest possible being. The moment they say the term "God" they are speaking of the greatest possible being, which as such must necessarily exist.

With this in mind, Anselm wondered what kind of person would utter the statement, "God does not exist." Unpacked, this statement negates itself, for it declares that God, which as the greatest possible being must exist, does not exist. What type of person contradicts himself in a single sentence? Someone who is not yet thinking clearly. Anselm observed that this must be what Psalm 14:1 means when it states that the person who says in his heart, "There is no God," is a fool. This person must be a fool because he can't deny God's existence without contradicting himself.

Perhaps you feel a bit schnookered by the argument so far. It makes perfect sense, yet you can't help but think that it's impossible to prove God's existence from a single idea in our own heads. We can't take room here to wade through the pros and cons of the argument, but even though numerous philosophers and theologians have criticized the argument, it has never gone away. Many significant scholars think that Anselm's argument still works.[2]

But whether or not you think it works is actually beside the point. The real legacy of Anselm's argument is not its attempt to prove God's existence but rather how it teaches us to speak about God. If God is "that than which nothing greater can be conceived," then we know there are certain things we must say about him. For starters, we must use only our best words to describe him. God must be righteous, powerful, loving, and kind—all the things that it is better to be than not to be. We may disagree about what items should go in the list (for example, evangelical theologians are currently discussing whether it is better for God to know the future or to learn about it as it comes, the way you and I do), but we all agree that the list must include all the great-making properties we can imagine.[3]

And of course, at the top of this list Anselm placed existence. One of Anselm's contemporaries argued that adding the phrase "greatest possible" before a noun does not necessarily guarantee its existence. We can imagine a greatest possible island but, despite the pictures in our vacation brochure, it doesn't necessarily exist in the real world.

Anselm replied that God is a unique case. He is not merely the greatest possible being in his category (such as islands), but the greatest possible being, period. And as the greatest possible being, he must, necessarily, exist. Anselm's point—and this is the staying power of his argument—is that as "that than which nothing greater can be conceived," God is qualitatively superior to anything in his creation. There is nothing that compares with the greatest possible being. He is in a class by himself—literally.

Say What?

Before we go on, I need to introduce you to a couple of new words. If words are the fuel of the mind (that is, we can only contemplate what we can name), then new words are often necessary to understand new thoughts. And since entertaining new thoughts is the essence of learning, you who are reading this book to learn something might feel cheated if you fail to enlarge your vocabulary.

Our first word is "metaphysics," a term that entered our vocabulary by a fluke of history. The great philosopher Aristotle once gave a series of lectures on the nature of reality. Since these lectures on reality appeared on the shelf after his lectures on physics, one of his students began calling this branch of philosophy "metaphysics," *meta* being the Greek word for "after." Thus the term "metaphysics" simply means the study of reality.

The second word, virtually synonymous in worldview discussions, is "ontology." This word comes from the Greek terms *onta*, which means "the really existent things," and *logos*, which means "the study of." So just like the term "metaphysics," "ontology" means the study of what is real. Be alert for the adjective "ontological," which appears frequently in this book. In using the term, I merely intend to indicate that in distinction from other philosophical categories, such as morality, I am speaking about the nature of reality.

Although the terms "metaphysics" and "ontology" may seem new, you are already familiar with the concept. Without consciously thinking about it, your mind continually makes ontological distinctions between things. For example, you easily assume that this book is real and that its reality differs from you. Unlike "Mike Wittmer" and "author of this book," which are two names for the same thing, you and the book are ontologically different.

Not only are you and the book two ontologically separate entities, but your metaphysical makeup is also different. Unlike the book, which is entirely material, you possess both a material body and an immaterial soul. Sometimes we attribute soulish qualities to a book, as when we say that *David Copperfield* moved or inspired us. However, everyone understands that such claims must be taken metaphorically, as vivid word pictures rather than as metaphysical descriptions of reality. We only mean to suggest that we deeply appreciated the contents of the book, not that the book is some living thing that audibly speaks to our soul.

Another familiar example of metaphysical issues involves what people commonly call "virtual reality." Besides the real world that we inhabit, technology has recently introduced a parallel world of computer-generated images. Reflective persons ask how this virtual world relates to the one we know. In what ways is virtual reality merely an extension of our world, and to what extent is it a separate world altogether? For instance, what ontological status should we assign to a film star who only exists in a computer? Is she real? Why or why not? Such ontological questions will continue to surface in our culture's ethical deliberations. Even as I write this, the U.S. Supreme Court has issued a ruling that allows the distribution of computer-generated child pornography on the grounds that the children involved are not real, so no one is actually victimized by this type of voyeurism.

Where Do You Draw the Line?

Armed with this new vocabulary, we are now prepared to address the big questions of life. Consider the question, "Where do you draw the line?" This is the most fundamental point of the Christian worldview. We must get this right, for if we are wrong here, we will be confused at every other point. Simply stated, the Christian worldview asserts that there is an ontological distinction—indeed, an ontological chasm—between the infinite Creator and his finite creation. Christians are metaphysical dualists, for we believe that there are primarily only two kinds of reality in the world: God, who is in a class by himself, and everything else (Fig. 2.2).

Sadly, many people who claim to follow the Christian worldview draw their line in the wrong place. Rather than draw a horizontal line separating God from his creation, many Christians think and live as if there is a vertical line separating two contrasting parts of God's creation. They believe that the fundamental ontological distinction lies

Figure 2.2: The Ontological Distinction between God and Creation

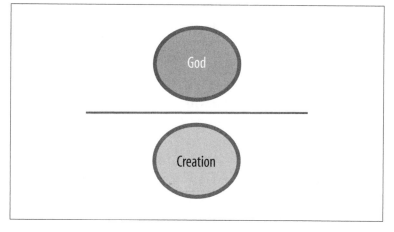

not between God and creation, but between the physical, or material, world and spiritual, or immaterial, reality (Fig. 2.3). They mistakenly equate Paul's use of the term "flesh" with matter and assume that it is their physical body that holds them back in their Christian walk.[4] If only they could rise above the animal passions of their physical nature, they would be free to nurture their good souls that constantly desire nothing but the higher activities of the heavenly, or spiritual, realm. So they believe that a tug-of-war exists within them

Figure 2.3: Misplaced Metaphysical Dualism

Physical, material world	Spiritual, immaterial world
Temporary	Eternal
Earthy	Heavenly
Lower nature	Higher nature
Flesh: hinders piety	Spirit: helps piety
Evil?	Completely good

between their unblemished, godlike spirit and the dark, somewhat evil side of their physical nature.

For example, listen to how many Christians rationalize their fall into sin. "I'm sorry. I never intended to hurt your feelings—sometimes my mouth gets carried away and I say things I don't even mean." Or "I didn't want to sleep with her, but she was so beautiful and so available, I just couldn't help myself." Or "I never meant to gain this much weight; I guess I've been eating more than I thought."

Notice that in each case the person claims that his heart remains pure. Deep down inside, where the "real" person resides, he always and still does mean well. His intentions are honorable, but his noble mind is too easily overpowered by the quick tongue, intense passion, and strong appetite of his bad body. If only he could rise above the gravitational pull of his physical nature, he is quite certain that his inherently good spirit would freely choose what is right.

Fortunately for them, most Christians who think this way also believe that their good souls are only temporarily trapped inside the prison of their bodies. At death they will finally shed this alien, material nature and be free to be nothing but the good soul that has always been their true core. For now, the best they can do is attempt to starve their physical appetites while stimulating their good, spiritual side to rise above their bodies, if only for fleeting moments here and there, and contemplate the heavenly reality that is their true home.

The next chapter explains why, though this horizontal dualism between spirit and matter has enjoyed a long run in the church, it is actually a pagan idea. Here I only want to point out how it prevents us from noticing the more foundational, vertical duality that exists between God and his creation. When we elevate one element of creation above another (such as spirit over matter) we tend to make the superiority absolute. We easily think that there is something intrinsically valuable about our immaterial nature that trumps our physical side, so we assign it qualities, such as immortality and inviolable goodness, that belong to God alone. Rather than recognize that both elements belong to creation, we seek to push our spiritual nature into the Godhead. After all, we remind ourselves, God himself is spirit.[5]

This line of thought is dangerously wrong. Although God is spirit and we possess a spirit, the ontological distinction between God and us implies that there will always be an infinite difference between the uncreated, eternal Spirit of God and our created, contingent spirits that each moment depend on God to hold them in existence. Indeed, the chasm between God and our spirits is infinitely greater than the difference between our spirits and our bodies. Because our spirits and bodies both exist in the realm of creation, they will always have more in common with each other than any similarities they might share with the uncreated God who made them. In sum, the fundamental line we draw to separate reality must never run through any two parts of creation but must always be a horizontal line that separates the entire creation from its Creator.

How Well Did You Do?

With this in mind, look again at the exercise that began this chapter. Most people successfully arrange the rock, rose, and donkey in ascending order, with some disagreement about whether angels or humans should be higher on the scale. (For the record, I place humans beneath angels on account of Hebrews 2:7, which states that people were made "a little lower than the angels."[6] I am aware that unlike humans, Scripture never says that angels are created in the image of God. But then again, it also never says they are not. Theologians tend to disagree about this. Both Thomas Aquinas and John Calvin assert that angels are made in the image of God, while Herman Bavinck—a Dutch theologian of the early twentieth century— suggests they are not; otherwise, he says, Jesus Christ, the perfect image of God, would have come to earth as an angel.)[7]

Whatever you decide about humans and angels is fine with me. The main point is that although we can rank the various elements of creation and conclude, for instance, that even the person with the lowest IQ remains superior to the smartest animal, yet the largest difference in reality does not lie here. The most fundamental ontological distinction is the chasm between all creatures and the uncreated God who made us (Fig. 2.4).

The infinite God is utterly transcendent, wholly other than the world he has made. He dwells on an entirely different plane of reality, a fact that makes him more real than we are. What does that mean? It's hard to say from our creaturely level of existence, but I suspect it has something to do with the inviolable, necessary existence of God. Unlike you and me, who exist moment by moment by the sheer mercy of God, God himself must necessarily exist.

Think about it: Our lives are radically dependent upon God. We did nothing to bring ourselves into existence, and we can do nothing to keep ourselves there. Before our creation, we did not exist at all. There was no "I" to bring into existence, for God's act of creating us is what first caused there to be a "me." And despite our years of growth and accomplishment, we have done nothing that requires God to keep us around. He was entirely happy before he created us, and he would remain completely contented should he decide to allow us, or even the entire universe, to pass from existence. Every part of

Figure 2.4: Answer to Exercise

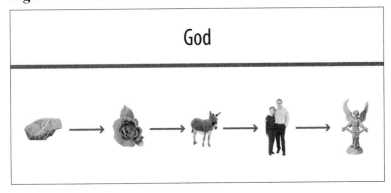

creation, from best friends to root beer floats, continues to exist only because God wants it to. Should God ever take his mind off us—should he ever for one moment stop affirming our existence—we would dissipate faster than soft butter on a hot griddle.

Furthermore, just as we were powerless to bring ourselves into existence, so we are utterly unable to take ourselves out. We may commit suicide and take ourselves out of this life, but we will continue to exist somewhere so long as God chooses to hold us in existence. Thus our lives are entirely dependent on God. Only he determines when our lives begin, and only he determines whether and when our lives should end.

Unlike our radically contingent existence, God must necessarily exist. God never came into existence, for he always was. And God can never go out of existence, for he will always be the same being that he has been up to this moment. The living God depends on no one or nothing outside of himself for his existence. He possesses what theologians call *aseity*, an innate ability to sustain his own existence. In this way our supremely independent God is the most real being imaginable, for while the reality of our universe depends completely upon him, he relies upon no one but himself.

When to Say You Don't Know

This ontological distinction between God and creation has important implications for the Christian worldview. Besides reminding us to use our best words when we speak about God, it also assures us that every question we raise about him will eventually end in mystery. But rather than throw up our hands in exasperation, threatening to give up our faith in God because we cannot completely understand him, we should remember that the very fact that we cannot comprehend him is a sure sign that we are speaking about God.

God, who is the pinnacle of truth, never asks us to believe anything that is irrational. There are no contradictions in the Christian faith. However, because we are dealing with a God who inhabits a transcendent level of reality, at every turn we are confronted with truth that is suprarational. No matter how carefully we study the Bible and logically piece together our theology, there will always be something left over, something we can't easily understand, when we're done.

Consider the doctrine of the Trinity, the Christian belief that the living God consists of one essence and three persons. This is not irrational, for we do not say that God is one and three in the same way. For instance, to say that God is one essence and three essences or one person and three persons is an obvious contradiction that no one should believe. But to say that God is one and three in different ways, such as one essence and three persons, is not a contradiction and thus remains an eligible belief.

Not that it is easy to understand. Everyone who has ever contemplated the Trinity would concur with Augustine, who after writing the definitive work on the Trinity bowed his knees in fear that he had misrepresented the living God. Of course we cannot comprehend the Trinity, but that is no surprise, given that God dwells above and we live down here, on the creaturely level of reality. And because the ontological distinction between God and creation will always exist, we will probably never understand the Trinity any better, even in the next life.

Or consider the story of Christmas. Each December we celebrate the unfathomable mystery that God himself became one of us. Numerous questions surround his birth. How can a virgin conceive a child? How can the God who holds the universe in existence fall asleep in his mother's arms? How can the single person of Jesus Christ possess both a full divine nature and a full human nature? Wouldn't these two natures often be at odds? For instance, was Jesus able to sin or not? Did he know the future, such as when he would return to judge the world, or not?[8] How could he grow in wisdom if, as God, he already knew everything?[9] How could the eternal God enter time?

These questions, good ones all, are signs that we are approaching the boundary between God and his creation. Because we inhabit the lower, creaturely level of this dualism, there should be many such questions that we can't begin to answer. They may be entertaining brainteasers, appropriately aimed at the poor fellow fielding questions from his ordination council, but in the end we have to admit that we just don't know. That's okay, for the same ontological distinction between God and creation that prevents us from knowing the answers also informs us where the answers lie and why we can't know them. The answers lie with God, and we can't know them because we're not him.

The remainder of this book uses God's special revelation—the Bible—to develop the fundamental perspectives of the Christian worldview. We will pursue every facet of our worldview as far as Scripture takes us, but no farther. There will be times, perhaps often, when the mystery surrounding our topic will force us to leave a question open. Don't be disturbed when this happens, figuring that surely an author with more brains or guts would come up with something. Rather, remember the chasm that exists between us and our Creator, and accept the mystery as evidence that we are right on track.

3

Where Are We?

GENESIS 1

God saw all that he had made, and it was very good.

GENESIS 1:31

I gravitate to Christian bookstores the way retirees flock to Florida. Especially here in Grand Rapids, home to several Christian publishers, I have spent hundreds of hours and many more dollars browsing through their informative books and inspiring music. Christian bookstores provide an invaluable service to the body of Christ, and I am a frequent and satisfied customer.

Still, I wonder whether some of their wares are entirely necessary. The retailer in my neighborhood has stocked its shelves with Christian picture frames, paperweights, appointment books, business card holders, jewelry boxes, key chains, candles, mugs, spill-proof cups, and even a complete set of china. If you can imagine it, someone has stamped a Bible verse on it and is selling it to well-meaning believers who think owning Christian things is a terrific way to express their faith.

An entire corner of the store is devoted to Christian clothing. Over there you can find Christian T-shirts and ties that announce the wearer to be either "Cross-training," "Cross-eyed," or a patron of "Abread-crumb & Fish" (think Abercrombie & Fitch). Against the other wall is a collection of Christian toys and games. There you can purchase Christian playing cards, race cars, and a doll that recites the Lord's Prayer when its hands are pressed together. Next to that is the full armor of God, which, complete with plastic sword, shield, and helmet, claims to instill the character of Ephesians 6 into young combatants.

Nearby is the Christian spin-off of Monopoly. Bibleopoly looks like the real game, except that instead of trying to snap up properties so you can build hotels and drive your competitors out of business, the object is to be the first person to purchase the bricks and steeple needed to build a church. Chance cards are replaced with Faith and Contingency cards, and instead of going to jail, unfortunate players are sent to meditation. Of course, the secular streets on the real Monopoly board have been replaced by biblical towns, with sites connected with Jesus' life—Nazareth, Bethlehem, and Jerusalem—occupying the higher rent districts. ("Rent" is not the right word here because players who land on their opponent's space are required to pay offerings). The game ends when one of the players obtains a steeple and, with the other players joining him in celebration, selects a name and holds a grand opening for his new church.

Perhaps most troubling are the packs of Testamints, those little pieces of white candy that come emblazoned with gold crosses. The display announces that these Christian breath mints provide two benefits. First, they may be a means of evangelism, for the person who gratefully accepts the mint may inquire about the cross on its cover. Second, should you find no takers for your free mint, this Christian candy is still useful for your own spiritual encouragement. Apparently just knowing that the mint in your mouth is emblazoned with a golden cross will draw you closer to Jesus in a way that a regular Certs never could.

It's tempting to dismiss this galaxy of Christian merchandise as just another example of niche marketing in America's vast capitalistic system. Just as there are specialty shops for woodworkers, birdwatchers, and big and tall people, so there should be stores that supply specific products to Christians. I'm not questioning the need for Christian retailers, for we certainly need access to Bibles, books, and quality Christian music. However, I am wondering whether some of what is sold there does more harm than good.

Though well-intentioned, Christians who buy such sanctified trinkets seem misinformed. If they possessed a fuller understanding of the Christian worldview—in this case a healthier appreciation for the world God has made—the market for this Christian paraphernalia would appropriately decline. As we will learn in this chapter, purchasing Christianized candy, clothes, toys, and games is not only a questionable use of money, but, on a deeper level, may also be an indication of bad theology.

Start at the Beginning

In chapters 1 and 2 we explained the structure of worldviews and the ontological distinction between God and creation, both of which remind us of our dependence on God's revelation. Now we come to the heart of the book, looking at the content of this divine revelation in order to articulate the central elements of the Christian worldview.

As we begin, the first thing we notice is that God's self-disclosure in Scripture is not some abstract outline to be memorized but is instead a wonderfully engaging story to be savored and enjoyed. Specifically, the biblical story occurs in three major movements: Creation, Fall, and Redemption. Genesis 1–2 records the creation of the world, Genesis 3–11 recounts the fall of Adam and the subsequent collapse of the world into sin, and the rest of Scripture explains God's redemptive solution to the mess that people have made of this world.

Although this largest portion of Scripture, Genesis 12 through Revelation 22, addresses the final act of redemption, it presupposes that its readers understand the opening acts of creation and fall. Indeed, we cannot begin to comprehend redemption until we first understand the damaged creation that the gospel intends to repair. Like any good story, miss the earlier plot development and the ending will make little sense.

Have you ever walked in on the closing scene of a movie? You watch the final car chase, shoot-out, or climactic kiss, but it doesn't mean much to you. Why? Because you didn't see the scenes that led up to the final smooch. Yet your wife, who has just lived through the near misses and desperate longings of the lonely lovers, is working through her second box of Kleenex. The kiss means so much more to her because she watched the entire movie. Granted, some of us guys could watch the entire chick flick and still not get it, but in general what I'm saying is true. Miss the earlier plot development of a story and you have little chance to understand its ending.

To use another analogy, think of the story of creation as the theological foundation for our Christian worldview. If you have ever suffered through foundation problems in your home, or have known someone who has, you know that few sounds keep one awake at night like the creaks and groans from a faulty foundation. It begins as a barely noticeable crack in the basement wall, then it slowly widens, sending its jagged fingers zigzagging across the lower reaches of your home. Although a casual visitor might not notice anything amiss, you know that if you don't soon take drastic, costly measures, you could lose your home.

Likewise, it is good for us every now and then to revisit our theological footer and check for cracks in our doctrine of creation. Even small problems there, if left unattended, will cause exponentially larger difficulties upstairs, in our understanding of the fall and redemption. In short, to the extent that we misunderstand the story of creation we will also be confused about the gospel.[1]

Starting on the Wrong Foot

The early church was well aware of this risk, for its largest challenge came from a religious group whose misconception of creation led them to also misconstrue sin and salvation. This group, called the Gnostics, essentially reinterpreted the teachings of Christ through the lens of their Greek philosophy. Their subsequent worldview made great inroads into the church, attracting so many new believers that it was an open question whether the nascent Christian faith would even survive.

The Gnostics were an eclectic bunch, borrowing shamelessly from Christianity, Judaism, and Greek philosophy. While various Gnostic teachers believed different things, they all viewed the material world with suspicion. They declared that the one true God is too high and pure to be contaminated by our lower, physical reality. Indeed, it besmirches his character to say that he is the Creator. Thus, when Gnostics read the Old Testament, they concluded that the God presented there must be an inferior god. He not only created the physical world but also claimed to possess physical characteristics such as hands, eyes, and hind parts. Such a material being could not be the one, true, high God.

The Gnostics' suspicion of the material world led them to fuse the first two movements of the biblical story, creation and fall, into a single event. They typically explained creation by saying that once upon a time a dissatisfied spiritual aeon refused its place among the harmonious aeons and fell, creating the material world. This aeon then sprinkled the earth with sparks of divinity, or souls, which became immersed in matter. Since people are essentially divine souls trapped within evil bodies, the goal of life is eventually to escape from our physical bodies and rejoin the high God in the heavens. Each soul can accomplish this only as it disdains its body by depriving its physical appetites and learns the *gnosis*, the secret knowledge that shows the path to liberation.

The Gnostics who most threatened the survival of the church were those who claimed that Jesus Christ was sent by the high God to earth to teach this divine *gnosis*. They didn't believe that Jesus was fully God and fully human, for the one true God cannot become entangled with matter. Many of these "Christian" Gnostics leaned toward the heresy of Docetism, claiming that Jesus was merely a divine phantom that only seemed to be human. Others suggested that the divine Spirit of Christ entered the human Jesus after his birth and departed from him just before his crucifixion. In this manner they thought they could protect God from contamination with matter and the pain and suffering that so often accompanies it. Either way, the Gnostics were quite sure that Jesus was not both divine and human.

Nevertheless, the Gnostics believed that Jesus was God's messenger. If a person denied his bodily desires and listened to Jesus' secret knowledge, then at death his enlightened soul would eventually escape the prison of this physical world and return to its true home in the heavens. Here is how one fourth-century Gnostic text depicts the secret knowledge that Jesus relayed to his disciples. Its magical formula, guaranteed to elude the heavenly beings who blocked the soul's ascent to God, consisted of various geometric shapes, numbers (such as 1119), names (such as Zozeze), and incantations (such as "Retreat Yaldabaoth and Choucho, archons of the third aeons, for I invoke Zozezaz Zaozoz Chozoz"), all of which must be signed and said at the appropriate moments to complete the journey.[2]

Correcting Gnosticism's False Start

While Gnosticism seems like some far-out, ancient version of New Age philosophy, it posed quite a threat to the New Testament church. Recognizing that the gospel itself was at stake, the apostle Paul firmly rejected it. At least twice in sacred Scripture he takes straight aim at incipient Gnosticism and its heretical view of creation. For instance, he gave this advice to a young pastor:

The Spirit clearly says that in later times some will abandon the faith and follow deceiving spirits and things taught by demons. Such teachings come through hypocritical liars, whose consciences have been seared as with a hot iron. They forbid people to marry and order them to abstain from certain foods, which God created to be received with thanksgiving by those who believe and who know the truth. *For everything God created is good, and nothing is to be rejected if it is received with thanksgiving*, because it is consecrated by the word of God and prayer.[3]

Paul declares that what seems on the surface to be a great act of piety, depriving the body so the spirit is free to contemplate higher realities, is actually demonic. This is not authentic spirituality, for true godliness will respect and appreciate all the works of God, including this physical world that he has made. Therefore Paul encourages Timothy to celebrate creation, reminding him that as "a good minister of Christ Jesus" he should "point these things out to the brothers."[4] Faithful pastors will remind their people to enjoy, not run from, creation.

Or consider Colossians 2:8. There Paul warns the church to "see to it that no one takes you captive through hollow and deceptive philosophy, which depends on human tradition and the basic principles of this world rather than on Christ." At the end of the chapter he explains what these "basic principles" are:

> Since you died with Christ to the basic principles of this world, why, as though you still belonged to it, do you submit to its rules: "Do not handle! Do not taste! Do not touch!"? These are all destined to perish with use, because they are based on human commands and teachings. Such regulations indeed have an appearance of wisdom, with their self-imposed worship, their false humility and their harsh treatment of the body, but they lack any value in restraining sensual indulgence.[5]

Again, the Gnostic lifestyle appears to be eminently pious. What could be more spiritual than suppressing physical appetites in order to meditate on heavenly things? But Paul refuses to be fooled by appearances. He observes that these Gnostic rules and regulations have never helped anyone become more righteous. Only Jesus Christ, not self-imposed duties, can restrain our evil lusts. And as Paul hinted to the Colossians in an earlier chapter, Jesus Christ will never lead his followers to denigrate creation, for he himself is the Creator. In Paul's words, "For by him [Jesus] all things were created: things in heaven and on earth, visible and invisible, whether thrones or powers or rulers or authorities; all things were created by him and for him."[6] Because Jesus Christ is the Creator of this physical world, his followers must celebrate, not condemn, creation.

Here is the point: Paul, perhaps the greatest missionary ever, devoted his entire life to preaching the gospel. His passion for the promise of redemption is unmatched in the history of the church. Yet it was this very commitment to the gospel that prompted him twice to take time in sacred Scripture to correct the Gnostic view of creation. Paul knew that any cracks left in one's theological foundation would fester and widen into huge fissures in the upper story of redemption. Paul was committed to the gospel, but he knew that the gospel only makes sense within the context of creation. If his listeners were wrong there, they didn't stand a chance to understand the gospel.

Here's why: As we will learn in chapter 11, the gospel story of redemption represents God's restoration of creation. God refuses to allow our fall to ultimately destroy his good creation, and he graciously comes to earth to put away sin and restore the world to its original goodness. To understand this work of restoration correctly, we must first properly distinguish between the original creation and its fall. If we confuse these initial movements of the biblical story, we will undoubtedly misunderstand what redemption intends to restore. We will think that redemption intends to correct what doesn't need fixing, and we will overlook the obvious problems crying out for resolution.

In the case of Gnosticism, its belief that our created bodies belong to the fall led it to long for deliverance from this material world and ignore the deeper issue of our sin against God. Thus its confusion of the fall with creation completely altered its understanding of redemption. To prevent this from happening with his audience, Paul went out of his way to lay the proper, biblical foundation of creation. He knew that if his listeners started with a Gnostic attitude toward creation, they would never understand the gospel he was proclaiming.

Not only Paul, but also the apostle John firmly rejected Gnosticism as heresy. John's number one opponent was Cerinthus, a Gnostic teacher who believed that the divine Christ had entered the human Jesus after his birth and departed before his crucifixion. In this way the high God was kept free from the pains and weaknesses of the flesh. John recognized that Cerinthus's position struck against the fullness of the incarnation, so he responded to his enemy in John 1:14. Speaking of Jesus, John wrote that "the Word became flesh and made his dwelling among us."[7]

The Word became flesh. Have you ever read the Christmas story as an affirmation of creation? That is precisely how John saw it. The Son of God not only created this physical world but also chose to become part of it. God himself has acquired a physical body. There is no stronger way to say that matter is good. How dare we suggest that the material world is somehow evil or beneath us? If matter is good enough for God, then whether we know it or not, it is plenty good for us.

Not only Paul and John, but also the Apostles' Creed, the church's first and most foundational statement of faith, specifically targeted Gnosticism's low view of creation. This important declaration of faith, accepted by all Christian churches, arose from the early church's baptismal creeds. Each church in this formative period required new converts to recite its statement of faith before receiving baptism and joining its fellowship. Since Gnosticism was the largest threat to the early church's survival, the leaders of the church carefully inserted statements into their baptismal creeds to weed out the heretics. To prevent any Gnostic from joining their assembly, they consciously wrote confessions of faith no Gnostic could stomach.

For instance, no Gnostic would ever declare, "I believe in God the Father Almighty, Maker of heaven and earth," for they believed that the high God could not contaminate himself with matter. For the same reason they would also choke on these words: "I believe in Jesus Christ, his only Son our Lord, who was . . . born of the virgin Mary, . . . suffered . . . , was crucified, died, and was buried . . . and rose again from the dead." These statements imply either that God has joined the physical world or that he has suffered because of this union. Because Gnostics considered both assertions to be blasphemy, they could not sign on to this creed and receive baptism into the church.[8]

Thanks to these early baptismal creeds, every Christian knew that those who held a lower, Gnostic view of creation were excluded from the life of the church. They were heretics on the most fundamental point, for they tripped over the creed's opening line, "I believe in God the Father Almighty, Maker of heaven and earth." They could never become baptized members of the Christian faith, for their misinterpretation of creation distorted their understanding of sin and salvation in Christ. The early church knew what many contemporary evangelicals have apparently forgotten: If we're wrong about creation, we don't stand a chance to ever understand the gospel.

One More Time, from the Top

We find the correct view of creation in Genesis 1. There we read that God, the toughest critic imaginable, announced no less than seven times that his work of creation was "good." Finally, when he was all done, God stepped back and smiled approvingly at the world he had just created. Where before there had been nothing but a void, now there was a fragrant, colorful world pulsating with life. God looked at it from the side, from the back, from all possible angles and decided that he wouldn't change a thing. "It's good," he said. "It's very good."[9]

I'm not sure that we always believe him. Although the Gnostic story of dissatisfied spiritual aeons and magical incantations eventually proved too incredible for popular belief, there remains an element of Gnostic thought that the church has never completely shaken off. We might not believe their story, but like the Gnostics, we often are far too suspicious of this material world.

Granted, the fall has occurred, so we now live in a broken world. But the fall, no matter how perverse, is not strong enough to squeeze out all of the good in God's creation. This world is certainly evil, but it is not completely evil. We must never take our sin more seriously than we take the goodness of God's creation. God's actions always outweigh our own. Nothing that puny people ever do can overthrow anything that God does. Almighty God created the world good, to a great extent it remains good, and one day soon God will restore it to its original created goodness, a goodness that it will never lose—ever. As the classic hymn proclaims,

> This is my Father's world—
> O let me ne'er forget
> That *though the wrong seems oft so strong,*
> *God is the Ruler yet.*
>
> This is my Father's world!
> The battle is not done;
> Jesus who died shall be satisfied,
> And earth and heav'n be one.

While many churches still sing this hymn of praise for creation, we unfortunately sing other songs that seem to disparage this material world as if it, not sin, were our problem. For instance, we sometimes sing that "all this world's empty pleasures will soon pass away." Not true. All this world's sinful pleasures will pass away, but most of this world's pleasures aren't empty. And why would we think they are? God created this world for us to enjoy, and he himself announced that he did a pretty good job. We do him no favors when we insist on proclaiming how empty this life is.

Not only our songs but also many of our sermons put down creation. Well-meaning preachers warn us not to get too attached to this world—which will all burn up anyhow—but to invest our time and money in the only thing that matters: saving souls. As one pastor put it, it may not be quite a sin to golf, fish, garden, live in a house, or hold a job, but if we really want to serve God, then we will use most of our time to pursue "spiritual values." After all, Matthew 6:33 says to "seek first" the kingdom of God, and it's hard to do that when you're fishing or planting tomatoes.

Can you see how many inroads Gnostic attitudes have made into evangelical churches? If this physical world is the problem, then what is the solution? To get out of this place, just as the Gnostics believed. But if the problem is not this earth but our sin, then the solution is to remain engaged in the world, leading fully human lives as we follow the perfect human, Jesus Christ, who came to this world to cross out our sin and save the planet.

Rightly Dividing the Word of Truth

The Gnostic suspicions that we bring to Scripture often prevent us from reading it correctly. For example, consider 1 John 2:15, which instructs us to "not love the world or anything in the world. If anyone loves the world, the love of the Father is not in him." Many people who read this too easily assume that by "world" John means the joys and attractions of our physical environment. Thus they think that John is warning us against becoming too attached to material things. He wants us to turn our backs on the charms and cares of this physical existence and long for the Father, who will one day whisk us away from this planet.

However, this interpretation can't possibly be correct. Remember that the apostle who is writing here is the same person who in John 1:14 went out of his way to praise creation by telling Cerinthus that God himself became flesh. Why would John turn around now and disparage this physical world? Unless we wish to conclude that John (and Holy Scripture) is contradicting himself, we must look for another definition for "world" than its obvious, physical meaning.

Fortunately, another definition is not hard to find, for John himself continues in the next verse to explain what he means by "world." He writes, "For everything in the world—the cravings of sinful man, the lust of his eyes and the boasting of what he has and does—comes not from the Father but from the world." Observe that John's three-fold description of the world—"cravings," "lust," and "boasting"—are *ethical* rather than *ontological* terms. In other words, they describe sins, not various aspects of reality. The world John is warning us about is not the universe of beautiful things, but the sinful manner in which we often respond to what attracts us (that is, we crave and lust after something and then boast about our accomplishment when we unjustly acquire it).

For example, the beauty of a young woman is a good thing, and in its appropriate, married context is intended to be maximally enjoyed by her lover. However, the same beauty that brings honor to God when celebrated within marriage can also be misused by those who lust after and ultimately seduce someone who is not their spouse. In each case the ontological beauty of the young woman remains unchanged. The difference is entirely ethical: One man marries the woman and praises God for her beauty while another sins against her and God by initiating an affair.

Likewise, John is not encouraging us to avoid the beauty of our physical, material environment—for we couldn't if we tried. As embodied human beings, we can't help but live on this physical planet, so we might as well enjoy it. John is warning us not to love the sin that is so prevalent in this world of fallen people. Surrounded by sinners who selfishly abuse God's created goodness and then boast about their exploits, we must determine to obey God and thus fully enjoy the creation as he intended. Our problem is sin, not matter; sin, not stuff.

Or consider Colossians 3:2, which instructs believers to "set your minds on things above, not on earthly things." At first glance, this seems to obviously implore Christians to put aside their physical cares and concentrate solely on more "spiritual," otherworldly realities. No doubt this passage has inspired many well-intentioned preachers to urge their congregations to disregard this temporary, material world and live solely for heavenly rewards that last forever. Some involvement in this world is inevitable, for we all need to secure food and shelter. However, the deeply spiritual among us will secure these necessities as quickly as possible so we can turn our attention to eternal, heavenly matters.

While this is a popular interpretation of this passage, on second glance it seems highly unlikely. As we observed earlier in this chapter, the verses immediately preceding Colossians 3:1–2 refute the errors of Gnosticism. If Paul concludes chapter 2 by protecting the goodness of creation, why would he begin chapter 3 by commanding Christians to put aside this physical world? Unless Paul is contradicting himself in adjacent paragraphs, we must locate a different meaning for "things above" and "earthly things" than a straightforward, ontological definition.

Fortunately, a different definition is not far away. Immediately after instructing the Colossians to set aside "earthly things," Paul explains what he means by that term. He writes,

> Put to death, therefore, whatever belongs to your earthly nature: sexual immorality, impurity, lust, evil desires and greed, which is idolatry. Because of these, the wrath of God is coming. You used to walk in these ways, in the life you once lived. But now you must rid yourselves of all such things as these: anger, rage, malice, slander, and filthy language from your lips. Do not lie to each other, since you have taken off your old self with its practices and have put on the new self, which is being renewed in knowledge in the image of its Creator.[10]

Just as we observed with John's description of "world," so we see here that Paul is using "earthly things" as an ethical rather than an ontological category. The elements he includes—immorality, impurity, lust, evil desires, greed, anger, rage, malice, slander, filthy language, and deceit—have one thing in common: They are all sins. None of these words suggests that we should avoid earthly things simply because they are earthly. Instead, we are to avoid the debauchery that sinful people on earth frequently commit. It is this sinful activity, not the earth itself, that we are to set aside.

If "earthly things" denotes an ethical rather than ontological category, it should be no surprise to find that Paul uses "things above" in the same way. Immediately after instructing the Colossians to put to death the sins that belong to their "earthly nature," he urges them to put on their "new self," which is marked by the "things above." Paul writes,

> Therefore, as God's chosen people, holy and dearly loved, clothe yourselves with compassion, kindness, humility, gentleness and patience. Bear with each other and forgive whatever grievances you may have against one another. Forgive as the Lord forgave you. And over all these virtues put on love, which binds them all together in perfect unity.
>
> Let the peace of Christ rule in your hearts, since as members of one body you were called to peace. And be thankful. Let the word of Christ dwell in you richly as you teach and admonish one another with all wisdom, and as you sing psalms, hymns and spiritual songs with gratitude in your hearts to God. And whatever you do, whether in word or deed, do it all in the name of the Lord Jesus, giving thanks to God the Father through him.[11]

Notice that none of the terms in Paul's list of "things above"—compassion, kindness, etc.—implies lifting our eyes from the distractions of this physical world. Rather, they all represent Christian virtues that we can and must exercise amid our life in this world.[12]

So despite our first impression, Paul is not advising the Colossians to meditate on ethereal, "spiritual" realities. Instead, he is strongly urging them to stay involved in this planet, modeling such godly lives that they bring at least a corner of Christ's heavenly kingdom to earth.

This is why he concludes by imploring them to conduct their entire earthly lives for the honor and glory of God. As we will learn in subsequent chapters, "whatever you do, whether in word or deed" is broad enough to include every aspect of our existence, not merely the particularly spiritual or religious activities we readily associate with the Christian life.

Here is the point: When reading Scripture, we must continually ask ourselves whether the author is speaking ontologically or ethically. As we saw in 1 John 2 and Colossians 3, the context of the passage in question will always yield important clues. If we confuse ontology with morality, as many readers do when they interpret these passages, we will never be able to understand our Bible or even life itself.

For instance, those who take "world" in 1 John 2:15 and "earthly things" in Colossians 3:2 in an ontological sense will mistakenly think that their main problem is their physical environment. So in Gnostic fashion they will continually strive to rise above the material world and meditate on "spiritual" things. In time they may turn themselves into pretty good angels, but they will also become a sorry excuse for human beings.

By contrast, if we rightly understand that John and Paul are speaking in ethical categories, then we can freely celebrate every aspect of our humanity, including its extremely important physical side. We will recognize that God does not want us to rise above our humanity and join the angelic host, but calls us to follow the perfect human, Jesus Christ, who, as far as we can tell, still inhabits a physical body. So rather than run from creation (which would be sin), we will run from sin as we stay plugged into creation. We will recognize that the goal of life is to become fully human (living each day without sin), not superhuman (living each day without any provision for our physical needs). In short, we will learn the liberating truth that the story of creation frees us to be ourselves, the very people our Father created us to be.

This Is (Still) My Father's World

What specifically does this mean for us? Simply this: Because we know that this creation is the good gift of God, we are not only permitted but encouraged to enjoy it *as is.* Unlike those who think that worldly objects are somehow enhanced by stamping Scripture verses on them, Christians who understand the goodness of this world celebrate the freedom to enjoy God's creation *as is.* We no longer need to sanitize secular items with our sanctified slogans to make them suitable for Christian consumption. As children of the heavenly Father, we refuse to relinquish our right to enjoy his creation *as is.* We concede that we now live in a fallen creation, but despite the sin that is present here, this place remains our Father's world. As such, he expects us to enjoy it *as is.*

Our children seem to naturally understand this. I love to watch my children play—to see their eyes light up as they shoot down a slide, overcome with the sheer joy of being alive. We honor God when we bring that same enthusiasm to every corner of creation. For example, take nature. I understand that we all have different temperaments and that some people are happier indoors than out. But the point remains the same: No one should enjoy the outdoors as much as a Christian. We know that nature comes from the hand of God, and though tarnished by sin, it retains much of its created beauty. So a walk in the woods, planting a garden, a picnic in the park—these all become opportunities to enjoy and give thanks to God for his beautiful world.

Or consider the arts. Because we know that the ability to draw and paint, write and sing all belong to the goodness of God's creation, we are able to fully participate in the arts. No one should enjoy a good book, painting, or symphony like a Christian.

We can enjoy every good form of artistic expression—including bluegrass!—even when the art is not making a distinctively Christian point. It's wonderful to use the arts to creatively spread the gospel.

But the point is that even when they do not, even when a piece of art is "secular," we may still enjoy it as a vital piece of God's good creation.

I am not encouraging participation in sinful forms of artistic expression. The fall has extensively damaged creation, and in few places is that more evident than in the arts. Certainly we should avoid any music, movie, or visual art that stirs up sin, such as pride and lust. My point is only that we don't need to stamp Christianity on something before we can enjoy it. In fact, our feeble attempts at baptizing creation tend to cheapen both it and the gospel.

Printing "cross-training" or "cross-eyed" on a T-shirt trivializes both the cross (do we really want to compare Jesus' suffering to a type of exercise or astigmatism?) and ordinary T-shirts (which are perhaps not as good as those with religious slogans). The same holds true for spill-proof cups emblazoned with John 4:14—"whoever drinks the water I give him will never thirst"; key chains that parody milk advertisements with the probing question "Got Jesus?"; dinner plates that claim to be "Home Grown and Heaven Bound"; and stuffed ducks wearing rain gear on account of recurring "Showers of Blessing" (honestly, I could not make this stuff up). Rather than improve creation, such silliness only distracts from the goodness that is already there while mocking the gospel it seeks to advertise.

Many preachers make a comfortable living warning people to give up certain pleasures because God says they're wrong. While that message certainly has its appropriate place in view of the fall, the opening movement of the biblical story conveys an equally important counterbalance. Enjoy creation! Our first responsibility as humans is to find pleasure in our Father's world.

When I go home for Christmas, I often spend whole days in my father's wood shop, marveling at how quickly a rough piece of lumber can be transformed into an artistically crafted shelf or picture frame. It is therapeutic—not just because it is a break from my normal job, but also because I am working with God's creation.

Where are the places you connect with God's creation? It may be sinking your fingers into a mound of topsoil, jogging down a tree-lined avenue, or plopping a lure into some promising weeds at water's edge. Wherever and whenever it happens for you, take a moment to thank God for his beautiful creation. Thank him for putting you here. Enjoy, celebrate, and, yes, even indulge in this, your Father's world.

4

Who Are We?

GENESIS 1 – 2

So God created man in his own image,
in the image of God he created him;
male and female he created them.

GENESIS 1:27

P lastic would be fine." I cringed slightly and turned away as I said it. I hoped that she hadn't noticed—I certainly didn't mean to be rude, but it was just too painful to look her in the face. My cashier looked like a page from *National Geographic*. She was sporting various rings in what appeared to be the most uncomfortable places: in her nose, on her eyebrow, and all the way up her ear. She may have had one on her tongue—I didn't have the heart to look again and find out.

If I had overcome my waves of sympathetic pain and hung around to speak with her, I suspect she might have offered several reasons for her impressive collection of jewelry. Perhaps she thinks they look nice and most of her friends are wearing them. If pressed, she might concede that they are a means of gaining attention, to stand apart from the crowd and be noticed. Perhaps it's a way to rebel against her parents—the fact that her mother absolutely detests her nose ring is half the fun. But most of all, though I'm unsure whether she would agree with me, I secretly wonder if all this facial piercing isn't just another stage in her quest to find herself. She just doesn't know who she is anymore.

No wonder! When it comes to their identity, today's young people are besieged with a barrage of conflicting messages. On the one hand, our culture wants men to be aggressive and athletic and women to be sexy and slim. But these ideals are so completely unattainable for most of us that we can only hope to reach them by cheating—usually through steroids for the guys and eating disorders for the girls.

Even worse, just as we're wracking our bodies to approach the Western ideal, our culture warns us not to give in to its stereotypes. Rather than become a dominating force that demands attention, wouldn't it be great if our guys could be soft and a tad mushy—more like Hugh Grant and less like Sylvester Stallone? So we encourage men to embrace their emotions, celebrate stay-at-home dads, and generally cultivate their feminine side. Likewise, rather than become beautiful playthings for their macho men, wouldn't it be wonderful if our girls could break through the glass ceiling and occupy leadership roles? So we encourage our girls to go out for sports, celebrate "Take Your Daughter to Work Day," and generally cultivate their masculine side.

And just in case anyone should doubt whether they have the strength to satisfy these conflicting cultural demands, we reassure them that the indomitable human spirit is able to achieve most anything it desires. We tell them to aim high, dream big, and attempt the impossible. As long as they think positive thoughts, they can become whatever they choose to be. As a popular song explains, "When it seems that hope is gone, / look inside you and be strong, / and you'll finally see the truth, / that a hero lies in you."[1] So up with people!

But then these fired-up souls attend science class, where they learn that they are merely the product of chance mutations that stretch across eons of years. There is no God. Everything, including themselves, can be entirely explained by a series of physical cause and effects. So their indomitable human spirit, their unique personality, even the passion they bring to life are merely the product of chemical reactions going off inside their brain. There really is nothing that ultimately distinguishes them from their pet, a tree, or even the chair they're sitting in. Everything is material, and all matter is equal.

So what does it mean to be human? According to our culture, not much. We may be the most highly advanced members of the food chain, but in the end we're still only part of the chain. We live, we die, we return to dust. Where is the meaning in that? Given what many young people understand themselves to be, we shouldn't be surprised that some behave outrageously. If they acted consistently on what they're told is the utter futility of being human, they would probably attempt to end their lives. Perhaps the reason they don't is because deep down they know better than to believe what our culture tells them. They may not know how or why, but there is something special about being human, isn't there?

The Climax of Creation

The previous chapter began our study of creation with this important point: Creation is good. We must never nod toward the Gnostic mistake that this physical world is somehow evil or beneath us. This world is a beautiful place in which to live. It was very good when it left God's hand, it remains good despite our sin, and it will one day soon be restored to its original goodness. We may enjoy and celebrate this good creation because, despite our sin, it remains "our Father's world."

This chapter examines the most important part of this good creation, at least from our perspective, as it explores what it means to be human. Indeed, the Genesis account gives us reason to think that God himself considers us to be his most important creatures. First, as we'll see, it is extremely significant that of all God's creatures, we alone are said to bear the image of our Creator. Second, it's probably not mere happenstance that God created us last. As John Calvin observes, it's as though God prepared a hospitable world just for us to inhabit and enjoy.[2]

Finally, even from a literary point of view it's easy to spot the significance that the author of Genesis 1 gives to humanity, for the narrative of creation screeches to a halt in verse 26. The previous days of creation rapidly record God's work. For example, Genesis 1:3–5 quickly tell us that God spoke light into existence and called it "good." But when the story of creation begins to describe humanity, it slows way down—as if the author wants his readers to reflect on the wonder of their creation. Listen carefully to the first recorded words that God ever spoke about us:

> Then God said: "Let us make man in our image, in our likeness, and let them rule over the fish of the sea and the birds of the air, over the livestock, over all the earth, and over all the creatures that move along the ground." So God created man in his own image, in the image of God he created him; male and female he created them. God blessed them and said to them, "Be fruitful and increase in number; fill the earth and subdue it. Rule over the fish of the sea and the birds of the air and over every living creature that moves on the ground."[3]

The Humility of Being Human

Genesis 1 and 2 paint a colorful and intriguing picture about what it means to be human. As we discuss the various aspects, it may help to frame our portrait of humanity with these two thoughts: humility and honor. Because we are created in the image of God, we have value and significance that far surpass all other creatures. However, before we take ourselves too seriously, we should remember where we come from.

Genesis 2:7 describes our creation in these words: "The LORD God formed the man from the dust of the ground and breathed into his nostrils the breath of life, and the man became a living being." An intriguing element of this verse is the striking similarity between the Hebrew term for man, *'ādām*, and the word for ground, *'ādāmâ*. God wants us to remember where we came from, so he uses a similar word for us and the ground. The *'ādām* comes from the *'ādāmâ*. Every time Adam heard God call his name ("Hey, dustboy, dirtbag"?), he would remember that he's nothing but well-designed dirt. It's actually worse than that. Not only are we made from dirt, but scientists tell us that our bodies are 60 percent water. We are dirt and water thrown together: one big pile of mud!

The point is that there is a vital connection between us and the ground. There is a connection physically because we are made from dust. But there is an even more important theological connection. Ever wonder why God cursed the ground rather than Adam after Adam sinned?[4] Or why is there so much pain in God's voice when he cried out to Cain, "What have you done? Listen! Your brother's blood cries out to me from the ground"?[5] The same dust that had produced Abel was now drinking up the blood from his untimely end. This is not the way it's supposed to be.

Ever wonder why, when God becomes so fed up with the sinfulness of people that he regrets ever making them, he decides to destroy not just people but the entire earth with a flood?[6] Or why, when God renews his blessing with Noah's family, he doesn't limit his blessing to just people but also includes the animal kingdom and even the earth itself?[7]

We're Already Home

There is a physical and theological connection between us and the ground. The lot of the earth is thrown in with us. As we go, so goes the earth. With this in mind, perhaps you can begin to accept the biblical truth—startling to some—that we belong on this planet. In short, we are earthlings. We were made to live here. This world is our home.

For too long, many evangelical Christians have mistakenly believed that the goal of life is to escape the bounds of earth. (Shades of Gnosticism?) It began early for most of us. Our first memories of Sunday school likely include the song, "Somewhere in outer space, God has prepared a place, for those who trust him and obey." The chorus consisted of a rocket countdown from ten to blastoff, at which point we gleefully jumped into the air in mock simulation of the future launch we were encouraged to expect.

As we grew older, it was only natural that our favorite songs would include "This world is not my home, I'm just a-passin' through" and "I'll fly away," the latter speaking of our departure "like a bird from prison bars has flown." Our Father's world is now a prison? The world that God prepared for us is not where we belong, but is merely a rest stop on the way to a better place? In light of what we learned in the previous chapter, I hope you can see why these well-intentioned songs are more Gnostic than Christian.

The plain truth of Genesis 1 and 2 is that we were made to populate the earth. As we have observed, we who are the children of God may rightly anticipate joining our loved ones in heaven when this life is over. However, nowhere does Scripture hold out heaven as our ultimate goal. Instead, it informs us that heaven is merely the first leg of a journey that is round-trip. The Christian hope is not that someday we get to join our Christian friends and family in the presence of God, but that God will bring our loved ones with him when he returns to live with us on planet earth. In short, we earthlings were made to live here—on this planet. This is where we belong. We're already home.

Of course, there is a sense in which this world is not our home. Paul proclaims that "our citizenship is in heaven," and Peter reminds us that we are "aliens and strangers in the world."[8] But here again, as we have noted, we will never properly understand these statements unless we discover whether Paul and Peter are speaking in *ontological* or *ethical* categories. In other words, are they asserting that this world is a foreign place in some physical, substantive sense or simply because its sinful, rebellious spirit prevents our righteous character from feeling at home here? It seems that both have in mind the latter, for in those same passages Paul contrasts his heavenly citizenship with sinners who live as *enemies of the cross* of Christ, and Peter immediately urges his fellow "aliens and strangers" to "abstain from *sinful desires*"—both of which are ethical, not ontological, concepts.[9]

So we may conclude that this world is not our home, but only if we're speaking in an ethical rather than ontological sense. *Ethically*, the righteous children of God should never feel comfortable in this world of sin. The daily news reports of robbery, rape, murder, and their consequent cover-ups should remind us to cry out, as Christ taught us, for God's heavenly kingdom of righteousness to come quickly to this earth. However, no matter how evil this world becomes, we must never forget that *ontologically* we belong here. We were made from the earth so that we might live here forever. In this ontological, though not ethical sense, we're already home.

The Honor of Being Human

So that's the humility of being human. We were made from the dust of the ground, so regardless how wealthy or successful, how beautiful or glamorous we become, we must remember that we are never more than highly cultured clods of dirt. The upside, the honor of being human, should utterly shock us. Imagine! God takes clumps of clay, fashions them into a human being, and then claims that this erect statue of earth is in his divine image. But that's precisely what the story says: "So God created man in his own image, in the image of God he created him; male and female he created them."[10]

According to Scripture, it is this *imago Dei* alone that separates humanity from the animals. Our souls don't make us superior to the animals, for as anyone with a loyal dog can attest, animals also seem to possess an immaterial nature (for example, my poodle wags her tail and barks excitedly when I come home because on some deep level she is genuinely excited to see me). True enough, unlike my poodle, whose afterlife is never addressed in Scripture, I know that my soul will continue to live even after I die. But note that there is nothing within my soul that makes this necessary. It only continues to exist because God chooses to keep it in existence. He could just as easily keep my poodle around and annihilate me.

In sum, what separates us from the rest of creation is not some higher, divine element that we possess and they lack. As we learned in chapter 2, both we and the animals, soul and body, exist entirely on the level of creation. What elevates us above the other creatures is the simple truth that we, not they, are said to bear the image of God.

This "image of God" is a tantalizing, puzzling phrase to nail down. Every Christian theologian agrees that people are created in the image of God, but no one has been able yet to explain entirely what that means, at least to the satisfaction of all the others.[11] Nevertheless, despite some loose ends that will inevitably follow, we can still survey what the Scriptures generally mean when they declare that people bear the image of God.

Scripture informs us that the image of God, whatever it is, both remains and is lost at the fall. We know that the image remains, for its lingering presence is the reason Scripture gives for its admonitions against murdering or cursing people. Genesis 9:6 reads, "Whoever sheds the blood of man, by man shall his blood be shed; for in the image of God has God made man." At the other end of the Bible, James 3:9–10 concurs: "With the tongue we praise our Lord and Father, and with it we curse men, who have been made in God's likeness.... My brothers, this should not be."

Because even fallen people retain the image of God, we must do everything in our power to protect the value and dignity of human life, from the cradle to the grave. We must guard human life at conception, protesting the practice of abortion and actively providing support to young mothers with unwanted pregnancies. We must oppose all attempts to create human beings for the sole purpose of supplying spare parts for those who already exist, whether through the distant dream of human cloning or through the present opportunity of embryonic stem-cell research. And we should think twice before implementing the widely available reproductive technologies, both those that prevent and those that enable or enhance conception.

I am not suggesting that all reproductive technologies are wrong, but only that we should use them with great caution. We must carefully consider the practical and theological implications of any method available to us. For instance, does a particular form of birth control ever destroy a viable fetus? With regard to in vitro fertilization, is it appropriate to create an image bearer of God in a petri dish, is it moral to implant a half-dozen embryos in a womb with the assumption that only one will survive, and is it permissible to destroy or leave on ice the other fertilized eggs that are never implanted? We must take these questions seriously, for we are commanded by God to treat his image bearers responsibly.

Not surprisingly, medical ethics is hardly able to keep up with the exploding field of reproductive technology. For example, consider the up-and-coming technology of genetic engineering. Is it appropriate to change an unborn child's DNA in order to correct a cancer gene he inherited from his mother? If so, might we also tweak his genes to make him smarter, slimmer, and more handsome? If not, why not? What criteria determine which genes we may change and which ones we shouldn't? Even if we discover these criteria, how will we resist the pressure to give our child the best possible start in life, especially knowing that he will be competing against peers whose parents had no qualms about genetically enhancing their abilities?

The only reason such questions even matter is because people are created in the image of God. We would have no moral problem with altering the DNA of frogs and fish (though we might worry about unintended consequences), because neither of them bears God's image. But we must always treat humans with the greatest care, cautiously exploring the theological implications of technology before we implement it.

Regardless of how humans come into the world—genetically enhanced or entirely natural—we must continue to respect them for the image bearers they are. We should avoid movies, music, and video games that might desensitize us to violence and the great evil of wounding another human being. This wounding can be spiritual as well as physical. As James tells us, we must never gossip or slander fellow image bearers, for to do so violates their reputation and disrespects the God who made them. The same sin occurs when we indulge in lust. When scantily clad pop stars cavort across our television screens, begging us to turn them into sexual objects, we must remember that they are *imago Dei* and refuse to dehumanize them. As image bearers they deserve more respect than they apparently give themselves. All people, even fallen ones, retain the image of God and are uniquely special.

This respect for human life, originating at conception, continues throughout our lives right up to our moment of death. On the one hand, our respect for the *imago Dei* protects our right to die with dignity. We will not use extraordinary measures to keep blood flowing through bodies whose minds have stopped functioning. The quality of life matters as much as its quantity. On the other hand, we will resist euthanasia or physician-assisted suicide, for we remember that the people who die by those means still bear the image of God. As such, it is wrong to kill them for any reason, whether to ease their suffering or to avoid the expense of keeping them alive.

I recognize that this quick survey of life-and-death issues tends to oversimplify matters. Individual scenarios can raise unique concerns that may dramatically qualify the situation. Nevertheless, I believe this thumbnail sketch of medical ethics generally describes Scripture's high value on human life.

It is worth noting that many of our current abuses of modern medicine arise from the limitations of our culture's modern worldview. The same worldview that supported the development of modern science also stymies the ability of modern ethics to keep pace. If, according to that worldview, God does not exist,[12] then we cannot very well be created in his image. And if we are not created in his image, there really isn't anything uniquely special about us—we're just the top rung (so far) of the evolutionary scale. Therefore, since we readily abort, clone, and euthanize other animals, why not do the same with humans, who, though highly advanced, are only animals after all?

No. Scripture reminds us that all people, though fallen, remain uniquely special. We dare not treat any person, no matter how mentally or physically impaired, with less or even equal respect than we give to the rest of creation. That person, regardless of what she can or can't contribute to society, possesses value and dignity that far surpass all other creatures (nonhuman and perhaps angelic), for unlike them, she alone bears the image of her Creator God.

The Loss of the Image

While the image of God remains even in fallen people, Scripture also tells us that some aspect of the image has now been lost because of sin. Paul informs us that the Christian life amounts to recovering the image of God by growing into the image of the perfect human, Jesus Christ. In Colossians 3:10 Paul reminds Christians that they have already put off their old self of sin and "have put on the new self, which is being renewed in knowledge in the image of its Creator" (who, according to the next verse, is Christ). Paul says something similar in Ephesians 4:22–24, urging believers to consciously choose to "put off your old self" and "put on the new self, created to be like God in true righteousness and holiness" (this God, according to verse 20, being Jesus Christ).

Thus it seems that acquiring a new self is something that occurs at the moment of conversion *and* continues in a moment-by-moment decision for the rest of our lives. In short, we are commanded to grow into the image of Christ that we already are. We probably look a bit comical when, at our conversion, we initially put on the character of Christ. His perfect righteousness drapes rather loosely across our scrawny limbs, much like a young boy who has just been given the ill-fitting suit of his older brother. But just as that child will continue to grow into his older brother's hand-me-downs, so our Christian growth enables us increasingly to fill out the righteousness of Christ, our elder Brother. If we are diligent, in time we will become the renewed image we already possess.

The point in these passages is that the image of God, whatever it turns out to be, is lost by sin and recovered in Christ. Combined with Genesis 9:6 and James 3:9, any final description of the *imago Dei* must be able to account both for that element of the image that survives and that which is destroyed by humanity's fall into sin. In sum, the image of God in fallen humanity resembles something like a cracked mirror. If we look closely, we can still see the reflection of God in ourselves, but it is now distorted by the jagged edges of sin. We still bear the image of God, but it's not as crisp and clean as it once was.

So What Is the Image?

Since Scripture suggests that the image of God both survives and succumbs to Adam's fall into sin, how are we to understand this? A way that many have found helpful is to distinguish between *ontological* and *ethical* aspects of the image. (Are you wondering how you ever got along without this distinction?)

In general, the part of the *imago Dei* that remains in fallen humans is our ontological capacity. God has bestowed distinctively godlike capacities on people, such as our higher intellect, free will, conscience, and ability for logic and language. These capacities remain active even in fallen people, unbelievers as well as Christians, which is why Scripture suggests that the image of God survives the destruction of sin.[13]

And what part of the *imago Dei* is lost in sin and recovered by Christ? It mostly has to do with how we use our capacities (an ethical category). God has given us our godlike capacities for language and reflection so that we might enter into three distinct relationships. It is these three relationships that are damaged by sin and restored in salvation (Fig. 4.1).[14]

First, and this probably goes without saying, God created us in his image so that we might enjoy personal fellowship with him. Our higher intellects and free will enable us to freely love and obey our Creator in ways that lower-functioning mammals never can.

Second, God created us in his image so that we might enjoy personal fellowship with others. Take another look at Genesis 1:27:

> So God created man in his own *image,*
> in the *image* of God he created him;
> *male and female* he created them.

Notice that the first two statements say exactly the same thing, in reverse order, while the third line adds an explanatory tag. It replaces

Figure 4.1: The Threefold Image of God

Genesis 1:27–28	"God created man in his own image, in the image of God he created him"	"Male and female he created them"	"Be fruitful and increase in number; fill the earth and subdue it. Rule …"
This means that humans are properly related to	God	Other humans	The world
Because of this humans are	Religious beings	Social beings	Cultural beings
These aspects of human life should produce	Worship of God	Love for others	Joyful work in the world

the term "image" with the phrase "male and female." So what is the image? It is humans in relationship, particularly that between males and females. Just as each member of the divine Trinity is dynamically involved with the others, so males and females participate in the most intimate acts of fellowship. The result, according to Genesis 1:28, is that people bear fruit and multiply (that is, produce other people). This also images God, who, after all, is the Creator. In this way the act of marriage may be the closest we ever come in this life to reflecting the triune relationship of the Godhead and subsequently becoming an image of God himself.[15]

Third, God created us in His image so that we might enjoy a right relationship with the rest of creation. In Genesis 1:28 God commands Adam to "be fruitful," "increase in number," and "fill the earth." While these responsibilities are duties that people share with the animals (Genesis 1:22), two additional commands—to "subdue" and "rule over" the earth—are unique to humans.

What does it mean to image God by subduing and ruling over the earth? In the Ancient Near East, where Genesis was written, kings often erected statues of themselves in far-flung corners of their empires. These statues were intended to represent the king in his absence. In a sense, they were to rule the region on his behalf.

This practice continues in some places today. For instance, many cities in China have a statue of Mao Zedong near their town square. This statue represents the power of the government in Beijing. Regardless of how the Chinese people feel about their government in general or Chairman Mao in particular, they honor the statue. They know that it's not just a statue, for to disrespect the statue—say, by placing the flag of Taiwan in its hand—is to disrespect the government, which bears consequences. In short, just as a king or government might leave a replica of himself behind to rule in his stead, so God the Creator has left us, made in his image, to rule the earth on his behalf. We successfully image God when we prudently care for the world he has entrusted to us.

To summarize, God intends people to use their godlike capacities in three ethical functions, or relationships. Thus, to be human is to be in proper relation with God, other people, and the world. Sin has marred and well-nigh destroyed these relationships, but in Christ, the perfect human, they are restored.

Through his work on the cross Christ removes our sin and guilt and so repairs our relationship with our heavenly Father. Now we can once again commune with him, reflecting the divine fellowship that exists among the Father, Son, and Holy Spirit. Furthermore, the cross also repairs our relationship with each other. According to Paul, this is what it means to be the church—diverse people with not much in common except their love for the Lord Jesus Christ. Now "there is neither Jew nor Greek, slave nor free, male nor female, for you are all one in Christ Jesus."[16] Finally, Christ died on the cross to restore our relationship to his world. Where previously we had carelessly misused his creation, now we may responsibly rule this planet on our Father's behalf.

In brief, each of these three relationships is restored as we increasingly grow into the image of Christ. Because Christ is the perfect human, the one person who completely fills out the image of God, the more we become like him, the more human we become. In this manner the Christian life, far from transforming us into superspiritual, quasi-angelic beings, is actually a quest to recover our humanity. That, in a nutshell, is what the rest of this book is about.

Part Two

Why Are We Here?

CREATION IN GENESIS 1–2

5

To Love God

You have made us for yourself,
and our heart is restless until it rests in you.

AUGUSTINE

In a provocative episode of the television series *Everybody Loves Raymond*, the typically inept Raymond attempts to field his daughter's questions about the origin of life. However, when he pursues her questions a bit further, he finds that Ally isn't as interested in how babies are made as she is why they, or any of us, exist. She presses Raymond with these penetrating questions: "Why are we born? Why does God put us here? If we all go to heaven when we die, then why does God want us here first? Why are we here, Daddy?"

Caught off guard, Raymond puts aside his books on the birds and the bees and grapples with this more fundamental problem. After several awkward moments of fumbling and confusion, he finally blurts out that God put us on earth to ease the heavenly congestion. It must be crowded up there, so God created this planet as a temporary measure until he could free up more space for everyone. Raymond recognizes the silliness of his response even as he is saying it, and fully aware that he is overmatched, he feigns a sneezing fit and hurriedly flees the room.

The interesting part comes when Raymond shares this embarrassing encounter with the rest of his family. His pragmatic wife, Debra, doesn't know what to say either, but she is furious that her bumbling husband left their daughter with nothing more than a lame response about celestial overcrowding. She finally orders Raymond to go tell Ally that "God put us on earth to help each other. It's simple. It's direct. It's a good way for her to live her life."

Raymond rightly observes that this doesn't really answer the question, "Why did God make humans in the first place?" Pretending to be God, Raymond asks, "So what did God say? 'Hey, I'm going to put some humans on earth so they can help each other, or I could just skip humans altogether and just go hit a bucket of balls'?"

When they learn of Ally's question, the other members of Raymond's family adopt various philosophical positions. Speaking from a naturalist perspective (there is no God, for nothing exists beyond this natural world), Raymond's father brusquely pushes the question aside. He suggests that all this talk about the meaning of life is nonsense. He concludes, "Here's what life is: You're born, you go to school, you go to work, you die. That's it. That's all."

Raymond's brother, troubled by such an easy dismissal, takes a nihilistic view (nihilists—from the Latin term *nihil*, "nothing"—are typically naturalists who recognize that their worldview is utterly unable to account for any meaning in life). He wonders why there is anything at all. Why is there something rather than nothing, and why is he one of those somethings? He observes that a fruit fly lives for only a single day. Where is the meaning in that brief life? And if there is no meaning for a fruit fly, perhaps there is no meaning for us either. In the end, all this gloomy talk about the purpose of life just leaves him depressed.

Raymond's mother plays the naïve Christian. She hastily skims through the Bible, eventually plucking a proverb that has no relevance to the discussion at hand. Debra loses patience with this simplistic approach. She reminds her mother-in-law that "religious scholars spend their entire lives trying to answer this question. You're not just going to flip through the Bible and find the meaning of life."

The episode ends when Raymond and Debra, frustrated by the futile suggestions of Ray's family, decide to go upstairs and together take their best shot at Ally's question. However, when they enter her room, they immediately see that, unlike the rest of the family, Ally is not terribly disturbed by her question. She apparently has forgotten all about it, for she is now giggling happily as she tickle-fights her younger brothers. Ray and Debra watch their children play for several moments and then smile knowingly to each other, content that they have finally discovered the answer they have sought.

Thus, the point of the episode seems to be that there is no point in worrying about the meaning of life. If you do, you will only become distraught, like Raymond's nihilistic brother. There is no answer to the reason why, so we might as well follow the example of our children and learn to enjoy ourselves. As Raymond says to his wife as they kiss goodnight, "We've learned a lot from them [the kids] today. There is something to be said for childlike innocence."

This story represents the very best that our naturalistic, modern age can do with the nagging question about the meaning of life. In the absence of any meaningful response, it can only hope to distract us from pondering the question. Notice the sleight of hand in this story. The characters conclude that there is no answer to the meaning of life, and they pass this non-answer off as if it were an answer. This vacuous solution may satisfy a child's periodic questions, but it cannot calm the heart of serious thinkers who desperately seek the truth.

Fortunately, the Christian worldview does not share this limitation of the modern worldview. Although we cannot say completely why God chose to make something rather than nothing (creation is entirely his free choice) we can declare why, given his choice to create the world, he decided to make us. So rather than lose ourselves in modernity's feeble attempts to avoid life's momentous questions, we may turn to Scripture, particularly the opening chapters of Genesis, to learn the answer to the meaning of life.

There we discover that God created us in his image so that we might enjoy three deeply satisfying and productive relationships: with God, other people, and the earth itself. Because these relationships comprise the all-important meaning of life, we will use the next three chapters to examine each of them. Taken together, these chapters aim toward a rough sketch of the meaning of life, a sketch that despite its brevity may expand our wonder and appreciation for the broad scope and profound worth of human life within the Christian worldview.

"You Have Made Us for Yourself"

Despite its intriguing content, the episode of *Everybody Loves Raymond* seems to miss the obvious. Nowhere in its twenty-two minutes of pondering the meaning of life does anyone mention that perhaps God has placed us on this earth to know him better. If, as most of the characters assume, "God has put us here," then might not our purpose in life somehow involve him?

The church has always thought so. Its earliest theologians claimed that our primary reason for existence is to know and worship God, life's *summum bonum*, or highest good. They leaned heavily on Jesus' counsel that nothing, not even the whole world, is an equal trade for one's soul.[1] Instead, shrewd people will readily give up everything they own in order to obtain the pearl of great price, entrance into the kingdom of God.[2] Regardless of how much wealth and how many friends we are able to accumulate, if we do not know and love God, our life has been a bust. As Jesus was fond of saying, "Whoever finds his life will lose it, and whoever loses his life for my sake will find it."[3]

These familiar statements introduce the strange delight of being human. As God's creatures we inhabit a realm of existence that is unable to satisfy our deepest longings. As we learned in chapter 2, we dwell entirely on the creaturely plane of existence. We will never be God, never unite with a piece of him, but now and forevermore will remain on the ontological level of creation.

And yet, though ontologically we are meant to remain here, we are also made to transcend the bounds of this globe and enter into vibrant, personal fellowship with the Creator himself. We who belong to nature will only discover our deepest satisfaction in the realm of the supernatural. In Augustine's words, God has made us for himself, and our hearts are restless until they rest in him.[4] Or, as the Westminster Shorter Catechism famously begins, "Man's chief end is to glorify God, and to enjoy him forever."

As natural beings with a supernatural end, we are in the awkward position of being unable to achieve by and for ourselves the purpose of our lives. Because our deepest longings are supernatural, they can only be satisfied by something that transcends our natural world. We cannot get there from here, but must depend entirely on the supernatural coming from there to here. God himself must reach down to help us, supplying both the revelation that quenches our thirst and our ability to wholeheartedly embrace it. He must graciously prepare us, merely natural beings, for our supernatural end.

Although the natural world is unable to bring us to God, it remains a useful place for deciphering our need. Everywhere we turn in this world we find what Peter Berger calls "signals of transcendence," signposts that stoke our thirst for God.[5] Some pointers to God are unmistakable. No one can miss the presence of a higher power in the majestic flashings and rumblings of a summer thunderstorm, the vast expanse of a starry night, or the rush of euphoria from romantic love.

But sometimes our longing for God sneaks up rather quietly. As subtle as the warmth from a soft blanket, we often don't realize it was there until after it's gone. It may slip upon us while we're rocking an infant or carrying a sleepy child to bed, walking barefoot across a freshly cut lawn at dusk, sharing laughter and a meal with family and friends, staring into the glowing embers of a dying campfire, or watching convoys of ants cart a line of debris to their subterranean home.

It happens to me whenever one of my boys wraps his tiny arms around my neck, smashes his snotty nose against my cheek, and declares that he loves me and Mommy more than anyone else in the world. A wave of gratitude and humility washes over me, gratitude to God for such love and humility that he would heap such kindness upon me. Our embrace reminds me that God is the goal of our love, and I determine anew to direct the devotion of my little one toward our heavenly Father.

Often it's not a single moment but a long period of time that reminds us of God's presence and our need for him. It's what many married couples experience at their fiftieth wedding anniversary. As they reflect on their shared history, they are struck by how completely their lives have merged into one. After thousands of meals and kisses goodnight, they now speak the same language, share the same interests, laugh at the same jokes, and oddly for many, have even begun to share the same facial features. They just look like they belong together.

If we reflect on these signals of transcendence, whether spectacular or simple, we may recognize that they fill us with both intense pleasure and profound sadness. In their grasp, we involuntarily gasp with delight at the sheer joy of being alive while we simultaneously ache for something more. We sense that these wonders of life are merely scratching an itch. We relish the temporary relief they bring, but in the end they only inflame our yearning, reminding us that the true meaning of life must be found beyond them, higher up and further in.

But rather than pursue this itch to its source, many people prefer to just continue scratching. Although they suspect they will never be satisfied until they rest in God, yet, shaped by the flattened ontology of the modern world, they choose to behave as if this life is all there is. As long as they stay inordinately busy, losing themselves in their work or chasing new and exciting moments of pleasure, they can largely ignore the hollow shell that their lives have become.

Even many Christians, though we readily volunteer that knowing and loving God is the chief reason for our existence, remarkably invest precious little time reading his Word, speaking to him in prayer, or telling others about him. Instead, like our modern neighbors, who don't even claim to know God, we tend to satiate our lives with amusements, possessions, and other luxuries that preoccupy us with lesser things. In our shortsightedness we often allow television, sports leagues, and the daily news cycle to distract us from what ultimately matters.

As long as we stay active, our constant scratching thinly disguises the itch at the center of our lives. But the moment we slow down, taking time to examine our condition and the limited value of our endless activity, our dull ache returns. Once again we are forced to choose: Shall we continue scratching, or shall we return to God, the one Person in the universe who can satisfy our cravings?

An Evangelical Overcorrection

This need for right priorities is appropriately the topic of many sermons and Bible studies, which, following a central contour in Scripture, caution us that even the good things of this life may conspire to divert our attention from following Christ. As Paul wrote to the Philippians, "I consider everything a loss compared to the surpassing greatness of knowing Christ Jesus my Lord, for whose sake I have lost all things. I consider them rubbish, that I may gain Christ."[6] Like Paul, we must vigilantly resist modernity's pressure to focus exclusively on this present, natural world. This life is not all there is. With the rest of humanity, we yearn for a fulfillment that comes from God alone.

Nevertheless, as is true of any good thing, it is possible to overplay this hand. In our desire to avoid the dangerous shoals of modernity's truncated view of life, we must be careful lest we overcorrect and fall off the other side. We may rightly criticize modernity for only taking our present life into account, but we can easily err in the opposite direction.

Specifically, too many Christians think that this life is nothing more than batting practice for our future, heavenly existence, so the only things that matter here are those few objects we can take with us into our real life that is yet to come. Although it approaches the question from the opposite perspective, this simplistic response, like *Everybody Loves Raymond*'s naturalistic solution, is evasive in its own way. It also fails to supply a satisfying response to the meaning of life.

This "spiritual" approach typically declares that the only things that ultimately matter in life are objects that last forever, such as the Word of God and souls. Since everything else will eventually burn up when the earth passes away, wise Christians will avoid too much contact with these earthly things and instead will invest their resources and energy in the only two things that really matter. As one pastor put it, "The only reason we are still on this planet is to lead more souls to Christ."

Personal evangelism is a vital part of the Christian life. Certainly Christians should look for and create opportunities to share the good news of Christ with lost people. However, it just isn't true that this is the only reason we remain on this planet. Personal evangelism does not comprise the sole meaning of life. And those who think that it does, if they are consistent, will drive themselves crazy. Just as people who take naturalism seriously must eventually fall into the despair of nihilism, so those who embrace this super-spiritual form of Christianity will eventually fall into a similar, though exceedingly pious, despair.

Think about it. We spend most of our time on tasks that are not considered "spiritual." We brush and floss our teeth, mow the lawn, buy groceries, take our children to the park or zoo, read the newspaper, bake a cake, wash the car, press our pants, watch a movie—all of which we do not so much because we are Christian but because we are human. Even full-time evangelists and missionaries must devote time to these merely human activities. Thus we are in deep trouble if leading souls to Christ is the only reason we remain on this planet, for most, perhaps 99.9 percent of what we do, is not that.

It's no wonder that many Christians leave church services feeling more than a little bruised. We often exhort them to lay aside earthly cares and concentrate on the one or two things that really matter: reading their Bibles and leading lost souls to Christ. They desperately want to do so, but they sense that their weekly schedule allows precious little time for intense Bible study and evangelism. They spend entire days on the job, either at work or at home with their children, and spend their evenings on routine maintenance around the house, running teens to band practice, and perhaps watching a little television. Thus they conclude that they are utterly unable to integrate the morning's sermon into their daily routine, and they feel pretty bad about it.

Fortunately, the guilt they feel is only temporary, for it soon dissipates in the afternoon heat of Monday's activities. Perhaps if they had a spiritual job like their pastor, they could invest their entire lives in things that "really matter." As it is, they must get by in the real world, where opportunities for evangelism are sometimes as scarce as dinnertime calls from someone other than a telemarketer. So they soon forget about Sunday's apparently irrelevant sermon, until the next Lord's Day rolls around and the preacher goes after them once more.

God Is Number One

Is there a way out of this endless cycle of guilt and irrelevance? Is Scripture really this unrelated to daily life, or does it speak to our normal routines in powerful ways that this singular focus on "eternal matters" regularly misses? The meaning of life, according to Scripture, certainly involves reading God's Word and leading others to Christ, but it also includes much more than these "spiritual" activities. Scripture casts its vision for life so widely that it requires a broad structure, what we are calling a worldview, to comprehend it all.

As we saw earlier in this chapter, our relationship with God is the most important facet of our life on earth. Nothing compares to knowing and serving the one true God of the universe. Nevertheless, this relationship with God is not most important in the way many people think.

To hear them talk, many Christian leaders assume that we make God the Lord of our lives by making everything else second rate. Accordingly, we should lavish the lion's share of our energy, time, and money on spiritual activities such as personal devotions, prayer, missions, evangelism, discipleship, and church attendance. Then, once these spiritual duties have been satisfactorily met, we may use any leftover resources for other, secular matters, such as family, work, friends, recreation, the arts, and spectator sports (Fig. 5.1). As one pastor explained,

> The bottom line is that we are to put spiritual values above temporal values. Serving God and being obedient to him ought to be more important to us than anything else we do, including fishing, golfing, hunting, gardening, our career, clothes, houses, lands, etc. These things are not wrong but they are not to be the primary focus and priorities of our life. God wants and demands first place!

It is difficult to argue with this pastor, for of course the kingdom of God is more important than any of the things he listed. But why must he leave the impression that its "spiritual values" are in opposition to our earthly concerns? Rather than view life as a struggle between "temporal" and "spiritual" values (which implies with Gnosticism that our problem is ontological rather than ethical—that is, our problem is that we are temporal, not that we are sinners), why not view our temporal, earthly endeavors as opportunities to pursue kingdom values? Then activities like fishing, golfing, and gardening

Figure 5.1: Misunderstanding the Preeminence of God

---

1. God

2. Family
3. Work
4. Friends
5. Recreation
6. Arts
7. Athletics

---

are more than merely "not wrong," neutral escapes for those seeking a diversion from spiritual values. Instead, they provide fresh opportunities for believers to extend the kingdom of God in the world (see chapter 11).

We have already mentioned another obvious flaw with this hierarchical approach: Except for a few extremely devoted monks, this lifestyle is completely unrealistic. Most people have family, friends, jobs, and other matters that prevent them from devoting their entire lives to spiritual pursuits. They couldn't follow this spiritual approach even if they wanted. Those who try simply set themselves up for failure and guilt.

But what if, rather than view God's preeminence as an obligation to rank everything else as a distant second and below, we recognize that giving God first place demands that we remain active in every other area of life? Then seeking first the kingdom of God will not mean that we ignore daily matters so we may focus exclusively upon him, but it will mean that in every area of life we passionately strive to honor God. This view recognizes that because God the Creator has made every area of life, his preeminence necessarily includes rather than excludes each aspect of our existence. Rather than think that God's primacy means that nothing else matters, it is precisely because God is number one that everything else does matter.

Thus, rather than understand God's primacy as the top item on a list, we may view it as the hub of the wheel of life. Every aspect of life, from friends and family to art and athletics, must be permeated with love for God (Fig. 5.2). Rather than divide life into the spiritual things above and the secular things below, we realize that even the "higher" things, such as worship and evangelism, may be conducted for selfish, sinful reasons and that the "lower" things, such as changing a diaper or vacuuming the carpet, may be done for the praise and honor of God.

In this view, what we are doing doesn't matter as much as how and why we are doing it. A full-orbed Christian worldview does not bother to discriminate between important and unimportant matters, but instead encourages all believers to do the best they can, for the glory of God, with whatever assignments fall their way. As Paul encouraged the Colossians, "And whatever you do, whether in word or deed, do it all in the name of the Lord Jesus, giving thanks to God the Father through him. . . . Whatever you do, work at it with all your

Figure 5.2: A Proper Understanding of the Preeminence of God

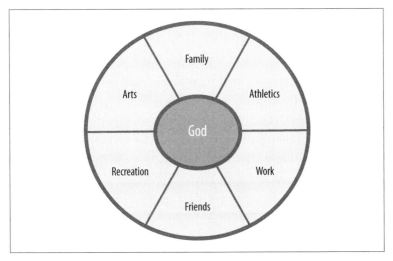

heart, as working for the Lord, not for men."[7] Or, as Martin Luther instructed his people, "Leave the works in one class. Consider one as good as another. Fear God, and be just, as has been said. And then do whatever comes before you. This way all will be well done even though it is no more than loading manure or driving a mule."[8]

The Mysterious Christian Life

Do you see the paradox in this chapter? On the one hand, it says we must prevent the things of this world from choking our love for God; on the other hand, it suggests that we rightly demonstrate our love for God through our active participation in the world. We properly obey God when we care for our families, our bodies, and our jobs. However, the same families, bodies, and jobs that provide opportunities for obedience may also become idols when they receive the attention and allegiance that belongs to God alone. So what is a Christian to do? How can we negotiate this minefield, seeking to honor God by our service in the world without allowing our concern for the world to replace and ultimately dishonor God?

This is a provocative question, one that will follow us throughout this book. Rather than offer a hasty, superficial response here, let me stimulate your thinking with an observation from Herman Bavinck. He notes that Jesus himself uses analogies that depict this dual responsibility of the Christian life. On the one hand, Jesus describes the kingdom of heaven as a treasure hidden in a field or a pearl of great price whose worth far exceeds anything else in this life.[9] According to this analogy, it is worth giving up everything we have for the sake of the gospel. We must not allow anything, regardless how good or important, to choke our primary love for God and his kingdom.

However, Jesus also uses another analogy, comparing the kingdom to yeast that leavens an entire lump of dough.[10] Assuming that the lump of dough represents the world, this analogy cautions us against shunning the world for the sake of the gospel. It is not enough to love God more than the world; a true disciple of Christ will also love the world for the sake of God.

According to Bavinck, this uneasy tension between the gospel as pearl and the gospel as leaven will not go away until Christ returns to consummate his kingdom. Until then, we must affirm both sides of the paradox: The God who is more important than anything in the world sends us into the world to transform it for him. God's preeminence means that nothing can be elevated to his level. But his preeminence also means that nothing can be dismissed. Nothing is as valuable as God, but because of God, everything is now valuable.[11]

Bavinck is correct. This paradox of pearl and leaven does seem inevitable on this side of Christ's return. If we do not struggle with this tension, it probably means we have already capitulated to one extreme or the other, either forsaking God for our love of the world or ignoring the world out of a purported love for God. Both extremes are unlivable, comic distortions of the true meaning of life. So we can be glad for the tension we feel. It suggests that we are right on track, safely negotiating between the God-denying extreme of modernity and the world-denying extreme of an overly spiritualized evangelicalism.

6

To Serve Others

"Love your neighbor as yourself."

MATTHEW 22:39

"Teacher, which is the greatest commandment in the Law?" Of all the questions ever asked to test Jesus, this one seemed the easiest. Anyone who knew anything about the law would predictably recite the Shema, the Jewish confession of faith found in Deuteronomy 6:4–5. And Jesus did. Recalling the words that every Jewish child had memorized, Jesus replied, "Love the Lord your God with all your heart and with all your soul and with all your mind. This is the first and greatest commandment."[1]

But then—and this might have been the tricky part—Jesus kept going. If his answer had been only this reference to the Shema, the Pharisees listening in could have legitimately clucked their disapproval. Anyone familiar with the Old Testament would also know that the God presented there, though passionately interested in his own worship, is equally concerned that his people care for one another. (Consider the Ten Commandments, four of which address our relationship with God and six of which concern our relationship with others.) Consequently, although his interrogator asked for only the greatest single command, Jesus felt obliged to give him two. Jesus reminded him that the second command, which is virtually equivalent to the first, is "'Love your neighbor as yourself.' All the Law and the Prophets hang on these two commandments."[2]

Four centuries later, Augustine, the church's greatest theologian, caught the spirit of what Jesus was saying when he observed that everything written in Scripture is meant to teach us how to love either God or our neighbor.[3] A millennium after him, a converted Augustinian monk named Martin Luther declared that the entire Christian life amounts to serving our neighbor. In his monastery Luther had devoted every waking moment to securing his own salvation. But once he learned that his salvation was a gift from God and that he no longer needed to earn it, he suddenly realized that he had a lot of time on his hands. What better way to show that he fully understood the undeserved grace that God had given him than to freely offer his help to others?[4]

The trajectory is unmistakable. The one truth that everyone seems to agree on, from Moses through Jesus and on to Augustine and the Reformers, is that it's virtually impossible to please God without loving our neighbor. Indeed, as the apostle John indicates, a sure sign that we are a child of God is that we love our closest neighbors, our brothers and sisters in the family of God.[5] Considering this close tie between loving God and loving others, it seems appropriate to follow the last chapter's discussion of loving God with this chapter's study of the second function of our *imago Dei:* our responsibility to serve our neighbors.

Where Is My Neighbor?

The church's consistent emphasis on loving others may be a bit disturbing to twenty-first-century Christians, for we inhabit an increasingly technological world that introduces us simultaneously to far too many and far too few neighbors. Globally, technology has made nearly everyone in the world our neighbor, for it connects us to people and their stories on the other side of the earth. From the comfort of our living rooms we learn about another civil war in Africa, an earthquake in central Asia, damaging floods in a rural Chinese province, forest fires in Australia, or the latest round of futile talks between the Israelis and Palestinians, Indians and Pakistanis, or North and South Koreans. Aid organizations such as the Red Cross, Compassion International, and Samaritan's Purse alert us to the poverty and suffering of people whom we have never even met—and probably never will.

Reflective Christians rightly worry about their responsibility to these impoverished families. If, as Jesus intimated in the story of the Good Samaritan, any person in need is our neighbor, then how can we not open our hearts and purses to heal their plight? On the other hand, it is easy to become overwhelmed by the sheer volume of requests. There are so many of them, each with a compelling story that cries out for attention. With the entire world within reach, where do we begin? If we help everyone who justifiably needs our aid, what will be left for us?

Unfortunately, this global glut of neighbors is not our only problem when it comes to loving others as ourselves. The same technology that makes everyone our neighbor on a global scale also threatens to leave us with too few neighbors on the local level. Many of us can breeze through an entire day with almost no personal interaction with another human being. Each morning the drawbridge to our castle opens just long enough for us to slide out of our driveway and, without leaving our vehicle, remotely close the garage door behind us. As we jockey for position in the morning commute, we barely notice that the cars with which we are competing are also driven by lone individuals isolated from the rest of us. If we stop for gasoline or groceries, we probably use a self-service pump and a U-Scan checkout line.

Our lonely commute over, we conceal ourselves inside our cubicles and boot up our computers. Equipped with the Internet, these amazing boxes (when functioning properly) enable us to transfer funds, purchase airplane tickets, chat with friends, plus do lots of other stuff the boss doesn't need to know about—all without ever making eye contact with another human being. Depending on our line of work, we may have more or less interaction with other people throughout our day, though it is likely that over the last ten years technology has reduced our face time with others. Rather than speak directly with another human being, we now send emails, leave voicemails, or dutifully pound the numbers on our phone's keypad as we painstakingly make our way through the maze of a company's automated answering system.

Even when we do finally make contact with another person, our efficient, disciplined culture teaches us to get the information we need and hang up quickly. Those employees who can process the most claims, see the most patients, or sell the most policies are handsomely rewarded. Those who dawdle, dabbling in small talk with a client they barely know, are a luxury most aggressive firms cannot afford. There just isn't time for the meandering, social interaction that other, less productive cultures enjoy.

Our isolation is even more intense when we arrive home. Most modern homes have replaced the front porch with an imposing garage, complete with the aforementioned remote-control drawbridge. So rather than relax outdoors with a community of neighbors, sipping lemonade and swapping stories until dusk settles and mosquitoes swarm over our lawns, we tend to scurry inside to the safety of our family rooms. There the flickering screens of our technological age continue to isolate us from others, substituting sitcom and chat-room relationships for the flesh-and-blood friendships of previous generations.

Thus it seems that our modern world has dealt us a double and paradoxical blow. The same technological hand that makes everyone our neighbor has also left us with few or none. We probably know the first names of many more people than Jesus, Augustine, or Luther ever met. But in large part because we are acquainted with so many people, we really don't know any of them that well.

All of this raises an interesting point. If we are rapidly losing community in our neighborhoods and social networks, then how are we able to follow Jesus' command to love our neighbors as ourselves? How can we obediently serve others we rarely see? Is it even possible to live as a Christian in a world without neighbors?[6]

Peace on Earth

To address this structural problem of the modern world, we must first understand the biblical vision for our social networks. Only by grasping God's plan for the world—and our role in that plan—can we begin to answer where and how we should love our neighbor. God's hope for the world is ably expressed in the Hebrew prayer of blessing that Jews and Christians still use to encourage one another: "The LORD bless you and keep you; the LORD make his face shine upon you and be gracious to you; the LORD turn his face toward you and give you peace."[7]

The word translated "peace" is the Hebrew term *shālôm*, a word so important to the Jewish psyche that, much as Hawaiians say "aloha," this beleaguered people use it for both hello and goodbye. In so doing, they wish upon the person they are greeting a thorough repose that comes from being at peace with one's friends and potential enemies. But this absence of conflict is not an end in itself. The term *shalom* also connotes the deep satisfaction and security that arise from such open and mutually enriching relationships. It describes the sense of well-being and wholeness people feel when all is right with the world. In the words of Neal Plantinga, *shalom* means "universal flourishing, wholeness, and delight." It expresses the way things ought to be.[8]

This concept of prosperity through peace is aptly illustrated in the life of King Solomon, whose very name, $sh^el\bar{o}m\bar{o}h$, is derived from the term $sh\bar{a}l\hat{o}m$. God told King David to name his son "Solomon" after shalom, for God would "grant Israel peace and quiet during his reign."[9] God kept his word, so that by the time Solomon dedicated the first temple, he could claim that "now the LORD my God has given me rest on every side; and there is no adversary or disaster."[10]

In large part because of this period of peace, Israel enjoyed more prosperity during Solomon's reign than any time before or since. We are told that "King Solomon was greater in riches and wisdom than all the other kings of the earth."[11] His wealth completely overwhelmed visitors such as the queen of Sheba. When she beheld the luxurious splendor of Solomon's palace, she exclaimed that "in wisdom and wealth you have far exceeded the report I heard. How happy your men must be! How happy your officials, who continually stand before you and hear your wisdom!"[12]

Solomon clearly understood that the continued prosperity of his empire depended on his ability to keep the peace. In an eloquent psalm he wisely asked God for the ability to lead his people with justice and righteousness, for he knew that his society must guard the rights of all its citizens to experience the shalom of God.[13] If Israeli society continues to "defend the afflicted" and "save the children of the needy" from their wicked oppressors, then "the righteous will flourish" amid an "abundance of peace."[14]

This abundance of shalom was evident in God's original creation, when Adam and Eve kept the peace and prospered in all three of their created relationships: with God, each other, and the earth. First, Adam and Eve flourished in their regular communion with God. They had opportunities to learn firsthand from the Person who created this pulsating universe of beauty and to thank him for the privilege of living here. Second, Adam and Eve enjoyed the deepest intimacy two humans have ever known. Uninhibited by the need to hide any painful or embarrassing secrets and certain that they could fully trust themselves to each other, they were free to explore each other's body and soul in ways that even our most celebrated lovers have not begun to consider.

Third, Adam and Eve took great delight in living on this planet. Adam never felt more alive than when he was naming the animals, planting tulip bulbs, or pruning back pear trees so they would bear more fruit. His job was made easier by the shalom that permeated this good creation. Lions snuggled up against his neck and purred like kittens, wolves and sheep played harmless games of hide-and-seek, and stately cedars and pines soared skyward, casting a fresh, fragrant scent over the garden floor.

Here, in God's original design for the natural world, we find that he intends for all of his creatures to blossom and prosper together. God did not mean his creation to be a zero-sum game, where one species thrives at another's expense. Instead, he created a tightly calibrated ecosystem in which individuals and species need each other to maximize their potential.

This interdependence is evident throughout nature. It occurs when bees pollinate flowers, collecting enough grams of nectar in the process to fuel their flight home and create a comb of honey in their hive. It happens when earthworms digest old leaves and garbage, growing fat from our waste and leaving a trail of organic mulch behind. It is especially apparent in the symbiotic relationship between people and plants. Through the "miracle" of photosynthesis, the green leaves of plants and trees produce oxygen for us to survive, while we return the favor by exhaling the carbon dioxide they need to thrive.

Perhaps in part to prevent us from running amok and steamrolling over the rest of creation, God made us dependent on it. The human race will only survive and flourish to the extent that we honor the delicate balance between us and the rest of creation. We need oxygen to breathe, honey to eat, and fertile soil and pollination for our flower gardens. In turn, trees, bees, and earthworms rely on the carbon dioxide, flowers, and waste that we provide. We may not be especially fond of earthworms and honeybees, but it would be awfully difficult to have flowers without them.

We catch a glimpse of this interdependence of shalom in Scripture's story of creation. God commands humankind to serve creation by exercising authority over it—to "subdue" and "rule" over the other creatures. Then he informs Adam that the herbs and fruit trees of creation will return the favor. In response to Adam's careful cultivation, the earth itself will yield plump, juicy fruit for him to enjoy. It is this interdependent ecosystem that God then pronounces to be "very good." Not merely each individual creature considered separately, but the entire system taken together—permeated with the interconnectedness of shalom—is what pleases God. It's as if he pumps his fist in exaltation: "Yes! This is good. This is very good."[15]

Prince of Peace

Unfortunately, this shalom of creation was soon shattered by the sin of Adam and Eve. They broke the peace when they disobeyed God and followed their own desires. And since rebellion against God is always accompanied by animosity toward others, it wasn't long until their sin had spoiled the other relationships within their world. As we will learn in chapter 10, the trajectory of human sin ricochets into the farthest corners of creation, destroying first ourselves, then human society, and finally the animals and even the earth itself. No aspect of shalom is spared from the careening path of sin.

This spoiling of shalom is frequently lamented by the Old Testament prophets, but perhaps nowhere more persuasively than in the eloquent speeches of Isaiah. Isaiah opens his book by informing the people of Judah that God has rejected their worship. He has had enough of their "meaningless offerings," considers their incense "detestable," and is frankly weary of their religious feasts.[16]

Why? Not because these religious duties are badly performed. The priests who offer the sacrifices follow the very letter of the law.

Rather, God is upset because the same people who piously present themselves before him are maliciously mistreating others the moment they leave the temple. According to Isaiah, these wicked people regularly take advantage of the defenseless orphans and widows among them. Instead of protecting these powerless people, they accept bribes from their oppressors in order to unjustly rule against them in court. In this way the wealthy become richer still on the backs of the already impoverished.[17] It is this blatant disregard for shalom, the well-being of others, that so incenses God. "What do you mean," he asks, "by crushing my people and grinding the faces of the poor?"[18]

So God declares that he will judge his people. Very soon he will pay them back for their mistreatment of the poor among them.[19] He will topple the "proud and lofty," sending them scurrying for cover like rats desperately searching for a hole to duck into.[20] He will punish his people by completely destroying the nation and carrying any survivors into exile.[21]

But though the immediate future looks bleak, Isaiah looks far enough ahead to glimpse a ray of hope. He envisions a day when God's chastened people will return to the land to be governed justly by the Prince of Peace.[22] This fighter for shalom will not only restore proper order to society but also remove the debilitating sin of its members by suffering in their place. In the words of Isaiah, the coming Messiah "was pierced for our transgressions, he was crushed for our iniquities; the punishment that brought us *peace* [shalom] was upon him, and by his wounds we are healed."[23]

Isaiah's expectation of shalom is fulfilled in the angels' announcement to the stunned shepherds. With Isaiah's vision clearly in mind, the heavens over Bethlehem rang, "Glory to God in the highest, and on earth *peace* to men on whom his favor rests."[24] Jesus Christ, the long-awaited Messiah, has come to restore universal flourishing, wholeness, and delight to every corner of his sin-damaged creation. As a favorite Christmas hymn powerfully puts it:

> No more let sins and sorrows grow,
> Nor thorns infest the ground;
> He comes to make His blessings flow
> Far as the curse is found.

Joy to the world!

Specifically, Isaiah expects that the coming Prince of Peace will restore wholeness to all three of our created relationships. First, those who enter his kingdom will find a renewed shalom with God. Isaiah predicts that one day

> the mountain of the LORD's temple will be established
>   as chief among the mountains;
> it will be raised above the hills,
>   and all nations will stream to it.
>
> Many peoples will come and say,
>
> "Come, let us go up to the mountain of the LORD,
>   to the house of the God of Jacob.
> He will teach us his ways,
> so that we may walk in his paths."[25]

The day is coming when all people will be God's people, flourishing in the knowledge and obedience that comes from a restored walk with him.

Second, just as rebellion against God leads to animosity toward others, so our return to God will prompt reconciliation with others. Isaiah explains that submission to the Prince of Peace will reestablish shalom among the nations, for "they will beat their swords into plowshares and their spears into pruning hooks. Nation will not take up sword against nation, nor will they train for war anymore."[26] In the absence of international conflict, governments will divert defense funds into economic development and so improve the lot of their people.

Yet the coming Messiah will not only establish peace *between* societies but also renew peace *within* society. The main mission of the Prince of Peace is to restore shalom to human society by raising the down-and-outers. Using words that Jesus will later apply to himself on the day he begins his ministry, Isaiah writes:

> The Spirit of the Sovereign LORD is on me,
>> because the LORD has anointed me
>> to preach good news to the poor.
> He has sent me to bind up the brokenhearted,
>> to proclaim freedom for the captives
>> and release from darkness for the prisoners,
> to proclaim the year of the LORD's favor.[27]

When the poor, the brokenhearted, and the captives receive the promise of flourishing wholeness offered in the gospel, then

> Justice will dwell in the desert
>> and righteousness live in the fertile field.
> The fruit of righteousness will be *peace;*
>> the effect of righteousness will be quietness and
>> confidence forever.
> My people will live in *peaceful* dwelling places,
>> in secure homes,
>> in undisturbed places of rest.[28]

In sum, when justice and righteousness once again permeate human society, all people will enjoy the satisfying prosperity of shalom.

Third, besides restoring shalom among people and between them and God, the peace that Christ brings also reinvigorates the rest of creation. Isaiah declares that the earth itself will now be lifted from the curse of sin. He asserts that when "the Spirit is poured upon us from on high," then "the desert becomes a fertile field, and the fertile field seems like a forest."[29] Even the animals will return to the shalom they knew before sin entered the world. After a lengthy description of the coming Messiah,[30] Isaiah details the peace that he will bring to the animal kingdom. He writes:

The wolf will live with the lamb,
    the leopard will lie down with the goat,
the calf and the lion and the yearling together;
    and a little child will lead them.
The cow will feed with the bear,
    their young will lie down together,
    and the lion will eat straw like the ox.
The infant will play near the hole of the cobra,
    and the young child put his hand into the viper's nest.
They will neither harm nor destroy
    on all my holy mountain,
for the earth will be full of the knowledge of the LORD
    as the waters cover the sea.[31]

To summarize: the entirety of God's original creation, from the highest human to the lowest larva, enjoyed shalom—the universal flourishing, wholeness, and delight that only comes when every creature is playing its part in the interconnectedness of creation. When sin spoiled this shalom, Jesus Christ, the Creator of this once-perfect world, responded by returning to the world he had made in order to remove the curse of sin and save the planet. His kingdom brings the recovery of shalom. People, animals, and the earth, formerly at odds with one another, find that once again they are connected by fruitful bonds that enable them and every corner of creation to thrive and prosper.

Brighten the Corner Where You Are

What does Isaiah's vision of this coming shalom mean for us? We now know that what Isaiah portrayed as one appearance of the Messiah must be divided into two distinct advents. Jesus Christ first came to earth two thousand years ago to remove the guilt of our sin and inaugurate his kingdom in the world. But though his death on the cross and resurrection guarantee his final victory, he will not completely eliminate evil and restore shalom throughout his entire creation until he comes again at the end of the age.

We who live in this awkward pause between Christ's first and second advents must resist two equal and opposite temptations. On the one hand, we must not think that in some triumphalistic manner we will usher in the fulfillment of Christ's kingdom. Regardless of how diligently we strive to make this world a better place, we will never fully succeed in removing sin and righting all wrongs. Only God can repair this broken world, and so we must wait for Christ to return to earth and make all things new.

On the other hand, just because we will not ultimately succeed in restoring shalom in our lifetime does not mean we should throw up our hands in despair. We may not be able to correct every slight and meet every need, but we can still make headway. We can bring a slice of shalom to our corner of the planet, to our sphere of influence, and so become a sign or firstfruit of the kingdom that Christ is bringing. We must wait for Christ's return, but it can be an active rather than passive waiting. While we wait, why not choose to participate in activities that herald the coming shalom?

Simply put, regardless of our prospects for immediate success, we who follow the Prince of Peace must seek to increase the net gain of shalom in the world. We who pray "thy kingdom come" must also be willing to work for it. Certainly this involves preaching the gospel, announcing to all people the good news that Christ has died for their sins and has thus made it possible for them to return to God. But it also includes practicing the gospel, demonstrating by our lives that the kingdom is near.

At the very least, we signal the arrival of the kingdom when we cultivate the virtues we learned in kindergarten: mind your manners, wait your turn, be kind, play fair, say "please" and "thank you," and share toys. In our grown-up world we repair the fabric of shalom when we inquire about our friend's day and then intently listen to her response, leave words of encouragement with those who least expect it, remember and use the names of people we've just met, let another finish the story that we are dying to tell, speak the truth even when it embarrasses us, prepare a home-cooked meal for a harried family, give up our seat to an elderly gentleman or young child, turn off our cell phones in restaurants and waiting rooms (and church!), hold the door for the person trailing behind us, allow another car to merge into our lane, speak courteously to the staff, return the video rewound, leave the toilet seat down, and politely ask the telemarketer to kindly never call us again.

I don't mean to imply that everyone who shows such consideration for others is necessarily announcing the arrival of Christ's kingdom. Obviously, many people who display such kindness are not even Christians. Yet, thanks to what theologians call God's common grace, non-Christians are able to overcome the selfishness of their sin and perform a great deal of moral good. Very different is the case with Christians who show such kindness, not from guilt or to earn the approval of others, but ultimately because they seek to spread shalom and thereby display their submission to the reign of Christ. For such people, these minor acts of consideration contain much spiritual value.

Nor am I suggesting that these small courtesies are the primary way we signal the arrival of the kingdom. I only begin here because these trivial matters, frequently overlooked by many, may be more important than we think. According to Jesus' account of the final judgment, it is fairly small matters that ultimately separate the children of God from those bound for hell. The saved sheep on God's right hand are there because they gave hospitality—food, drink, clothes, and shelter—to "the least of these" among them. The goats are condemned because they didn't.[32] While this passage need not imply that we can work our way into God's good graces, it does indicate that those who receive the grace of God thankfully respond by doing good works. Small acts of kindness will not automatically make anyone a Christian, but genuine Christians will take pains to practice them.

Indeed, it is just this attention to detail that separates genuine believers from hypocrites. The most offensive people on the planet are those who profess to be godly but consistently mistreat the "least of these" in their lives. In large part, this is why Jesus rails against the Pharisees. They pretend to be the spiritual elite, yet they "devour widows' houses" and "tie up heavy loads and put them on men's shoulders." Their lack of compassion has made them children of hell, "whitewashed tombs" which, though beautiful on the outside, are full of deadness and decay in their heart.[33]

With Liberty and Justice for All

Thus the little acts of shalom building are important. But so are the larger, global opportunities to restore flourishing and delight to those in need. Many evangelical Christians have typically been slow to confront and solve the significant social issues of our day. In part because we fear falling into the trap of liberalism's "social gospel," we tend to focus only on people's spiritual needs. Too much concern for their physical or social well-being may distract us from the deeper issues of the soul, so we had better stick solely to gospel preaching and let someone else, perhaps the government or secular aid agencies, care for people's other, less important problems.

A recent sermon reminded me of our reticence to address the need for shalom in the world. The sermon opened with a PowerPoint slide depicting the current chaos in the Middle East. Beneath the scowling faces of Palestinian leader Yassar Arafat and then-Israeli Prime Minister Ehud Barak, the pastor related the devastating acts of terrorism and retaliation that had occurred during the previous week.

Whereas a mainline or liberal pastor may have made this story the focus of his sermon, this conservative pastor smoothly segued from the crisis in Palestine to a similar battle that rages within every human heart. "Just as there is no peace in the Middle East," he intoned, "so there will be no peace in our hearts without Christ." The rest of the sermon never returned to the Israeli-Palestinian conflict, but focused exclusively on how each of us can attain our very own "peace of God, which transcends all understanding."[34]

This moralistic, individualistic approach to the world's problems is typical of my experience in church. My conservative upbringing has seldom used world events for anything more than object lessons, moral stories that we can apply to our individual lives. (Mainline pastors browse *Newsweek* for sermon topics; conservative pastors read it for illustrations.) We are not really interested in solving the world's problems but are content to learn a few life lessons from its misfortune. While I am not endorsing those churches who have replaced the gospel with social programs, I wonder whether our conservative, individualistic approach isn't also missing the gospel in its own way.

Specifically, we must recognize that the same shalom that gives peace to my own heart intends to permeate every piece of life on every part of the planet. As agents of shalom, we must begin to think beyond mere spiritual needs and our narrow neighborhoods and listen to the full-bodied cries for shalom scattered across the global village. Like the Jewish exiles living in Babylon, God calls us to care for the overall health of even our unbelieving neighbors. Though they lived as strangers in a foreign land, God commanded his people to "seek the peace and prosperity [shalom] of the city to which I have carried you into exile. Pray to the LORD for it, because if it prospers, you too will prosper" (literally, "in its shalom you will have shalom").[35]

Seeking the shalom of the city means remembering that all people have been endowed by their Creator with certain inalienable rights, such as the right to earn a living wage, dwell in safe neighborhoods, freely participate in society, and access clean drinking water and basic medical care. Wherever these basic rights are denied, shalom is broken and God's image in the world is sullied. So it should matter to us when Palestinian suicide bombers blow up Israeli buses and pizza parlors, religious and political dissenters languish in Chinese and

Cuban jails, Saudi women are deprived of their dignity and educational opportunities, and AIDS spreads like wildfire across the population of South Africa.

We should especially care about those situations that we can help solve. For instance, we should encourage our government to flex its muscle in the Israeli-Palestinian conflict, using its clout to broker a deal that justly serves both sides. Whether or not we believe that peace will ever be achieved in this part of the world until the return of Christ, we still have the responsibility to work for it.

Loving our neighbor may also prompt us to pressure dictatorial governments in the Middle East, driving them to an open political process that will give millions of disenfranchised Arabs a genuine stake and say in their countries' future. As we learned on September 11, 2001, it is really in our own best interest to do so, for happy young Arab men do not blow themselves up to make a political point. According to the rules of shalom, the aid we lend to others has a way of looping back and blessing us. As Jeremiah reminded the Jewish exiles, everyone benefits when social networks are satiated with shalom. So earnestly seek the shalom of our increasingly global community, "for in its shalom you will have shalom."

But though we must think globally, we will perform most of our actions locally. We may not provide for every needy person in a distant country (though we may be able to help some), but we can aid the needy ones in our vicinity. We can volunteer at the city rescue mission, regularly serving on days other than the photo-op holidays of Thanksgiving and Christmas. We can donate our services to the local pregnancy center, tutor a child, babysit for a single mother, or coach Little League.

Besides this type of individual attention, we may potentially help even greater numbers of people through our analysis and action on the larger, structural systems of our society. For example, we should regularly monitor our government's tax code to make sure it justly balances our need to reward the wealth-producing members of society and assist those willing workers to pull themselves out of poverty. A society of shalom handsomely repays the efforts of its successful risk-takers while also maintaining a sufficient safety net for those who fall.

Furthermore, we who wish to keep the peace should also be sensitive to institutionalized forms of discrimination, vigilantly rooting out racism and sexism in our communities so that all people, regardless of their individual profile, have equal opportunities for success. It is this line of thinking that leads many Christians to support the civil rights and right-to-life movements. In these ways and more, we who follow the Prince of Peace seek to restore justice and shalom to human society so that every image bearer may experience at least a portion of the flourishing, wholeness, and delight that God intended.

The New Community

We are now better prepared to address the questions raised at the beginning of this chapter. How do we serve Christ in a world where globally everyone is our neighbor and locally few are? One response, which I have presented here, is to think globally and act locally. We should always keep the large, global picture in mind, monitoring trends and evaluating how our actions inadvertently help or hurt others on the other side of the world. But though we follow and seek to influence the global picture, most of our concrete, specific steps for shalom will occur within our local communities. There, in our personal touch with our fellow image bearers, lies our greatest opportunity to advance shalom.

These local networks include the neighborhood in which we reside, the colleagues we work alongside, and the family within our home. While these are all important, our greatest opportunity to promote shalom lies not in our neighborhoods, offices, or even our homes, but in our local churches. Jesus Christ established his church as a beacon, a beachhead for shalom within this dark world of war and division. His supreme passion is for his people to enjoy the fruitful unity that comes from the shalom of God. On the evening before his death, Jesus' final prayer in the Upper Room was for his followers to "be one, Father, just as you are in me and I am in you. May they also be in us so that the world may believe that you have sent me."[36]

Paul applies this passion for peace to ethnic and religious strife, explaining that Christ has overcome centuries of animosity between Jews and Gentiles, reconciling them to each other as he reconciles each to the Father.[37] So now "there is neither Jew nor Greek, slave nor free, male nor female, for you are all one in Christ Jesus."[38]

This unity among individual believers—church community—is a recurring emphasis throughout Paul's writings. For instance, in Romans 12:1 Paul exhorts the Christians in Rome to present their bodies (plural) as "a living sacrifice" (singular).[39] More than merely commanding individual believers to offer their individual selves directly to God, Paul may also be imploring individual Christians to join their uplifted selves with others in the church so that together they may form a single, united offering to the Lord. It is good to praise and serve God individually, but it's even better when individuals unite and "with one heart and mouth . . . glorify the God and Father of our Lord Jesus Christ."[40]

To this end Paul devotes the rest of his letter to the Romans to explaining how this is done. He urges the believers there to use their distinctive gifts to serve the body (12:3–8), humbly honor and care for one another (12:9–16), live peaceably with all people (12:17–21), support and submit to the governing authorities (13:1–7), love others (13:8–10), allow diversity of opinion about matters of Christian freedom, protecting the weak while not condemning the strong (14:1–23), and patiently bear one another's burdens, seeking to benefit their neighbor rather than themselves (15:1–13). Perhaps inspired by this commentary on community, Paul concludes the book with an entire chapter of personal greetings to the fellow believers he loved in Rome (16:3–16).[41]

Consider also Ephesians 4:11–16, where Paul observes that Christ gave gifted people to the church, not merely so that individual believers could improve their personal relationship with God, but so that the entire body together might "reach unity in the faith and in the knowledge of the Son of God and become mature, attaining to the whole measure of the fullness of Christ." Paul seems to imply here that spiritual maturity does not occur in isolation, with individual Christians acting independently in their love and service to God; rather, we must all grow up together, only able to know and love God as we learn to serve one another.

This interdependent nature of spirituality is radically different from the prevailing view among many evangelical Christians. Despite the growing number of churches that include the word "community" somewhere in their title, we still tend to think of spiritual growth as an independent, do-it-yourself project between us and God. We attend church, not primarily so we can contribute to the health and growth of the body, but so the worship, fellowship, or sermon may minister to us. Should we consistently fail to "get something out" of our time together, it won't be long until we shop for another, more promising community of faith, often changing churches several times in one lifetime.

Against this type of self-centered religion, Paul argues that we need the church, not merely for the inspiration it lends to our individual lives, but because we cannot be whole, complete Christians apart from the community of Christ. We cannot grow in Christ so long as we are isolated from our brothers and sisters, for genuine progress only occurs when "the whole body, joined and held together by every supporting ligament, grows and builds itself up in love, as each part does its work."[42]

In short, each person will only flourish and find delight in God to the extent that the entire body experiences shalom. Our spiritual health depends both on receiving help from our brothers and sisters and giving our gifts to serve them. As Paul reminded the Corinthians, just as we rely on each member of our physical body to pull its weight, so we need each person in Christ's body to honor and care for the others and thereby sustain a healthy body that functions as God intended.[43]

To summarize: Although we may never fully succeed in restoring shalom to our selfish world, there is at least one place where we should expect to find the flourishing, wholeness, and delight that comes from genuine community. Christ intends his church to be a herald of shalom. When this collection of diverse individuals chooses to sacrificially serve one another in the name of the Prince of Peace, we silently announce to a troubled world that the kingdom of shalom is present in our midst. In this way we proclaim the gospel of Jesus Christ, proving by our conduct that sin does not have the last word, but just as shalom once permeated the original creation, it has come to Christ's church and will come again to his world.

To Responsibly
Cultivate the Earth

The LORD God took the man and put him in the Garden of Eden
to work it and take care of it.

GENESIS 2:15

I was a junior in high school when I first realized that I wanted to
give the rest of my life to serve the church. My calling into vocational ministry did not come with any bright lights or inner voices,
just an unmistakable sense that any other line of work could not possibly matter so much as proclaiming the gospel of Christ. Others
might settle for second best; I was going to use my gifts to count for
eternity.

During my college years this dream edged closer to reality.
Fueled by intimate friendships, a regular dose of inspiring chapels,
life-changing mission trips, and perhaps more than a few raging hor-
mones, my twenty-something kindling caught fire for God. I was ide-
alistic enough to believe that I could capture a large portion of the
world for Christ, and young enough to try.

But when my campus exuberance came home for summer vacation, I sometimes discovered that reentry into my parents' atmosphere could burn off even my most zealous enthusiasm. Convinced that nothing else mattered in life but leading other people to Christ, I struggled to make sense of a world of mortgages, home maintenance, and small talk. Not always perceiving that my parents had certain obligations that forced them into a routine, I sometimes wondered why they weren't more excited about spiritual things. Why didn't they strike up conversations with lost people or pass out tracts? Didn't they care that their neighbors were going to hell?

In my immaturity I silently questioned my parents' commitment to Christ. Why was Mom so obsessed with keeping house? Just like Martha, it seemed that she was always busy folding another load of wash or peeling potatoes.[1] And why must Dad be so meticulous about his truck? Doesn't he care about laying up treasure in heaven, where neither moth nor rust corrupts?[2] If my parents really loved God, wouldn't they let some of these things slide so they could focus on what counts for eternity?

I have never wavered from the initial commitment I made in high school. After more than twelve years of higher education, I became an ordained minister and a seminary professor. However, along the way I also married, took out a mortgage, and picked up a hobby or two. In short, I have become like my parents.

Sometimes I feel the poorer for it. If only I had kept my original zeal for Christ, I might today be on the mission field, living by faith. Instead, I am leading an all-too-common life, where concern for the lost must make room for annual performance evaluations, parent-teacher conferences, and a slew of other mundane tasks.

This chapter is about the possibility that my misgivings are mistaken and that my parents, not me, were right after all.

Our First Command

In chapter 4 we learned that the meaning of human life arises from our creation in the image of God, an image that places us in relationship with God, each other, and the earth. Chapters 5 and 6 explored these initial two relationships. Now we examine a third opportunity to reflect our Creator as we responsibly cultivate his creation.[3]

This area of responsibility is frequently overlooked by evangelical Christians, perhaps because we fear that too much emphasis on the earth may distract our attention from our more important duties to love God and serve others. However, as we will see, our responsibility to cultivate the earth is connected to these prior two relationships in important ways.

For starters, this duty is directly related to God because it is the first command he ever gave us. As we learned in chapter 4, God commanded his freshly minted humans to "be fruitful," "increase in number," "fill the earth," "subdue it," and "rule" over the rest of creation. These five directives to govern and develop the original creation are what theologians call the "creation mandate" or "cultural mandate." It is the first command God ever gave us, and he has never taken it back. If you are a human being, this cultural mandate applies to you. It is a large reason why God placed you on this planet.

In Genesis 2:15 God elaborates on this command: "The LORD God took the man and put him in the Garden of Eden to work it and take care of it." Notice that this instruction preceded Adam and Eve's fall into sin. This strongly suggests that labor is not a consequence of sin; we would be expected to work hard even if the fall had never occurred. In fact, work turns out to be a very godlike activity, for Genesis 2:2 declares that God himself diligently labored to fashion our world during the first six days of creation. In sum, we work because God works, and we are created in his image.

Let's take a closer look at these two commands to "work" (ʿābad) and "take care of" (shāmar) the garden. God did not create a static world. He didn't want his pristine creation to remain the same, but commanded Adam and Eve to make it better. I'm always a bit surprised that God didn't take the safe route, content to merely warn

Adam and Eve not to mess things up. He could have said something like this: "Children, here's a wonderful world for you to enjoy. Have all the fun you want, just don't break anything!"

But he didn't. God created a stunning Garden of Eden in the midst of a beautiful earth, placed Adam and Eve there, and then told them to change things. But how could they improve an already glorious world? By developing it in a distinctively human fashion: Plant the geraniums over there, learn what grows best where and what they most enjoy eating. God wanted Adam and Eve to participate in his ongoing work of creation, to take the raw materials of a perfect world and arrange them to produce the highest possible benefit.

This task continues today. We call it the development of culture. Cultures advance as people learn to cultivate the resources of God's creation, learning how to grow more wheat with less energy, pounding the earth's metals into automobiles and musical instruments, and mastering the lengthy process of turning the extra wool on a lamb into a hand-knit sweater.

Where does your job fit into this picture? How does what you do enable you or others to exercise dominion over the earth, cultivating its resources for the profit of both humanity and the earth itself? If you can locate your occupation within this process, you will discover a divine nobility in your tasks. You will no longer work with one eye on the clock, motivated only by your paycheck, but will realize that in your job you are cooperating with God. God has humbly chosen to complete and care for his creation through you. To paraphrase Martin Luther: "God milks his cows by those farmers he has assigned to that task."[4]

God also commanded Adam and Eve to guard or take care of his creation. They must not carelessly destroy the earth as they develop its resources, but even as they mine its treasures they must remember their obligation to protect it.[5]

These twin responsibilities to "cultivate" and "keep" the garden (NASB) act as guardrails to keep us on track as we cultivate the goodness of God's creation. On the one hand, we must not so over-protect the earth that we turn it into a museum, for this would forsake our obligation to develop its raw materials. On the other hand, we must not recklessly overuse creation that we waste and pollute its valuable, and sometimes irreplaceable, resources.

Just knowing this dual-sided responsibility will not necessarily make our specific decisions any easier, for well-informed and well-meaning people may still disagree about whether it is appropriate to drill for oil in the Arctic National Wildlife Refuge, restrict the size and number of gasoline-powered engines on our highways, or convert acres of arable farmland into suburban subdivisions. Nevertheless, though we may disagree with the views of any specific position, the dual command to cultivate and protect creation still provides the talking points on which the conversation can move forward.

So That's What the Reformation Was About

The significance of this cultural mandate was largely lost until the time of the Reformation. Although the early church fought valiantly to defeat Gnosticism, it never did entirely overcome its deep attraction to Greek philosophy, particularly that of Plato. Plato held to a spirit-body dualism that was strikingly similar to Gnosticism. Like the Gnostics, he believed that our eternal souls formerly inhabited an ethereal, heavenly world. At birth these souls entered our bodies, where they remain trapped inside these physical prisons until death releases and returns them to their celestial home. Consequently, Plato taught his students to value the eternal, spiritual world and disdain this temporal, material existence. He said that the goal of life is for our souls to rise above our bodies and contemplate the spiritual world from which they came.

Plato's spirit-body dualism significantly impacted the early church. For instance, it motivated readers of Scripture to dig beneath the plain, historical-grammatical meaning of the text to uncover a deeper, spiritual meaning below. It encouraged the more zealous types to forsake the physical world entirely, or as much as they could, and become lonely monks intent on nothing but their individual spiritual growth. And it implied that physical pleasures, such as the act of marriage and the enjoyment of material goods, are at worst evil and at best distractions from the most important things in life. Rather than indulge in these base pleasures, those who are deeply devoted to God would take vows of celibacy and poverty.

This Platonic dualism was at least partially conveyed to the Middle Ages by Augustine, the most important church father since New Testament times. Augustine had dabbled in Neoplatonism before his conversion, and though he successfully checked most of its wrong beliefs at the door, he unknowingly carried remnants of its unconcern for creation into his Christianity. He passed this along to the rest of the church, which understandably (and in most areas of his thought, correctly) sought to follow his example.

All this to say that by the sixteenth century the medieval church had more than a millennium of Platonic influence under its belt. It believed that marriage is legitimate—a sacrament even—but that celibacy is the ultimate Christian ideal. Possessions are permissible, but poverty is better. It is okay to hold a normal, nine-to-five job, but even better to be a monk who invests his entire day, every day, in prayer and spiritual contemplation. With these views, the church transformed Christianity into an add-on religion. The normal, ordinary life is tolerable, but those who really want to please God will always go one better. They will seek to move beyond the ordinary, relinquishing some aspect of their humanity in order to reap the more desirable spiritual benefits.

It was precisely this type of add-on Christianity that raised the Reformers' ire and ignited the Reformation. Against the church's insistence that only spiritual callings ultimately mattered, Martin Luther left the monastery and got married. Although Luther barely knew the former nun whom he was marrying (and those who did tried to dissuade him, saying that while marriage was a good idea, "for heaven's sake, not this one"), he said he wanted to go through with the wedding for three reasons: to please his father with grandchildren, to spite the pope, and to seal his witness to the Reformation faith before he died. (He expected to be burned at the stake within the year.)[6]

Though this is admittedly not the most romantic story in the annals of love, Luther wished to prove by his life that an ordinary married life is equal, if not superior, to his previous life as a monk. No longer should devoted followers of Christ imagine that they must endure a superhuman, angelic existence. In the words of Herman Bavinck, rather than continue the medieval call to rise beyond this world, the Reformers urged their followers to change it. In this way they sought a "Reformation of the natural."[7]

Called to Serve Others

The Reformers recovered the importance of the natural world by emphasizing our various vocations, or callings from God. ("Vocation" comes from the Latin *vocare*, which means "to call.") They explained that our formative calling occurred when God, through the power of the Holy Spirit, compelled us to follow his Son, Jesus Christ. This foundational calling, first heard at the moment of conversion, continues to command our complete commitment throughout our lives. In the words of Os Guinness, this calling is "the truth that God calls us to himself so decisively that everything we are, everything we do, and everything we have is invested with a special devotion, dynamism, and direction lived out as a response to his summons and service."[8] Unlike the medievals, who thought that the best way to answer this call was to join a monastery, the Reformers observed that this primary calling contains within it a plethora of secondary vocations that require our continued presence in the world.

For example, the Reformers would say that my various vocations include my obligation to God to be a faithful husband, father, brother, friend, church member, professor, author, neighbor, citizen, home-owner, and so on. Each one of these vocations describes a specific responsibility that I have before God to care for his world. Together they represent the complete way that I obey God's primary call on my life. As I faithfully fulfill these duties before the face of God, I answer the call of Jesus Christ, who has redeemed me and then placed me into his service. This is why Bavinck declared that the Reformation was a "Reformation of the natural." Rather than instructing godly people to flee this evil world, the gospel urges Christians to remain engaged in the world so that they might reform their various vocations for the glory of God.

Because our love for God is inextricably bound to our love for neighbor (as we learned in the previous chapter), one vital way our vocations honor God is how they benefit others. Each item in my personal list of vocations above implies, rather directly, a relationship with other people. "Husband" implies that I have a wife, just as "son" suggests parents, "author" readers, and so on. As I carefully tend to these vocations, I am not only serving God, but through his various callings on my life am also serving others.

For instance, I serve my family when I bring home a paycheck, play with my children, and do odd jobs around our home. I serve my parents and siblings when I stay in touch, pitch in when they need a hand, and remember their birthdays and anniversaries with a punctual card (I'm still working on that one). I serve my community when I make time to chat with my neighbors, write informed letters to the editor for the local newspaper, and pick up the fast-food trash that passing diners discard in my yard. And I serve the body of Christ when I prepare well for a Sunday morning message or instruct my students how to do the same.

Just as I answer these callings to serve others, so I benefit when others use their vocations to help me. For example, consider all of the effort that goes into a humble peanut-butter-and-jelly sandwich. It's relatively easy for me—I simply go to the cupboard, open a couple jars, and slap two slices of bread together. But it's so convenient only because hundreds, perhaps thousands, of others have faithfully fulfilled their personal vocations on my behalf.

I can't possibly list them all, but there are the growers of the peanuts, strawberries, wheat, and whatever other ingredients go into making peanut butter, jelly, and bread. Then there are the factories and mills that process the ingredients, the truckers who haul the loaves and jars to town, and a store full of stockers and cashiers who sell them to me. I might add those organizations that mined and smelted the stainless steel for my knife and processed the paper for my plate, together with their transportation systems. Each of these groups represents businesses with administrators, secretaries, financial officers, purchasing and marketing agents, and human resource personnel. If I could somehow add it all up, I'd probably be dumbfounded by the number of hands that either directly or indirectly contributed to my midmorning snack.

The Reformers noticed this reliance on others and praised God for it, for they believed that those who use their vocations to serve us become the hands of God in our lives. As Luther explained in his Large Catechism, "Our parents and all authorities—in short, all people placed in the position of neighbors—have received the command to do us all kinds of good. So we receive our blessings not from them, but from God through them. Creatures are only the hands, channels, and means through which God bestows all blessings."[9]

Because we rarely think of these helpers as divine agents, Luther frequently calls them the "mask of God."[10] Although God could directly intervene in our affairs, giving us bread from heaven the way he bestowed manna on the Israelites, he typically chooses to conceal himself within our normal human vocations. Luther encourages us to recognize, through eyes of faith, that the many hands that serve us ultimately belong to God, just as surely as if he had miraculously made a PB & J sandwich appear on my kitchen table.

John Calvin agrees. After a lifetime of reflection on God's providence in our lives, Calvin inserted this single line into the final edition of his *Institutes*. He observed that "God's providence does not always appear naked, but by employing means, God is, as it were, dressed."[11] Like Luther's analogy of a mask, Calvin suggests that our human efforts are the clothes of God. Certainly God reserves the right to directly intervene in our world, using his naked, brute force to accomplish his will. However, most often God does not operate in such naked fashion, but chooses to conceal his working within human hands.

Calvin and Luther encourage us to recognize the invisible world that lies behind our various vocations. My particular callings have value because through them I become the hands of God to someone else. Likewise, the help I receive from them is God's way of blessing me. Even when our vocations lead us to spend an inordinate amount of time with inanimate things such as building houses, collecting garbage, or repairing roads, we are still serving other people. These callings are necessary because people need shelter, a place to deposit waste, and smooth streets to move from one place to another.

In this way, as we hinted at the beginning of this chapter, our obedience to responsibly care for the earth is intimately connected to our relationship with others. And since our love for others is directly tied to our love for God, our obedience to our particular callings in the cultural mandate is one important way that we love God.

Heigh-Ho, Heigh-Ho, It's Off to Work We Go

With this truth in mind, consider that specific vocation by which we earn a living (I mean to include housewives and mothers, not merely those lesser jobs that we must be paid to do). Why do we work? After some reflection, we might offer that we need to earn money to support our family and our local church. We might add that we hope to rub shoulders with unsaved people and share the gospel with them.

These are important reasons and even wonderful by-products of having a job, but they can't be the number one reason we go to work. If work is only good for earning money and finding evangelistic opportunities, then most of our jobs are unfulfilling most of the time.

Think about it. I don't want to disparage the money, for we need it to take care of our familial and church responsibilities. But is our time spent at work worth nothing more than its cash value? Some of us are stuck in jobs we don't particularly enjoy. We live for the weekends and the few hours of free time that we sneak in each evening. If we are working this hard at something we don't enjoy, merely for a buck, then we are mired in an extremely dismal existence.

Even those of us fortunate enough to have enjoyable jobs recognize, for that reason, that our work is worth far more than the income it generates. We work primarily not for the money but because our jobs seem to complete our humanity. As many early retirees and unemployed workers can attest, something more valuable than money—something truly irreplaceable—is lost when the daily rhythm of gainful employment is disrupted.

Or what about sharing the gospel? Again, this is a wonderful thing to do, and may God grant us all frequent openings to speak about Christ. However, if we're faithfully performing our jobs, we likely won't have lots of extra time to strike up spiritual conversations. Many of our jobs tend to isolate us from lost people; we spend much time at work riding alone in a car, sitting at a desk, screwing in parts on an assembly line, or cleaning Cheerios out of our child's ears. So if sharing our faith is the primary reason we go to work, most days we're just wasting our time.

Another, more serious problem with this approach is that people who seek to use their jobs primarily as witnessing opportunities tend to view their Christianity as something added on to life. They don't often ponder how obedience to Jesus Christ directly changes the way they work; they merely tack him on to their work. They typically don't view their jobs as a way to serve Christ, but think that they are only obeying Christ when they are talking about him with others. Wouldn't it be better if, rather than viewing Jesus as an add-on, we recognize that as our Lord he wishes to centrally transform the very way we conduct our jobs?

For instance, rather than plot our next evangelistic encounter, what if we ponder what it means to follow our crucified Christ as we close a deal, type a report, sort the mail, care for our employees, or prepare a lesson? For starters, one who has died with Christ will refuse to cut corners, but will build houses up to code even if it means that his bid comes in higher than his shoddy competitors'. She will always speak the truth to her clients even if it means losing their business. He will honor the promises he's made to his employees even when it hurts the bottom line. She will resist the temptation to "phone it in," but even though she's taught the course a zillion times, will continue to stretch for fresh insights and innovative ways to present the material.

When we allow Jesus Christ to change our work, he becomes so much more than someone we merely talk about at work. He becomes the reason why we work. Perhaps best of all, when others observe our commitment, the foolish way we deny ourselves for the sake of Christ, they are bound to wonder about us. Consequently, we will likely enjoy many more quality opportunities to speak about our faith in Christ than if we had come to work with only that goal in mind.

We're All Full-time Christians Now

The Reformers pressed home the logical implications of this renewed concern for our various vocations. They immediately recognized that all Christians now stand on a level field. We no longer need to bow in deference to pastors and missionaries, who alone have been called into "full-time Christian service." After all, if only pastors and missionaries are "full-time" Christians, then what does that make the rest of us—part-time, half-time, or worse?

It is true that pastors and missionaries possess a particularly high calling from God. There is no greater privilege or responsibility than to lead Christ's church. However, as significant as this is, they are not the only full-time Christian workers. If we do our work as unto the Lord, then our work pleases God just as much as if we were preaching a sermon or evangelizing in a Third World nation. Whether we are a lawyer, engineer, entrepreneur, or janitor, we must recognize that our job, too, is a calling from God.

This truth touches me in a personal way. When I was a toddler, my parents traveled to Guatemala on a short-term mission trip. They greatly enjoyed their time there, but after several months' reflection on their gifts and "fit" for mission work, decided against returning full-time. Some people, including their pastor, thought they were making a huge mistake. If they were completely committed to Christ, why wouldn't they give up everything, including their children, to serve God in a foreign country?

Despite this pressure, my parents recognized that one of their vocations was parenting, a responsibility they were not prepared to subcontract to another. (I don't mean to imply that missionary families who send their children to boarding schools are shirking their parental responsibilities. This is an individual decision that each family must make before God.)

Equally important, my parents decided they were just not cut out for mission work. My mother found her greatest delight as a stay-at-home mom, and my father thought his gifts were more suited to construction work. So for the next twenty-five years my parents devoted themselves to their vocations, my mother raising four godly sons and my father perfecting his trade until he became widely known as the best drywall finisher in northeast Ohio.

According to the Reformers, my parents' vocational choice is equally valuable before God as if they had become foreign missionaries. In a sermon on Matthew 6:24–34, Luther explained:

To serve God simply means to do what God has commanded and not to do what God has forbidden. And if only we would accustom ourselves properly to this view, the entire world would be full of service to God, not only the churches but also the home, the kitchen, the cellar, the workshop, and the field of townsfolk and farmers. For it is certain that God would have not only the church and world order but also the house order established and upheld. All, therefore, who serve the latter purpose—father and mother first, then the children, and finally the servants and neighbors—are jointly serving God; for so He wills and commands.

In the light of this view of the matter a poor maid should have the joy in her heart of being able to say: "Now I am cooking, making the bed, sweeping the house. Who has commanded me to do these things? My master and mistress have. Who has given them this authority over me? God has. Very well, then it must be true that I am serving not them alone but also God in heaven and that God must be pleased with my service. How could I possibly be more blessed? Why, my service is equal to cooking for God in heaven!"

In this way a man could be happy and of good cheer in all his trouble and labor; and if he accustomed himself to look at his service and calling in this way, nothing would be distasteful to him. But the devil opposes this point of view tooth and nail, to keep one from coming to this joy and to cause everybody to have a special dislike for what he should do and is commanded to do. So the devil operates in order to make sure that people do not love their work and no service be rendered to God.[12]

Like my parents, some of you may need to know that God is pleased with you and what you do for a living. To you, I say that as long as you are using your gifts to please him, to contribute to society and thus obey the cultural mandate, then you are a full-time servant of God. You don't need to apologize to anyone for not being in professional ministry. You are not a second-class citizen of the kingdom. When you do your job for Christ, whether it is filing papers, serving a customer, or scrubbing toilets, you please God.

Sometimes our capitalistic economy makes this difficult to see. In the name of efficiency we have constructed assembly lines where a person does the same repetitive job day after day, such as tightening the same number seven screw. This is not the ideal job; it is not the way God intended us to work. We who are able should strive to reorganize such dismal workplaces so that our fellow laborers can find outlets for their creativity and so better reflect the divine image they bear. But even if you happen to have one of the most tedious, dead-end jobs imaginable, you can still find value and dignity in what you are doing.

For instance, what does your number seven screw do? Let's say it holds the legs of a desk in place. Well, then, you're not just tightening the number seven screw, you're making desks. And why are you making desks? Because people need them. Every desk you put together for another person—not just because it's your job but because you seek to obey the God who commanded you to develop creation and contribute to your society—becomes obedience to the creation mandate. Every desk, every tightening of the number seven screw, is weighted with significance.

Career Counseling

With this Reformational, "worldly" perspective, how should we go about selecting a career path? Too many people settle on an occupation because of its salary, prestige, or benefits package. These are important factors, for we all need cash, health insurance, and the respect of others. But other, more important values should drive our decision.

For instance, what if we chose our career path based on our giftedness and interests (that is, what we are good at and what we enjoy doing)? What if we thought beyond ourselves, selecting our occupation based on how well it enabled us to contribute to society and serve others, especially "the least of these," as we together cultivate God's creation and seek to raise the level of shalom? What if we tried to match our skills and temperament with society's greatest needs? What if we asked whether our career adds something necessary and wholesome to others, or whether it actually detracts from the net gain of goodness in the world? What if we made certain that our career choice, whatever it is, could be easily balanced with our other vocational responsibilities, such as our obligation to church and family? Wouldn't these be better, more biblical criteria than how well a job pays, the size of its stock options, and how much vacation time we get?[13]

To illustrate, my present attempt at writing this book is a side calling that arises from my vocation as a seminary professor. Although filling a blank page with meaningful words is often a daunting and tiresome task, these first seven chapters have brought me deep joy and satisfaction. When friends ask how my book is coming, I usually respond that while it is hard work, I also think I have found a significant piece of my calling. The pleasure I take in a well-turned phrase—akin to the satisfaction of a musician who nails a difficult lick or a craftsman who caresses the smooth contours of his sanded shelf—leads me to think that perhaps I was born to write. Combined with my enthusiasm for the content of this book, I sense, at least for now, that writing is one important way I can serve others and fulfill my calling from God.

Of course, this initial belief may change if few people appreciate or pass along this book to others. Perhaps my estimation of this book and my writing ability is overrated. In that case my writing may still qualify as an *avocation*—a hobby or diversion that I do more for my own enjoyment than as a vocation by which I serve others. And that's okay. We all need hobbies that satisfy some of the creative aptitude and energy we rarely get to use in our central vocations. No single vocation can utilize all that we have to offer. This is why God gives us more than one, plus avocations on the side.[14]

Besides our need to turn inward and analyze ourselves, we should also look outward and, as the corporate body of Christ, encourage others to find and fulfill their vocations. Brothers and sisters in the family of God should regularly watch out for one another, feeling free to say, "Sue, you're really good at that. Have you ever considered pursuing a degree in that area?" or "Tom, how are you juggling your overtime with family time? Don't forget your obligation to God to be your children's father."

In sum, because we now recognize that our vocations matter to God, we must take them very seriously. Our vocations are more than a way to earn money or bolster self-esteem; they are a primary way that we serve God in the world. What the Reformers knew, and what we must learn, is that every corner of our existence matters to God. Does God care that we go to church, read the Bible, and pray? Of course he does. But he also cares deeply about how we raise our children, conduct our business, and spend our weekends. Even when we are not doing "spiritual" things, our actions, when done from obedience to God's cultural mandate, still count. The cultural mandate fills every aspect of our lives with meaning. To synthesize Paul's words in Colossians 3:17 and 23: "Whatever you do, whether in word or deed, work at it with all your heart. Do it all in the name of the Lord Jesus, giving thanks to God the Father through him."

To Savor the Works of Our Hands

"Remember the Sabbath day by keeping it holy."

EXODUS 20:8

From the indispensable microwave ovens, speed-dial telephones, and digital video recorders with commercial skip to fast food, frozen entrees, and instant anything (coffee, potatoes, etc.), never in the history of humanity have people possessed so many time-saving devices. It's a good thing, because never in the history of the world have people possessed so little time to save. Whether it's squeezing in a little overtime, volunteering on various community or church committees, or chauffeuring children to school, swim meets, and clarinet lessons, we are one exhausted country.

The upscale village of Ridgewood, New Jersey, had finally had enough. Tired of lugging little ones to the next essential activity, these parents decided to organize a family night on which all homework and extracurricular events would be canceled. It took an eighteen-member committee seven months of meetings to plan the event, but they finally found one evening—a Tuesday—that everyone—pastors, coaches, and teachers—could agree to leave free. Rather than race across town to the next event, parents and children spent this quiet evening at home, relaxing, playing games, and sharing a leisurely dinner full of laughter and conversation.[1]

While Ridgewood's example is commendable, I can't help but wonder if part of their exhaustion stems from either not knowing or not following the Christian worldview. Perhaps they would not have needed to schedule this special nonevent if they had realized that they already possess an entire day each week to slow down and catch their breath.

This day of rest is the second climax of the creation story. Like the first climax of creation, humanity, this day of rest is uniquely special not only because it is the final day but also because it is so different from the previous days of creation. God filled the first six days with his creative acts, but on this, the seventh day, he rested.

> Thus the heavens and the earth were completed in all their vast array. By the seventh day God had finished the work he had been doing; so on the seventh day he rested from all his work. And God blessed the seventh day and made it holy, because on it he rested from all the work of creating that he had done.[2]

Aren't you glad that the story of creation does not end after the sixth day? If it had, we might get the idea that life is nothing more than an opportunity to work, work, and work some more. Instead, Genesis' opening chapters present a more balanced view. The story of creation depicts the rhythm of life, a rhythm that alternates between the pulsating allegros of the workday week and the serene legato of the seventh-day rest.[3]

The Original Holiday

The Jewish notion of a "Sabbath" is grounded in this opening story of creation, for Genesis 2:2 states that God rested, or began to *shābat*.

This Hebrew term for rest means "to cease or desist." The sense here is simply that on the seventh day of creation God stopped the work he had been doing during the previous six days. It was literally a day off.

Exodus 31:17 elaborates on this break in God's activity, for there we learn that God not only stopped working on the seventh day, but in his rest "was refreshed" (NKJV). The Hebrew term for "refreshed" means to stop and catch one's breath.[4] Much as we use it today, the Hebrews metaphorically said that a person who works hard often runs ahead of his air. This is why he bends over and grabs his knees, panting heavily until his air catches up. Now refreshed, he is able to continue his work.

The imagery does not directly apply to God, for he does not have knees to grab and he never grows weary.[5] Yet there is a sense in which the seventh day refreshed him. It was a time to enjoy the works of his hands, to delight in the beauty of his creation, and to savor the perfect community that existed between him and Adam. Even God knows when enough is enough. His act of creation now complete, he handed this good world over to Adam for its cultural development. While God's providence would continue to govern his creation, the responsibility for teasing out the latent possibilities within creation rested on Adam.

This seventh-day rest that God took—is it a creation ordinance? Like the cultural mandate of Genesis 1:26–28 and 2:15, is this another rule or principle of creation that we must follow? Good Christians disagree. Many say no, this is not a creation ordinance because unlike the cultural mandate, there is no command here for Adam to rest. We must not hastily conclude that just because God rested on the seventh day, he expects everyone else to follow suit.

Others say yes, it is a creation ordinance—in large part because it is God who is resting. If rest and refreshment are important to God, then certainly they are most necessary for us. Although there is no direct command for us to rest, it is obvious that rest is built into the very structure of creation.

Furthermore, the day of rest is one of only three parts of creation that God specifically blessed. Earlier he blessed the animals and humanity, endowing them with power to be fruitful and rule over the earth.[6] There he blesses work; here he blesses rest. Just as his blessing intended that animals and people would successfully perform their respective tasks, so here his blessing empowers the function of the seventh day—it should be a day of refreshment, a day to catch our breath.

But God goes one step further. He not only blesses the seventh-day rest but also sanctifies it. To sanctify something means to set it apart, to declare that it is different, special. In Scripture we find sanctified things, such as utensils for the temple and the Scriptures themselves, which God calls "holy." The Scriptures are unlike any other writing; they are a holy book, for they are the very words of God. We also find sanctified places, such as Mount Sinai and the temple. No Israelite except Moses could touch the mountain when God was there, and no Israelite except the high priest could enter the Holy of Holies, because God was there. We also find sanctified people, such as the Levites and priests. These people were set apart for God's service in the temple.

Considering the many sanctified persons, places, and things, it is somewhat surprising that the first part of creation that God called holy, set apart, or special was not a person, place, or thing, but a time. God's week of creation included the creation of sacred time. He divided time, declaring that one day a week is holy and set apart for him.

Whether or not the seventh-day rest is a creation ordinance, there is no mistaking that God is making a statement here. Life is more than work. There must be a balanced rhythm between work and rest, labor and refreshment. Indeed, as a creature of the late sixth day, Adam's first full day on the planet was the seventh-day rest. He had just gotten started when it was already time for a break (a practice still followed by Michigan road crews).

Because the seventh-day rest is creation's final day, our refreshment seems to be the goal, the end toward which we work. Unlike the ancient Greeks, who argued that the sole purpose of rest is to renew our energy for the next task, the biblical story of creation implies that rest is an end in itself. Like God, we work hard so that we may enjoy the fruit of our labor.

You Deserve a Break Today

We haven't determined yet whether this seventh-day rest is a creation ordinance. To find out, it is helpful to examine how this day of rest functioned within the nation of Israel and then the church.

Israel certainly understood the importance of this day of rest, for it was included in the nation's Ten Commandments. When God cut his covenant with his people Israel, his top ten list included a mandatory day of rest every seven days. According to Exodus 20:8–11, the rationale for this rest arises from the story of creation.

> Remember the Sabbath day by keeping it holy. Six days you shall labor and do all your work, but the seventh day is a Sabbath to the LORD your God. On it you shall not do any work, neither you, nor your son or daughter, nor your manservant or maidservant, nor your animals, nor the alien within your gates. For in six days the LORD made the heavens and the earth, the sea, and all that is in them, but he rested the seventh day. Therefore the LORD blessed the Sabbath day and made it holy.[7]

According to this account, God's day of rest in creation provides a pattern for the Jewish people. Just as God sanctified his seventh-day rest, so his people must keep the day holy by resting every seven days. They have six days to labor, or ⁹*ābad*,[8] but the seventh day is a *shabbāt*, a day of rest to the Lord.

At the time this command was given, the day of rest was exactly that. It wasn't meant to be a distinctive day of worship. While priests would offer additional sacrifices on the Sabbath, there is no evidence that the average Israelite performed any special religious tasks. They didn't necessarily come to the tabernacle, offer sacrifices, or read long passages from the Law. Instead, the people used it as a day of rest, period.

And this day of rest was not just for themselves but also for their servants, animals, and even the non-Hebrews living among them. God's point is that one day in seven everyone deserves a break. They rest not in order to do anything, such as worship, but for the sake of refreshment and to catch their breath.

On a related note, God intends the Sabbath rest not only for his people and their animals but also for the earth. In Leviticus 25:1–7 he instructs Israel to give the land a rest. Every seventh year they must refrain from planting and pruning, content to eat whatever they have stored from previous years or whatever the land produces on its own.

Exodus is not the only place where Scripture records the Ten Commandments. It also lists them in Deuteronomy 5, where we find a different slant on this Sabbath command. Moses reminds the Israelites to

> "Observe the Sabbath day by keeping it holy, as the LORD your God has commanded you. Six days you shall labor and do all your work, but the seventh day is a Sabbath to the LORD your God. On it you shall not do any work, neither you, nor your son or daughter, nor your manservant or maidservant, nor your ox, your donkey or any of your animals, nor the alien within your gates, so that your manservant and maidservant may rest, as you do. *Remember that you were slaves in Egypt and that the LORD your God brought you out of there with a mighty hand and an outstretched arm. Therefore the LORD your God has commanded you to observe the Sabbath day.*"[9]

While most of this passage reads much like Exodus 20, it does offer a new rationale for the command. Rather than ground the Sabbath rest in creation, God now bases it on redemption. Resting every seven days is a way for Israel to remember that God has delivered them from the fields of slavery in Egypt (where weekend breaks were not allowed).

This redemptive addition to the Sabbath command is understandable, for, as we will learn in chapter 11, since redemption amounts to the restoration of creation, it should not be surprising that their goal turns out to be the same. Consider that the word for "slaves" in this passage is *ʿābad*—the same word used to describe Adam's serving the garden and the Israelite work week.[10] Thus, wherever one is laboring, whether in the garden of creation, the farms of Palestine, or the oppressive fields of Egypt, the goal remains the same—Sabbath rest.

A Test of Faith

In one respect, the Sabbath rest was the most important of the Ten Commandments, for it was not only a part of the covenant, but also the sign of the covenant. God instructed Moses,

> "Say to the Israelites, 'You must observe my Sabbaths. This will be a *sign* between me and you for the generations to come, so you may know that I am the LORD, who makes you holy.
>
> "'Observe the Sabbath, because it is holy to you. Anyone who desecrates it must be put to death; whoever does any work on that day must be cut off from his people. For six days, work is to be done, but the seventh day is a Sabbath of rest, holy to the LORD. Whoever does any work on the Sabbath day must be put to death. The Israelites are to observe the Sabbath, celebrating it for the generations to come as a lasting covenant. It will be a *sign* between me and the Israelites forever, for in six days the LORD made the heavens and the earth, and on the seventh day he abstained from work and rested.'"[11]

Along with circumcision, keeping the Sabbath day was a sign that Israel was the people of God. Anyone who worked on the Sabbath should be put to death, for it was a sure sign that they did not love God.

Isaiah explains the same thing in a positive way, encouraging the Israelites that

"If you keep your feet from breaking the Sabbath and from doing as you please on my holy day, if you call the Sabbath a *delight* and the LORD's holy day honorable, and if you honor it by not going your own way and not doing as you please or speaking idle words, then you will find your *joy* in the LORD, and I will cause you to ride on the heights of the land and to feast on the inheritance of your father Jacob."[12]

This passage portrays the direct link for Israel between the Sabbath and the Lord. Those who delight in their day of refreshment will also delight in God and enjoy his blessing.

Unfortunately, the sad history of Israel is that they frequently disobeyed God and desecrated his Sabbaths. The prophet Ezekiel explains how immediately after receiving the Ten Commandments, while they were still in the desert on their way to Palestine, Israel polluted the Sabbath day and received the judgment of God, forbidden entrance into the Promised Land.[13]

Later, after the Israelites were finally settled in their new country, the prophet Jeremiah warned Judah that its very survival depended on keeping the Sabbath day holy.[14] But they would not listen, and so they were taken into exile. Even after their restoration, when a chastened Judah returned to Jerusalem, the people still struggled to keep the Sabbath. Nehemiah became exasperated and threatened with force those who attempted to buy and sell on the Sabbath. "If you do this again," Nehemiah warned, "I will lay hands on you."[15]

Why did the Israelites struggle to keep the Sabbath, and why was it so important to God that he would destroy the nation when they violated it? These two questions have the same answer. It was important to God because the Sabbath demonstrated his sovereignty, his ownership, over Israel. Every week when the Israelites stopped their normal routine and took a break, their actions announced that God is Lord of all life, even their time.

Of course, this is why they struggled to keep it. Because people are fallen, they don't want to submit to God as Lord of all, especially their time. So the Sabbath rest became a sore spot between God and

Israel, a tug-of-war over who is the sovereign Lord of all life. More often than not, Israel gave the wrong answer—and suffered terribly because of it.

From Sabbath to the Lord's Day

This may be a fine survey of the Sabbath's purpose in the Old Testament, but how does it apply to us, the church of the New Testament? At first glance, not very much.

The Sabbath is the only one of the Ten Commandments not restated in the New Testament. For instance, though Jesus intensifies the command against adultery and murder to include lust and anger,[16] he makes no mention of the need to keep the Sabbath. In fact, the New Testament goes out of its way to explain that Christians are no longer obligated to observe the Sabbath day. According to Paul,

> One man considers one day more sacred than another; another man considers every day alike. Each one should be fully convinced in his own mind. He who regards one day as special, does so to the Lord. He who eats meat, eats to the Lord, for he gives thanks to God; and he who abstains, does so to the Lord and gives thanks to God.[17]

Paul seems to relegate the observance of special days, such as the Sabbath, to Christian liberty. He makes the same point more explicitly in his letter to the Colossians. After explaining that Christ's sacrificial death has eliminated the requirements of the law, Paul admonishes the church to "not let anyone judge you by what you eat or drink, or with regard to a religious festival, a New Moon celebration or a Sabbath day. These are a shadow of the things that were to come; the reality, however, is found in Christ."[18] Here Paul implies that the reason the New Testament does not reissue the Sabbath command is because it has been fulfilled in Christ.

For more on this, we turn to Hebrews 4:1–11, the primary discussion of Sabbath rest in the New Testament. In Hebrews 3 we are exhorted to persevere in our faith by fixing our minds on Jesus, the substitutionary atonement for our sins. The author then illustrates the perseverance we need by contrasting it with the Israelites, who failed to persevere during their journey to their promised rest in Canaan. Along the way they rebelled against God and so failed to achieve their rest.

In chapter 4 the author warns us to learn from their example:

> Therefore, since the promise of entering his rest still stands, let us be careful that none of you be found to have fallen short of it. For we also have had the gospel preached to us, just as they did; but the message they heard was of no value to them, because those who heard did not combine it with faith. Now we who have believed enter that rest, just as God has said: "So I declared on oath in my anger, 'They shall never enter my rest.'"
>
> And yet his work has been finished since the creation of the world. For somewhere he has spoken about the seventh day in these words: "And on the seventh day God rested from all his work." And again in the passage above he says, "They shall never enter my rest."
>
> It still remains that some will enter that rest, and those who formerly had the gospel preached to them did not go in, because of their disobedience. Therefore God again set a certain day, calling it Today, when a long time later he spoke through David, as was said before: "Today, if you hear his voice, do not harden your hearts."
>
> For if Joshua had given them rest, God would not have spoken later about another day. There remains, then, a Sabbath-rest for the people of God; for anyone who enters God's rest also rests from his own work, just as God did from his. Let us, therefore, make every effort to enter that rest, so that no one will fall by following their example of disobedience.[19]

While this is an exceedingly difficult passage, most commentators agree on the following four points.[20] First, this passage clearly states that rest is the goal of both creation and redemption. Just as God rested on the seventh day of creation, so Israel sought her promised rest during her deliverance from Egypt and so we pursue rest as the goal of our salvation. This double ground for rest in creation and redemption, the beginning and end of life, resoundingly underscores its central role in our lives.

Second, and this is a bit more controversial, the text seems to imply that in some sense our salvation rest is already here. In the author's words, "We who have believed enter that rest." Although our rest will not be complete until we run the course of this life, yet we who believe the gospel are already in the process of entering that rest. Our salvation, though its final fulfillment lies in the future, is already attainable.

Third, the gospel that supplies this rest is the good news that Jesus Christ has suffered and died on our behalf. Rather than trust our own works to earn our salvation, we rest on the finished work of Christ, who, according to Hebrews 2:9 and 17, has "taste[d] death for everyone . . . that he might make atonement for the sins of the people." Our good works, though essential evidence of our walk with Christ, cannot replace our more foundational faith in him. Salvation comes not to those who work harder but to those who learn how to rest in Christ, allowing his grace to forgive even their best efforts.

Fourth, if the Hebrew Sabbath is grounded on God's seventh-day rest (Exodus 20)—a rest that we ultimately receive when we rest in the finished work of Christ—then we might conclude, as Paul does in Colossians 2:16–17, that the Sabbath has been fulfilled in Christ. In sum, the Sabbath seems to be a type of Christ. Just as the Israelites stopped their work and rested on the Sabbath, so we stop trusting our religious or good works and rest in Christ. Our free salvation in Christ fills up the meaning of the Sabbath. That is why we no longer observe the Sabbath per se, but rather celebrate the Lord's Day.

Unlike the seventh-day Sabbath, we celebrate the Lord's Day on Sunday because the first day of the week is when Jesus arose from the grave. Also unlike the Sabbath, we are not such sticklers for complete rest. The New Testament indicates that the Lord's Day was a special day for the church to gather and worship. It is unclear whether the New Testament church also treated it as a special day of rest.

The Sabbath Today

So what is the point? There are reasons for believing that the Sabbath day is not a creation ordinance, and even better reasons for believing that it no longer applies to the church. Therefore, what role should the Sabbath play in our lives?

Here I defer to John Calvin, who presents what I believe is a balanced approach. He agrees that the Sabbath command has been fulfilled in Christ, yet he contends that there remains an important place in the Christian life for the Sabbath principle.[21]

First, it is obvious that rest is built into creation. Physical rest and refreshment are important. Although God does not command us to rest, it is instructive that he rested. If rest is important to God, it certainly should also be important to us. At the very least, we can agree that rest is a good idea. Modern life moves very fast. For many of us it is on the verge of becoming a blur. A seventh-day rest applies the brakes to our ceaseless activity, slowing life down just enough so that we can regain our bearings.

In light of this, we should expect Sunday to feel different from the other days. Ever wonder why we absolutely need a nap on Sunday afternoons and not on other days? Most weekday afternoons we crank it up a notch as we desperately seek to finish our assignments by quitting time. Not on Sunday. After feasting on a fine Sunday dinner, many of us drag ourselves to the couch for the sweetest sleep of our week. That is a good thing. It is a sign that we have slowed life down on this day, that we are grabbing our knees and catching our breath. We are being refreshed.

We must be careful here, for we don't want to make a new law, legislating where the Scriptures are silent. Romans 14 and Colossians 2 clearly say that we are not spiritually bound to keep the Sabbath. Christians aren't obligated to take naps on Sunday, especially if they're not tired. We must never imply that everyone or anyone *must* observe the Sabbath, for to do so would obscure our freedom in Christ and threaten the gospel itself. Christ has fulfilled the law. We must never impose its requirements on anyone, even with the best of intentions.

Nevertheless, though we must avoid the danger of legalism, we must also be careful lest we fall into the opposite human tendency of lawlessness. Those who casually dismiss the Sabbath because it is fulfilled in Christ will also miss the spiritual benefits its physical rest provides.

For instance, precisely because the Sabbath is fulfilled in Christ, it ably serves as a silent testimony to our faith in Christ. Rather than automatically discard the Sabbath because it is fulfilled in Christ, we may recognize in this day a wonderful reminder of our salvation. Our day of physical rest makes a fine type of our spiritual rest in Christ. Because our life is secure in him, we are free to relax. We do not need to work nonstop in order to make something of ourselves or to secure our place in history. We are already somebody. We are children of the King, secure in his love.

With this perspective, our day of rest becomes a weekly reminder that the defining questions of our lives are settled. Our lives are hidden with Christ. Without saying a word, our physical break announces to a harried world that we are resting in our risen Savior and Lord.

How about it? Do we have one day a week to rest physically and refresh ourselves? Sunday is the obvious choice, since for many of us it provides a natural break from our weekly responsibilities. Have we made the break, or do the commitments of the week continue to press in upon us, consuming increasingly larger chunks of our Lord's Day?

Protecting our day of rest must be intentional. There are too many distractions for it to happen by accident. For some of us, it is employers who make continued demands on our day of rest. The pressure to perform makes it almost impossible to say no. For others, it's our children. Soccer and football leagues now schedule their games on Sunday mornings.

That never happened when I was a kid. My father thought it was bad enough that my baseball team had games on Wednesday nights.

Every Wednesday at a quarter till seven, which usually fell during the third inning, I told the coach I was leaving for prayer meeting. I hated missing the rest of the game, and I was still in church when my victorious teammates, whooping and hollering from the bed of a pickup truck, rode past for their post-game ice cream cone. But my father was wise. Unlike the other parents who let their kids play on, he taught me what was important in life.

For some of us, the distractions may come from the last place we'd expect—our church. If we are not careful, we can become too involved in church meetings and activities that Sunday is anything but a day of rest. How do we feel at nine o'clock on Sunday evening? We should feel refreshed, ready to tackle another week. If not, it is time to evaluate our church commitments.

Second, besides physical rest, Calvin states that the Lord's Day is an opportunity for spiritual renewal. Because he's a preacher, Calvin asserts that in a perfect world the church would meet every day for worship and the preaching of the Word. But since our daily responsibilities make this impractical, God has given us one day in seven as a special day for worship.

This seventh day is a special opportunity to reflect on God's grace in our lives. In a sermon on the Sabbath, Calvin compares the Lord's Day to a high tower from which we may survey the terrain of our lives and remember just how good God has been to us. He says that if we take time for this on Sunday, we will be more disposed to live thankfully throughout the coming week, and if we don't, we should not be surprised to find ourselves living like beasts. The Lord's Day is a wonderful gift, an opportunity to stop the continual flow of life and remember what is important: the presence of our Father and his incomprehensible love for us.[22]

Despite these physical and spiritual benefits, I suspect that many of us Type A personalities will continually struggle to observe a weekly Sabbath. I typically approach Sunday afternoons with an impressive list of projects begging for my attention. But each Sunday, or nearly so, I fight the temptation to get a jump on the coming week (or catch up on the last one) and instead choose to stretch out on the couch, wrestle with my boys, and just be for a day. And each Sunday I'm awfully glad I did, for I begin my week refreshed, rejoicing in God, and close to my family.

There are many marks of the Christian life, signs that indicate how things are between us and the Lord. Here is an important one: How we are using the Lord's Day? It is a gift from God, grounded both in the original creation and in his Son's redemption, that offers both physical and spiritual refreshment. Feeling weary and worn out? Feeling far from God? Your answer does not merely begin this Sunday. It *is* Sunday. May it refresh you in the Lord.

Part Three

What Is Wrong with Me and My World?

The Fall in Genesis 3–11

The Original Sin

Therefore, just as sin entered the world through one man, and death through sin, and in this way death came to all men, because all sinned.

ROMANS 5:12

It is one of the more remarkable lessons of history: Every war that has ever been fought began without the benefit of a first shot. Though the corridors of time are littered with epic battles between families, nations, and kings, no one ever claims to have fired first. In the minds of the participants, every shot of every battle is merely a response to some previous injustice.[1]

For example, consider America's military operation in Afghanistan. We bombed the hideouts of Al Qaeda and their Taliban sponsors in order to exact revenge for their destruction of the World Trade Center and Pentagon and to prevent future attacks. For his part, Osama bin Laden claimed that he was motivated to kill Americans because we had established military bases in his Saudi homeland during the Gulf War. In our defense, we would never have come to Saudi Arabia had not Saddam Hussein directed his Iraqi troops to invade his neighboring country of Kuwait.

So does the blame for our terrorist crisis rest with Saddam? Not according to Iraq. In their view, Saddam was merely taking back what rightly belonged to his country. Britain had unjustly separated Kuwait from Iraq after the First World War to block Iraq's access to the Persian Gulf and prevent her from challenging Britain's dominance in the region. Now Saddam's desperately poor Iraq was merely recovering the wealthy territory that, according to the maps of the former Ottoman Empire, had always belonged to them.

From her perspective, Britain felt obligated to redraw the maps of the Middle East to protect her interests in the region. She had rebuffed her closest competitors, Germany, Russia, and the disintegrating Ottoman Empire, for control over this strategic area—rich with oil and essential trade routes to the East—and she was not about to carelessly allow other countries such as Iraq to threaten the flow of oil and trade that were so important to her prosperous way of life.

Of course, the nations Britain defeated had their own persuasive claims to the Middle East: Germany because of alliances made with the Ottoman Turks, Russia because Constantinople was her spiritual and cultural home, and the Turks because they had ruled the region for five centuries. Eventually, the claims and counterclaims of this part of the world run all the way back to medieval relations between Christians, Jews, and Muslims. Who was there first? Who has the right to be there today? Who is the aggressor, and who is merely defending their interests? It largely depends on whom you ask. The only certain fact in this corner of the world is that whoever initiates hostilities can point to centuries of animosity and injustice to justify their aggression. They're not firing the first shot—they're merely responding to what others have done to them.

This spirit of retaliation enables nations to defend their actions, regardless how brutal, to their own satisfaction. Of course they would prefer a more humane way to settle their differences, but given the national interests at stake, the iron fist of war often seems to be the best option. This annoying ability to rationalize, to vindicate our aggression in our own minds, has been around as long as there have been people. It began with the very first family and, as our turbulent world is too painfully aware, has never let up since.

The Mystery of Sin

Our previous chapters on creation have taught us some important truths. We've learned that creation is good. It was entirely good when it came from the hand of God, it remains good despite our sin, and one day soon its Creator, Jesus Christ, will return to restore it to its original goodness. We must never nod toward the Gnostic mistake that this physical world is somehow beneath us or a bad place to be. We also learned that as image bearers of God, we reflect our Creator when we cultivate the resources of this good creation and take a break to rest every seven days.

This rhythm of labor and refreshment should have continued forever. You and I should have been born into a perfect world: a world without suffering and tears, a world of exponentially increasing joys. We should live in a world where we never lock our doors, where farewells are never final, and where it never snows (I'm writing this in Michigan).[2] We should live in a world where everyone has a hundred best friends, where unbroken stallions offer free rides, and where juicy beefsteak tomatoes are picked fresh from the garden all year long.

But we don't. Something has gone terribly wrong. This world, with its break-ins, teary good-byes, frigid temperatures, lonely dinners for one, wild horses, and blossom end-rot, is not the way it's supposed to be. Like graffiti spray-painted across the Mona Lisa, our fallen creation is now a horrid amalgam of breathtaking beauty and crass ugliness. The world retains impressive reminders of its created beauty, but this beauty has now been buried beneath the unsightliness of sin.

This chapter examines our fall, or what went wrong with this perfect world.

Just what, not why. We do not know why Adam chose to sin. The first sin is an unsolvable riddle. Adam and Eve possessed perfect wills that had always chosen to obey God. What could make their perfectly good wills turn bad? We have no idea. It does not even seem possible, but somehow they turned their back on God and all the good they had ever known and chose evil.

We will never solve this mystery of sin, in large part because it is evil. Anything connected with the problem of evil, such as the presence of sin, the pain and suffering of the innocent, and the everlasting torment of hell, is not easily explained by any, including the Christian, worldview. Why did God permit the fall, why doesn't he protect the innocent victims of violence, and why doesn't he empty hell and save everyone? These questions, good ones all, are easier asked than answered. Like a misshaped piece to a jigsaw puzzle, evil's angular form is difficult to squeeze into any, including the Christian, picture of reality.

But this is what we should expect. If we could comprehend the presence of evil—its origin, purpose, and how and why God allowed it to enter his perfect world—then it wouldn't be quite so evil. A large part of what makes evil so bad is its inexplicable mystery. We will never be able to wrap our arms around it, never be able to declare, "Oh, now I get it! So that's why evil is here." Evil should never make sense. The moment we think we have explained it, intelligibly cramming it into our view of the world, at that moment we prove that we are no longer speaking about evil. Evil, just because it is so evil, resists fitting snugly into any worldview. It mocks any and all attempts to tame it, for a domesticated evil would not be evil after all.

So we will never entirely understand why the first couple sinned and why God permitted their fall to occur. Nevertheless, humanity's fall into sin is an important movement in the Christian story. Just as we cannot understand the Christian worldview without first comprehending the story of creation, so we will never make sense of this world without a healthy respect for the fall that has occurred here.

Of Snakes and Trees

To understand this original sin we must consider the chief characters and context of the story. Genesis 3:1 introduces the serpent who "was more crafty than any of the wild animals the LORD God had made." The Old Testament rarely supplies explicit descriptions for its characters. It prefers simply to tell the story and allow readers to learn about the characters from how they interact with others. But here, at the beginning of his story, the author makes a point of telling us that the serpent is crafty, or shrewd. He wants us to pay close attention to the serpent's words, for they may not mean what they seem.

God created a forest of beautiful and nutritious trees in the Garden of Eden, two of which—the tree of life and the tree of the knowledge of good and evil—were especially significant. "And the LORD God made all kinds of trees grow out of the ground—trees that were pleasing to the eye and good for food. In the middle of the garden were the tree of life and the tree of the knowledge of good and evil."[3]

The significance of the latter tree is explained in Genesis 2:16–17: "And the LORD God commanded the man, 'You are free to eat from any tree in the garden; but you must not eat from the tree of the knowledge of good and evil, for when you eat of it you will surely die.'" The Hebrew text emphasizes the certainty of death by repeating the verb, warning Adam that should he eat from the tree, then "dying you will die."

(The rumor that this tree of the knowledge of good and evil was an apple tree arises from a medieval pun. Monks poring over their Latin Bibles found it funny that the Latin term for "evil" *[malum]* is also the word for "apple." Thus, the running joke in the Middle Ages was that when Eve ate the *malum* [apple] she contracted *malum* [evil].[4] If you fail to see the humor here, project yourself into the confines of a medieval monastery. After a couple of weeks, you'd probably think it was funny too.)

In a garden overflowing with sturdy and stately trees, God tells Adam and Eve that there is only one that is off-limits. This lone tree becomes the small opening that the serpent will use to tempt Eve. Does that make you angry? Satan uses God's good creation to tempt Eve. He doesn't use his own material, for he has no material. He can only take the good things God has made and distort them for his own evil purposes.

Just like Adam and Eve, we live in world chock full of the goodness of the Lord. God made an abundance of good things for us to enjoy—and we should be content with them. We should be satisfied with our own spouses and houses, our own clothes and cars. Do other people have nice homes? Do other people have attractive husbands and wives? Sure they do. That should not be surprising, for they are all gifts from God. But our spouses and possessions are gifts also, and they're good too. We must not let Satan tempt us with the few things that are off-limits. God has created an entire garden for us to enjoy— so let's not obsess over that one fruit we can't have.

The tree of life appears to be the original fountain of youth, for it seems necessary to sustain Adam and Eve's physical existence. As long as they ate from the tree, they would continue to exist. This is implied in Genesis 3:22, which says God expelled Adam and Eve from the garden lest they eat from the tree of life and continue to exist in their sinful condition. It is also why the tree of life reappears in Revelation 22:2. Its presence at the end of the biblical story symbolizes that there will be no more dying on the new earth.

So the tree of life means exactly what its name implies: Whoever eats from this tree will maintain his physical existence. If the tree of life means what it says, then we should assume that the tree of the knowledge of good and evil also means what its name implies. Anyone who eats its fruit will gain moral discernment and wisdom—the ability to distinguish between right and wrong. We know this must be a good thing, for God said that Adam and Eve, having eaten from the tree, have "become like one of us, knowing good and evil."[5]

You may ask, what's wrong with that? If eating from the tree of the knowledge of good and evil makes one morally wise, why would God command Adam and Eve to stay away? That is exactly the same question the serpent asked. Now that we're thinking like the devil, let's look at the temptation itself.

Never Talk to Snakes

The crafty serpent approaches the woman with a clever question, "Did God really say, 'You must not eat from any tree in the garden'?"[6] Compared with what God said in Genesis 2:16–17, this is an outrageous question. There God commanded Adam not to eat from one tree—just one—and here the serpent blithely universalizes it to include the entire garden. The serpent knows that this is a heinous generalization, which is why he frames his statement as a question. A direct statement would too starkly oppose God's words and betray his intent. Eve would certainly be on to him. But a question—"hey, I'm only asking for information"—just might slip by her defenses.

How dare the serpent ask such a blatantly wrong question! All the good trees in the garden came from God. Because he warned them against eating from one—just one—suddenly he is a mean-spirited tyrant? What can the serpent offer that is any better? He can't even create. Since he can't do anything positive, all he can do is go negative and pick on the one person who can. The serpent cannot compete with God. All he can do is suggest that perhaps, just possibly, God is not so kind.

Eve's response is pretty good. She replies to the serpent, "We may eat fruit from the trees in the garden, but God did say, 'You must not eat fruit from the tree that is in the middle of the garden, and you must not touch it, or you will die.'"[7] Eve corrects the serpent's error of generalizing God's prohibition to include the entire garden. She informs him that she may eat from any tree in the garden except for the tree of the knowledge of good and evil, which she isn't supposed to even touch.

Some people believe that Eve's answer here implies an overly harsh view of God. God told Adam and Eve not to eat from the tree, and Eve, perhaps feeling constrained by this single prohibition, adds that her persnickety God would pulverize them if they even touch it. Personally, I doubt whether Eve is adding to God's command. If God had warned Adam and Eve not to eat from the tree, it is reasonable to conclude that he also didn't want them to touch it.

For example, when we tell our children not to eat any more snacks, we expect them to leave the goodies alone. Should we find them with one hand in the cookie jar, we are not likely to let them off on a technicality. We wouldn't say, "You're lucky you're only touching the cookies, because if you were actually chewing one, I'd have to discipline you." No, we typically hold them guilty whether or not they actually took a bite. Likewise, it makes sense for Adam and Eve to stay away from the fruit they were not supposed to eat. God would not have been amused to find them playing catch, passing the forbidden fruit past their mouths for pretend bites before passing off to their partner. He clearly wanted them to steer clear of this tree.

The original audience hearing this story would likely agree. It would have been obvious to any Jew that the tree of the knowledge of good and evil was something unclean. And Jews knew what to do with unclean things: stay far away, neither eating nor touching them. For instance, consider God's instructions concerning the cudless, and therefore unclean, pig: "You must not eat their meat or touch their carcasses; they are unclean for you."[8] So Eve responded as any good Jew would. Because the tree of the knowledge of good and evil is unclean, she must not eat or even touch its fruit.[9]

However, despite the correctness of Eve's words, her response is far from adequate. Her problem is not so much what she said but how she said it—her nonverbals. She should have denounced the serpent for even suggesting that God was mean. But she didn't. Her mistake was treating the serpent's line as a genuine question. She gave respect to a question that she should have ridiculed and in so doing disposed herself to eventually agree with the serpent.

This lie about God continues today, and like Eve, many of us openly consider it. We are often like the stoic Lutherans in Garrison Keillor's Lake Woebegone community who think that enjoying life and serving God are mutually exclusive options. Anyone who is serious about following God must give up all earthly pleasures; it's a necessary trade for us to get our rewards in the next life. And though we know the trade is worth it, we still try to sneak in some fun down here—and because we're sure that can't be what God wants, we feel guilty.

This is why our preceding chapters on the goodness of creation have been therapeutic for me. I grew up in churches that emphasized only the cost of following Christ. I was constantly reminded to resist the siren call of the world, to place my "all on the altar" and surrender my dreams for whatever God might want. Missionary conferences usually ended with the same probing invitation: Would I raise my hand, stand up, or go forward to publicly announce that, should God so choose, I was willing to leave my happy life and travel to some distant place to serve him?

While denying myself is an essential component of the Christian life, I also need to remember that God is the Creator of this beautiful world that he made for me to enjoy. God made all of the trees in the garden. Despite this, the serpent told Eve that God didn't want her to enjoy them. Likewise, God created everything good in our lives: laughter, romance, family, music, beauty, and chocolate. The serpent says that God doesn't want us to enjoy them—to do so might even be wrong. Do we believe him?

For some, it may come as a surprise that God has our best interests at heart. This is why we really don't trust God with our lives. We are afraid to commit for fear that he will hurt us—consign us to a life we don't enjoy just to test our commitment to him. If we tell him that we will go anywhere or do anything, he might send us to Togo, Timbuktu, or worse, to work with the junior high.

Can we believe that the good God who made us wants to place us in roles and locations where our gifts and desires will blossom? If we enjoy Africa or the junior high, then God may well lead us there. If we don't, we need not worry. God really doesn't want to make our life miserable. He wants us to find what we most enjoy—no doubt where our gifts best fit—and plug in there. God is on our side. He is pulling for us, not against us.

Sensing that Eve's resistance is weakening, the serpent becomes more aggressive. When he next speaks, he is no longer asking outrageous questions, but making outrageous statements. He alleges, "You will surely not die.... For God knows that when you eat of it your eyes will be opened, and you will be like God, knowing good and evil."[10] Notice that the serpent directly contradicts God's statement in Genesis 2:17, and with the same intensity. God emphatically said that eating from the tree would kill them; the serpent says just as emphatically that if Eve eats from the tree, she surely would not die.

Of course, we may be dealing here with a postmodern serpent. If cornered, he could have replied that both his and God's statements are correct, depending on one's definition of death. On the one hand, God is right to say that Adam and Eve would eventually die if they ate from the tree. On the other hand, the serpent is also right to say they would not perish, if that is taken to mean immediately, for Adam would continue to live until the ripe old age of 930. Anyway, the serpent did not bother to clear up this confusion, but left Eve to consider the apparent contradiction between his word and God's.

Eve should have been aware that the serpent could be lying, or at least wrong, for his first comment concerning which fruit she could eat was far off the mark. Since his only other statement has been wrong, why should she think he is telling the truth now? Knowing that Eve might not believe him, the serpent supports his argument with evidence. He invites her to inspect the beauty of the off-limits tree. God himself had said that eating its fruit would give moral discernment. What could be wrong with that? Absolutely nothing. Perhaps God does not want them to eat from the tree because he is selfishly protecting himself. He doesn't want Adam and Eve to become like him and to know what he knows, so he scared them away by warning that they would die if they eat from it. Again, there is an element of truth in the serpent's line. After Adam and Eve eat from the tree, God himself concedes that they have become like him, though—and this is what the serpent conveniently forgets—in a way that will ultimately destroy them.[11]

The Original Sin

Eve has just heard three outrageous claims against God. First, God does not want her to enjoy any of the trees. She answers correctly but gives this statement far more respect than it deserves. Second, God lied about the consequences of eating, for she would not really die. Third, God is selfishly trying to keep her down. These last two claims Eve respects so much that she doesn't even respond. She is now considering them.

But Eve isn't thinking clearly, for she has become autonomous, believing that she is able to decide for herself what is right and wrong, true and false.[12] Rather than obediently submit to God's word, Eve grants equal consideration to the serpent's interpretation of the tree. She elevates herself as the judge between God and the serpent, choosing to rely on her own mind to determine who is telling the truth. It is this move toward autonomy that is the nub of the fall. Once Eve sets herself up as judge over God and his explanation of the tree, eating the fruit becomes a foregone conclusion.

Eve has more than enough objective evidence to believe God's word. She knows that he is the sovereign Creator and gracious Provider of all good things. Her brief encounter with the serpent has already demonstrated that the serpent could be terribly wrong. She herself told him so. So why should she believe that the serpent is telling the truth this time?

Because Eve wants him to be right. She has a vested interest in the serpent's side. In her autonomy Eve's highest goal is to actualize herself—to be all she can be and grab all the power and happiness she can get. She will oppose anyone, even God, who gets in her way. So Eve looks at the tree and, relying on her own empirical and rational skills, she sees "that the fruit of the tree was good for food and pleasing to the eye, and also desirable for gaining wisdom." She decides that the potential benefits outweigh the risks, so she "took some and ate it."[13]

Eve is deceived, but she is not innocent. The serpent deceives her by playing to her autonomy, encouraging her to use her own empirical and rational ability to evaluate God's word and not let anyone, including God, get in the way of the wisdom and success she feels she deserves. In her selfishness Eve sets herself up to being tricked.

More amazing is the sin of Adam. He isn't deceived, for he clearly sees the wave of panic and fear that sweeps over his wife after she eats from the tree. But even though he knows the consequences, he somehow decides that it is in his best interest to give in to the frantic appeals of his wife. Adam's autonomy is so strong that he knowingly sides with Eve and voluntarily joins her rebellion against God.

And this is why it is wrong to eat from the tree. Certainly it is a good thing to have moral discernment, the knowledge of good and evil. But Adam and Eve seek this ability independently from God and his revelation. Rather than allow God to define what is good and evil, they take the job on themselves. As a result, they acquire a heightened sense of right and wrong, but they no longer know what goes into each category. We can see the effects in our world: Choice is good, carrying a baby is a burden; tolerance is good, absolutes are bad; money and power are the marks of success, humility and servanthood are for losers.

Our world knows what good and evil mean, but people do not always know what is good and what is evil. To know this we must answer the question, good and evil for whom? Before the fall, things were good and evil in relation to God. He is the highest, absolute standard by which all morality is measured. He revealed his will to

Adam and Eve so they could know it too. But since the fall, humanity has turned this question on its head. Rather than ask what is good for God, we ask only what is good for us. We focus on our own personal pleasure, calling good whatever enhances our happiness and evil whatever threatens it.

So our world is a mess. Each person plays god in his own life, deciding for himself what is right and wrong, good and bad. Of course, what may be good for me may not be so great for you, so we fight. And without an absolute standard to judge between us, morality is decided by whoever is the strongest. Might really does make right. Those in power make the rules, while those on the bottom attempt to sneak around them. Both sides use their own slant on good and evil to justify their actions, being thoroughly convinced in their own mind that they are in the right. As we learned in the introduction to this chapter, it is just this ability to rationalize and justify our own particular point of view that lies behind every war, especially the centuries of counterblows that continue to plague the Middle East. Now can we see why God told Adam and Eve not to eat from the tree? He was serious.

My Unoriginal Modern Sin

Can we find ourselves in this story of the fall? It is easy to stand outside the story and blame Eve for being so dumb, but God's Word invites us to enter the story and turn its light on ourselves. How often do we play the role of Eve? How many times do we reject God's will and do just what we want, when we want, only because we want to do it? How many times do we listen to the serpent and cave in to our own autonomy?

For instance, we are tempted to say something witty. We know it may hurt the other person, but it's just too funny to pass up. Or we are about to share some interesting information—technically it's gossip—but it will make us look so good if we share it. We begin to spin—

telling only the part of the truth that casts us in the best light and puts another in the shade. We make a promise we only barely intend to keep. We blow off or blow up at a child. We brush aside a plea for help.

Just before we do these things, in those moments when we catch ourselves, we are standing with Eve. If we decide we don't care that it is selfish, we're going ahead anyway, then we are listening to the serpent; we are reenacting the fall. If we are redeemed children of God, just how wrong is that? If Eve was dumb to listen to the serpent, then what should we make of ourselves, who so clearly see her demise but insist on following her anyway? Let's learn from her mistake and repent of our autonomy—all those moments we live for ourselves, disobeying God's Word and doing what we want just because we want to do it.

We will stop living for ourselves the moment we realize that God, our Creator, is good. He is on our side; we can trust him. So rather than waste time and energy lusting after the one tree that is off-limits, we will flood our lives with the entire garden of pleasures that God created for us to enjoy. The old hymn says it well: "Trust and obey, for there's no other way to be happy in Jesus, but to trust and obey." Disobedience ultimately arises from unbelief. Those who trust God, who really believe that he is on their side, will have little trouble obeying his Word. Trust, and we will obey.

10

The Fallout from the Fall

GENESIS 3 – 11

We know that the whole creation has been groaning
as in the pains of childbirth right up to the present time.

ROMANS 8:22

I took a deep breath and pushed open the door to my friend's room in the intensive care unit. There, lying on his back, was a form I did not recognize. The person in the bed was a swollen, bruised hulk of a man. His labored breathing rose and fell in rhythm with the whooshing sound of his ventilator. Various tubes, alternately supplying nourishment and removing waste from his body, protruded from his nose, throat, and side.

Embarrassed that I had intruded upon the death throes of a stranger, I hastily turned to leave the room. "Poor fellow," I thought to myself, "I wonder where they moved Joe?" Just then my eye caught sight of a recent photograph that family members had taped beside the door. It was him.

I stood in the doorway for a long moment, scarcely willing to believe my eyes. I looked at the photo, at the bed, then back again.

The figure in the bed looked nothing like the photo, nothing like the friend and mentor I had known for eight years. I was stunned by the suddenness of his demise. How could a seminary professor at the height of his powers deteriorate into an unrecognizable, helpless form in the span of just a few days?

The doctors said my friend suffered from a dissected aorta, the consequence of a genetic defect he had inherited from his father. I understand that. But why did this genetic flaw exist in the first place? What was its cause? In a word, sin. The sin of Adam and Eve unleashed a nearly incurable cancer upon the world, a cancer that from the first family until now has contaminated every last corner of creation. Thus, as we learn in this chapter, genetic defects are just the sort of thing we might expect to find in a fallen world. So my friend lay dying in a lonely hospital bed, another witness to the devastating power of sin.

Not the Way It's Supposed to Be

Most people who follow the news are painfully aware that something is terribly wrong with our world. Every news cycle is smattered with stories of children who lost parents or parents who lost children to car accidents, house fires, or disease. On any given day we hear stories of corrupt officials, dishonest business leaders, and mean-spirited politicians. Most days we also learn about the plight of the poor on the other side of the globe, such as the children in Africa who are needlessly dying because they cannot afford the miracle drug that can cure them—the same drug that pharmaceutical companies make and sell to wealthy Westerners who wish to remove unwanted facial hair.

Although most everyone can see that things are wrong, those who don't believe the biblical story of the fall don't know what to make of it. They often attribute the brokenness of this fallen world to creation, declaring that "death is just a normal part of life," "people are just naturally competitive," or "survival of the fittest—this is just the way life is."

Imagine how difficult it is for these people to make sense of our world. Because they don't believe the story of creation, they don't know that God made this world good—a beautiful place for us to enjoy forever. And because they don't believe the story of the fall, they can't explain how or why this world has become so bad. They suspect that the world, God's wonderful creation, has just always been this way. It's akin to happening on the scene of an accident and not realizing there's been an accident. They don't even know what they're looking at.

It is a tremendous advantage to know what is wrong with our world, for only when we know what's wrong can we understand how to fix things. This chapter surveys the low points of Genesis 3–11, the downward spiral of the world after its fall. This is the most depressing passage in all of Scripture, for here we see the fallout from Adam's sin. The world turns ugly in ways that neither he nor Eve could have anticipated when they disobeyed God and picked the fruit from the tree of the knowledge of good and evil. Adam's sin did not just affect him but, like a stone tossed into a pond, rippled out until it had destroyed the entire world.

There Goes the Neighborhood

For starters, Adam's sin immediately began to destroy human society, for as we learn in Genesis 3, his sin drove a wedge between him and Eve and between both of them and God. Sin had made them vulnerable. They had been naked from the moment of their creation, but only now did it become a problem—because now they had something to hide. They pathetically tried to cover up with a few oversized fig leaves and then scurried into the trees when they heard the footsteps of God approaching.

The voice of God broke the chilly silence with a question they had never heard: "Where are you?" Adam hesitated, fumbling for words, then he bravely replied that he was afraid because he realized he was naked. God expressed surprise: "Afraid? Naked? Adam, those words are not in your vocabulary. Who told you—did you eat from the tree?"

Cornered, Adam came out fighting, finger wagging (the other fingers desperately clutching his fig leaf). "It was the woman *you* gave me. Why did you give me someone you knew would drag me down? This woman of yours ate from the tree that you said not to, and then she gave it to me." God then turned to the woman, who, following the example of her loving husband, pointed down the chain to the serpent: "He deceived me."

So God wheeled on the serpent. I wouldn't be surprised if he grabbed the serpent by the throat, for the anger in his voice is palpable: "Because you have done this, cursed are you above all the livestock and all the wild animals! You will crawl on your belly and you will eat dust all the days of your life."[1] From now on the serpent will bite the dust, slithering along the ground like the most despicable animal that he has become.

(Isaiah 65:25 suggests that this curse is not going away anytime soon. In his vision of the new earth Isaiah informs us that even when all the other animals have been released from the curse of sin and become friends—"the wolf and the lamb will feed together, and the lion will eat straw like the ox"—yet "dust will be the serpent's food." Although God will one day set everything right and make all things new,[2] the one curse that will never be lifted, the one flaw that will never be fixed, is the custom of snakes to crawl along the ground. It seems that God wishes to leave this curse as a silent reminder to his children of the fall.)

Adam's sin did more than make his life with Eve a little less comfortable. His sin became a cancer on the human race. The fall began with him but it didn't stop there. Adam was unable to limit the damaging effects of sin to his own person. To his horror he found that the disease of sin passes on to one's children. It must have been pure agony for him and Eve to watch as the chilling fingers of sin wrapped themselves around the heart of their firstborn son. Who could have guessed that this tiny infant, the first baby the world had ever seen, would grow up to be a murderer?

Genesis 4 records how this came about. When God accepted Abel's sacrifice but rejected Cain's, a visibly agitated Cain sought revenge by killing his brother. But rather than soothe his anger, Cain's bloody hands only made him more belligerent. Remember how meekly Adam responded to God's question after the fall? God said, "Adam, where are you?" and Adam stuttered that he was hiding because he realized he was naked. He was afraid of God, but Cain was not. God asked Cain a similar question: "Where is your brother?" But rather than accept God's invitation to take responsibility for his deed, Cain curtly snapped: "I don't know. . . . Am I my brother's keeper?"[3]

Now it was God's turn to become angry. He replied, "What have you done? Cain, this is no time to be cute. The same earth from which I formed your brother now soaks up his blood. You have desecrated my creation. You've murdered your brother!"[4] Then God took the unusual step of placing Cain under a curse. Note that God was careful not to curse Adam and Eve; he cursed the ground instead. But Cain crossed the line. He did the unthinkable, so God cursed him. He informed Cain that because the ground had drunk his brother's blood, it would no longer yield its crops for him. It wouldn't even tolerate him. No patch of earth would stand his presence for long, but he would be forced to stay on the lam, a wandering fugitive on the earth.

Little Foxes Spoil the Vine

Consider what must have been going through the mind of Adam and Eve. No parent should ever have to bury a child. Anyone who has can testify that a heart broken in this way never heals. A parent may be able to get on with life, but she never gets over it. Yet as bad as this is, there may be one thing worse—when the child who dies is murdered by the hands of his own brother. We can hear the pain still lingering in Eve's voice when she declares about Seth, her newborn son, "God has granted me another child in place of Abel, since Cain killed him."[5]

Even worse than knowing that one son has killed another was Eve's knowledge that she was largely responsible. How she and Adam must have longed for a mulligan. If they could only return to the Garden of Eden and have one more chance at the serpent, how differently it would go. How many times did Eve turn the conversation over in her mind? How many nights did it keep her awake? If she could do it over, she wouldn't give the serpent the time of day but would immediately pick up a stick and beat his brains in. But there was no going back. She and her husband had to live with the consequences of their sin.

But who could have guessed: Such a small thing—eating a fruit—would degenerate into murder within one generation? How could such a small sin reap such large consequences? We saw earlier that Adam and Eve's sin was motivated by their autonomy. They wanted to do what they wanted to do, and no one, not even God, could cramp their style. Because every sin comes from autonomy, every sin, no matter how small it seems on the surface, conceals an iceberg of devastation below. Once Adam and Eve gave way to autonomy, they guaranteed that their sin would not remain small for long. Autonomous individuals will sin as large as they need to keep themselves on top. Autonomy for Adam and Eve meant eating a piece of fruit; autonomy for their son meant murdering his brother.

So Adam and Eve lived to witness the awful consequences of their sin. They lived long enough to see one son kill another. They lived long enough to hear Lamech's notorious song:

> "Adah and Zillah, listen to me;
>> wives of Lamech, hear my words.
> I have killed a man for wounding me,
>> a young man for injuring me.
> If Cain is avenged seven times,
>> then Lamech seventy-seven times."[6]

A descendant of Cain, Lamech goes one step further than his fore-father. There's a boastful swagger in his violent verse: He has indiscriminately killed an adult and a youth for as little as a wound. Unlike Cain, Lamech does not need God's protection but will take revenge into his own hands. If God promised to avenge Cain seven times, then Lamech would avenge any hurt to himself many times over.

Adam lived long enough to see his sin degenerate into the cesspool of Genesis 6. Placing Adam's 930 years into the genealogy of Genesis 5, we discover that the next person born after Adam's death was Noah. Since we know that the world in Noah's day was exceedingly evil, it's likely that Adam saw more than he wanted of the devastation his sin had brought upon the world.

The End of the World

Three consecutive verses in Genesis 6 contain three startling revelations. First, Genesis 6:5 states that "the LORD saw how great man's wickedness on the earth had become, and that every inclination of the thoughts of his heart was only evil all the time." At the creation, God approvingly declared that his work was "very good." Now, a few generations later, his originally good creation is full of people whose every thought of every day has become nothing but premeditated, calculated evil.

This sad state of affairs angered and deeply offended its Creator. Genesis 6:6 declares that "the LORD was grieved that he had made man on the earth, and his heart was filled with pain." The strong language here—a mixture of rage and anguish—is used elsewhere in Scripture to capture the intense emotion of a wounded party. The same word for "grief" appears when Dinah's brothers react in "grief and fury" to the news of her rape; when Jonathan responds to Saul's plan to kill David, rising from the table in "fierce anger" and refusing to eat; and when David laments the death of his son, crying out in agony, "O my son Absalom! O Absalom, my son, my son!"[7]

This profound pain draws God to an unbelievable conclusion: "So the LORD said, 'I will wipe mankind, whom I have created, from the face of the earth—men and animals, and creatures that move along the ground, and birds of the air—for I am grieved that I have made them.'"[8] Come again? Did we read that right? God is so set against his world that he will wipe out everything? Earlier, God joyfully breathed life into Adam, "the beasts of the earth," "the birds of the air," and "the creatures that move on the ground."[9] Now God vows "to destroy all life under the heavens, every creature that has the breath of life in it. Everything on earth will perish."[10]

It is impossible to capture the pain that must have driven God to such extreme measures. Perhaps it is something like what an innocent party feels during a divorce—the hurt and rejection run as deep as the original love and promise of the relationship. God was enraged at the world because he had hoped for so much more. There was the honeymoon period, when Adam led all creation to rejoice in the presence of its Creator. But since Adam's sin introduced evil into the world, the very things that once brought God so much pleasure—verdant landscapes, playful animals, and responsible humans—now brought him nothing but pain. God endured about as much as he could stand, and then he declared, "That's it! I'm destroying everything."

Here the rippling circles of sin have reached their culmination. Sin began with Adam and Eve, but it didn't stop there. It rippled out and ruined human society, shortly leading Cain to kill Abel and the entire earth to become "corrupt in God's sight" and "full of violence."[11] This is to be expected, for as we learned in the previous chapter, once people operate from autonomy, deciding what is right and wrong for themselves, fighting with one another becomes inevitable.

But sin didn't stop there. It rippled out until it damaged relations between animals and even the earth itself. They, too, endure the curse of sin, for as Paul reminds us, "The creation was subjected to frustration, not by its own choice, but by the will of the one who subjected it, in hope that the creation itself will be liberated from its bondage to decay and brought into the glorious freedom of the children of God. We know that the whole creation has been groaning as in the pains of childbirth right up to the present time."[12] Sin spoiled everything—and to such an extent that God decided to destroy the entire world (Fig. 10.1).

So God sent a great flood. We have so sanitized this story for children that I fear we have lost sense of its tragedy. Most pictures show Noah, a grandfatherly figure, smiling and waving beside pairs of giraffes, elephants, and zebras. I'm not suggesting that we fill our children's storybooks with graphic details of the flood, but for too long we have only thought of the flood as a children's story. We have forgotten that this was not a happy voyage for Noah and his family. They could hear the shrieks and cries from those drowning outside their boat. Noah likely heard the voices of his brothers and sisters and nieces and nephews. His daughters-in-law heard the desperate cries of their parents calling their names and begging to be let inside. This was no Carnival Cruise.

Figure 10.1: Sin's Swath of Destruction

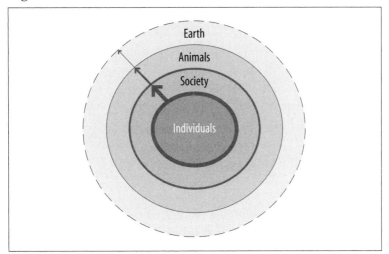

Far from being a happy tale, the story of Noah's Ark is about the end of civilization. It is a vivid reminder of sin's destruction and the lengths to which God will go to eradicate it. Sin has corrupted everything, so everything must go. Only after God has purged the earth of its evildoers can he start over, building a new civilization with the people and animals who took refuge with Noah, the lone righteous leader of his generation.[13]

Fatal Attraction

The fallout from the fall is as intensive as it is extensive. The cancer of sin not only ripples out until it ruins the entire world—proceeding from individuals through society to the rest of creation—but it also wreaks near-total devastation on each level. For instance, consider how sin destroys the identity and purpose of individual people. In chapter 4 we learned that what separates humanity from the rest of creation is that we alone bear the image of God. Specifically, this means that God has equipped us with certain capacities, such as the ability to think and speak rationally, so that we might blossom and flourish in our relationship with God, others, and the earth.

But Adam's fall into sin has deeply damaged each of these relationships. Rather than responsibly care for this creation, we make only halfhearted stabs in our vocations, doing as little as we can to get by and still receive credit. Rather than search for imaginative opportunities to encourage and serve our neighbors, we only befriend those whose personal assets promise to benefit us. And rather than joyfully offer ourselves as living sacrifices to God, we fixate on how our alleged obedience might boomerang and bring us bushels of divine blessings.

In all these ways and more, our fallen nature gives a wide berth to our autonomy. Whereas God intended each of our created relationships to be an opportunity for us to contribute to another, our autonomous selves have turned this upside down—for the most part caring only for the ways the other may benefit us. Ironically, the more we selfishly pursue this autonomous direction, the more we damage our true selves, for what should be joyful work becomes drudgery, what should be enriching community becomes social strife, and what should be invigorating worship turns into thinly veiled idolatry. In short, our commitment to autonomy succeeds only in distorting our humanity (figure 10.2).[14]

Ultimately, this damage to our humanity will result in our eventual death. Adam and Eve died twice on the day they sinned. They died spiritually when God banished them from the Garden of Eden and the unfettered fellowship they had previously shared with him. From now on their relationship with God must run through a blood sacrifice, whether it be the animals God slew to clothe them,[15] the spotless cattle slaughtered on Israel's Day of Atonement,[16] or the ultimate sacrifice of Jesus Christ for their sins and ours.[17] They also died

Figure 10.2: How the Fall Damages Our Image of God

Creation			
Genesis 1:27–28	"God created man in his own image, in the image of God he created him"	"Male and female he created them"	"Be fruitful and increase in number; fill the earth and subdue it. Rule …"
This means that humans are properly related to	God	Other humans	The world
Because of this humans are	Religious beings	Social beings	Cultural beings
These aspects of human life should produce	Worship of God	Love for others	Joyful work in the world
Fall			
Because of the fall, these image-bearing characteristics produce	**Idolatry, self-worship**	**Greed, selfishness**	**Laziness, sloth, or self-indulgence**
The consequences of sin are	**Alienation from God—Wrath**	**Alienation from others—Hate**	**Alienation from work—Drudgery**

physically, for their bodies began the slow process of deterioration that signaled their approaching demise. Though Adam's final day was nearly a millennium away, he eventually returned to the ground as promised, "for dust you are and to dust you will return."[18]

It is this double-sided death that Adam's sin passed on to his descendants, guaranteeing that, short of Christ's return, our lives on this earth will end in tragedy. I don't think I ever fully appreciated this truth until I saw my stricken friend struggle through his final moments of life. Until then, it was convenient for me to believe that sin was a bit of harmless fun, a guilty pleasure that I could indulge here and there without getting hurt. But the true nature of sin was exposed in that hospital room. My foolish delusions melted away, and I understood sin for what it really is—the enemy that will one day separate me from the loved ones I leave behind.

I left my friend's side angry with myself, wondering why, even though I am aware that sin is the mortal enemy that will eventually destroy me, I am still fatally attracted to it. Like mosquitoes drawn to the scented light of a backyard bug zapper, there is something within me—what Paul calls the "flesh" and what I am calling "autonomy"— that craves the noisy buzz and flashing thrill of death. Left to myself, I am powerless to fly to freedom, but will inexplicably and irresistibly continue to celebrate the very sin that even now is eating away at my body and soul.

But the good news of the gospel is that God has not left us to ourselves and our dangerous dance with death. Indeed, he is more disturbed by sin than we are and even now is working to reverse the fallout from the fall. The next chapter will examine the details of God's daring plan to rescue his creation from the ravaging cancer of sin. There we will learn that God is not content to stand idly by and allow evil to destroy his perfectly good creation, but will personally enter this world—becoming vulnerable himself to the suffering of sin—in order to take back what rightly belongs to him. To paraphrase Al Wolters's insightful comment: "God does not make junk," and though his beautiful creation is now frightfully deformed by the fall, he's not about to "junk what he has made."[19]

Part Four

What Is God's Plan for This World?

REDEMPTION IN GENESIS 12 – REVELATION 22

11

The Cosmic Reach of the Gospel

"God so loved the world. . . ."

JOHN 3:16

I n Victor Hugo's epic tale *Les Misérables*, the released convict Jean Valjean stumbles into town, haggard and hungry from his four-day trek to freedom. His fierce visage and prison passport frighten the townsfolk, and they pelt his bowed head with stones and insults as he wanders from house to house in search of a soft bed and warm meal. Finally, just when it seems he will collapse from cold and starvation, he knocks on the door of the bishop's residence. To his surprise, this man of God not only opens his home but brings out his best silver and china, calls him "Sir," and in general offers respect and hospitality that Valjean no longer thought he deserved.

Unfortunately, this single moment of grace is unable to overcome Valjean's nineteen years of forced labor in the galleys, and during the night the hardened convict steals into the bishop's bedroom and leaves with his expensive silver. He doesn't get very far but is arrested the next morning and returned to the bishop's home with the confiscated treasure. Valjean lowers his eyes in shame. How could he look the kind bishop in the face? The one person who had pitied him, who probably had saved his life, and he had returned the favor by taking advantage of his vulnerability. Even worse, this robbery had violated his parole. After a meager four days of freedom, Valjean would be locked up again, perhaps this time forever.

These thoughts leave Valjean completely unprepared for the bishop's response, who graciously informs the police that the presumably stolen silver was actually his gift to this poor convict. In fact, he reprimands Valjean for overlooking the silver candlesticks, which undoubtedly would fetch an additional two hundred francs. When the surprised police have left, the man of God turns to his gaping guest. "Jean Valjean, my brother," he begins, "you belong no longer to evil, but to good. It is your soul that I am buying for you. I withdraw it from dark thoughts and from the spirit of perdition, and I give it to God!"[1]

Valjean's numb heart could hardly process this extraordinary kindness, and after a period of intense wrestling, it leaves him a changed man. He vows that from now on he will imitate the bishop's faith, extending grace and second chances to those who need it most. So he establishes a new life in a poor town, where he single-handedly turns around the fortunes of a flagging factory and brings prosperity and hope to the grateful villagers. Besides guaranteeing that every willing person could have a well-paying job, Valjean generously funds hospitals, schools, and retirement programs. The more money he makes, the more he gives away, and the entire region benefits from his largesse.

Given his past, Valjean reserves a special place in his heart for people who desperately need a break. In particular, he responds to the dying wishes of one of his workers, a single mother who had unknowingly left her beloved daughter in the care of abusive foster parents. Valjean not only purchases this orphan's freedom but, though he is doggedly pursued by a legalistic policeman intent on making him pay for past sins, he devotes the rest of his life to providing this child with the happiness that her mother longed for but was never able to deliver.

You will have to read the book (which, of course, is better than the movie) to enjoy the narrow escapes and heroic efforts this pursuit of happiness entails. In all, *Les Misérables* presents a thrilling picture of the power of grace. Just as Jean Valjean responded to the bishop's kindness by devoting his life to others, so God graces each of us, not merely for our own sake, but so that through us he might reclaim the entire world.

The Empire Strikes Back

Let's review the story of the Christian worldview. It opens with *creation* (Genesis 1–2), the initial scene that shows that we were made to enjoy intimacy with God and others while we savor and develop this good earth. Unfortunately, Adam's *fall* broke our good world when he followed his autonomy and selfishly ate from the tree that God told him to avoid (Genesis 3–11). Adam's sin damaged not only himself but also the rest of creation. Like a stone tossed into a pond, the corrosive curse of sin rippled out to destroy the entire world: human society, the animal kingdom, and even the ground itself began groaning beneath the weight of sin. Life on earth degenerated so quickly that within a few generations God ordered a great flood to wipe out everything, save only pairs of every animal and a handful of people.

Now place yourself in God's shoes. What is your next move? I doubt you would scrap the world, admitting that it is broken beyond repair. If you did, wouldn't you be conceding victory to Satan? You would be admitting that Satan had won, for the sin he introduced has overpowered your good creation, making it irretrievably evil. No, if you are God, you will never concede that. Instead, you will forcefully strike back at Satan with your plan of *redemption* (Genesis 12–Revelation 22). Not content to merely snatch a few souls from this mess and leave everything else to the devil, you will not rest until you have redeemed every last corner of your good creation from evil's grasp.

According to Scripture, this is precisely what God is doing. As Peter proclaimed to inquiring crowds shortly after Pentecost, Jesus "must remain in heaven until the time comes for God to *restore everything*, as he promised long ago through his holy prophets."[2] Or as Paul explained to the churches in Ephesus and Colosse, God is using the cross of Christ "to reconcile to himself *all things*, whether things on earth or things in heaven" so that "*all things* in heaven and on earth" might be "together under one head, even Christ."[3]

In short, just as sin began with individuals and rippled out to contaminate the entire world, so grace begins with individuals and ripples out to redeem the rest of creation (Fig. 11.1). We humans are the bull's-eye of God's grace, the target of his redemption. But though salvation begins with us, the God who redeems us does not want us to keep redemption to ourselves. He wants us to share his grace with

Figure 11.1: The Recapitulation of Redemption

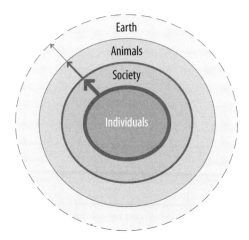

the rest of creation, redeeming society, the animal kingdom, and even the earth itself. God wants it all. In the words of Abraham Kuyper, "There is not a square inch in the whole domain of our human existence over which Christ, who is Sovereign over *all*, does not cry: 'Mine!'"[4]

"For God So Loved the World . . ."

God inaugurates this plan of redemption with his promise to Abraham in Genesis 12:1–3. The markers in the biblical text are so obvious that attentive readers can hardly miss them. For instance, the story of creation in Genesis 1–2 speaks of the blessing of God on Adam and the animals.[5] But the fall and the world's subsequent downward spiral, as told in Genesis 3–11, reverse this blessing. People and things are cursed, such as the serpent, the ground, Cain, Canaan, and ultimately the entire world.[6]

Against this dark backdrop of cursing and judgment, Genesis 12 opens with a renewed emphasis on blessing, as demonstrated in God's promise to Abraham:

> I will make you into a great nation
> > and I will *bless* you;
> I will make your name great,
> > and you will be a *blessing*.
> I will *bless* those who bless you,
> > and whoever curses you I will curse;
> and all peoples on earth
> > will be *blessed* through you.

This promise that "all peoples on earth will be blessed through you" is repeated often to Abraham, his son, and grandson.[7] God wanted the father of our faith to know that through him and his children God planned to set the world right, correcting the curses of the fall and restoring the original blessings of creation.

God gave the details of his plan for Abraham's descendants at Mount Sinai. As he prepared to establish his covenant with the Israelites, he told Moses to relay this message to his liberated people:

> "You yourselves have seen what I did to Egypt, and how I carried you on eagles' wings and brought you to myself. Now if you obey me fully and keep my covenant, then out of all nations you will be my treasured possession. Although the whole earth is mine, you will be for me a kingdom of priests and a holy nation."[8]

By "kingdom of priests" God meant that he intended his people to be set apart, special, and holy to himself. Just as individual priests must take care to purify themselves before they enter the presence of God, so the entire nation of Israel must be a people dedicated to the knowledge and service of the Lord. This is why we find so many precise commands for daily life in the book of Leviticus. God was particular about his people's diet, their sexual habits, and even their handling of infectious skin diseases and mildew, because they were not just any people.[9] They were his special nation, a kingdom of priests, so every aspect of their lives mattered.

God wasn't being persnickety, passing out random commands merely to try his children's patience. On the contrary, he wanted Israel to follow his laws because he knew that only in this way would their community blossom and flourish. He wanted Abraham's children to thrive in their three created relationships: with God, each other, and the earth itself. They would grow in their knowledge of God as long as they stayed away from idols.[10] Their society would prosper so long as they used honest scales,[11] gave interest-free loans,[12] observed gleaning laws[13] and the Year of Jubilee,[14] and generally looked after the poor and needy among them.[15] And their animals and soil, refreshed from a Sabbath rest every week and every seven years respectively, would outperform the beasts and ground of surrounding nations.[16]

In this way Israel would fulfill a second priestly function. Not only would she be a "holy nation," but her conspicuous prosperity would attract other nations to the glory of her Lord. She would be a model, a living witness to the flourishing and delight that occurs when a nation experiences the blessing of God. Other nations would observe her affluence and, confessing that Israel's Lord must be the one true God, would seek to join her community. Thus God planned for this "kingdom of priests" to become his intercessors—his chosen link to bring other people to himself.

Unfortunately, Israel never did live up to God's challenge. She foolishly abandoned her living God for impotent idols that she could see and touch. She callously trampled on the defenseless faces of the desperate poor. And, in her quest for ever-increasing production, she even refused to give the earth its required rest.[17] In response, God replaced his intended blessings with the curses of the covenant.[18] Rather than prosper as the people of God, Israel would languish in a barren land until the day when other nations, decidedly unimpressed with Israeli society, demolished her towns and led her survivors into captivity.

But even though Israel failed miserably at her mission, the Old Testament prophets refused to give up on the dream. Isaiah and Micah share nearly identical visions of a future when many nations will stream to Israel's God, saying: "Come, let us go up to the mountain of the LORD, to the house of the God of Jacob. He will teach us his ways, so that we may walk in his paths."[19] Isaiah was even willing to name some of these nations, claiming that Egypt and Assyria, two perennial enemies of Israel, would eventually join her as the people of God.[20]

Yet, given Israel's stubborn unfaithfulness, just how would God pull off this plan? Isaiah predicts that although Israel as a nation will be cut down, yet God will cause a green shoot to sprout from its dead stump.[21] This tender shoot will blossom into a sturdy sapling, a fruitful Branch that will conquer evil and restore shalom to humanity's three created relationships: with God ("he will delight in the fear of the LORD"), with others ("with righteousness he will judge the needy, with justice he will give decisions for the poor"), and with the rest of creation ("the wolf will live with the lamb . . . ; and a little child will lead them").[22] This restoration of the entire person will be true for all people, for on that day "the earth will be full of the knowledge of the LORD as the waters cover the sea."[23]

". . . That He Gave His One and Only Son"

This tender shoot announced its arrival into our world of hurt when Jesus Christ stood up in his hometown synagogue and applied a prophecy from Isaiah to himself. He read:

> "The Spirit of the Lord is on me,
>   because he has anointed me
>   to preach good news to the poor.
> He has sent me to proclaim freedom for the prisoners
>   and recovery of sight for the blind,
> to release the oppressed,
>   to proclaim the year of the Lord's favor."[24]

And then, with "the eyes of everyone in the synagogue . . . fastened on him," Jesus issued the challenge that would change the course of history. Defying the forces of evil that had introduced sin and suffering into the world, he told his assembled townsfolk: "Today this scripture is fulfilled in your hearing."[25] Game on!

The Jewish villagers who heard Jesus' announcement would no doubt agree with Isaiah's assessment of their pain. They knew plenty of poor, blind, and oppressed people, most of whom were victims of "the system." These townsfolk rightly resented the plundering Romans and the Jewish traitors who accommodated them. If they could only get free of their oppressive political and religious bureaucracy, they just knew that most of their problems would be solved.

Jesus pitied the poor, trapped in a hopeless cycle of hard work and harassment, and he spent much time healing the sick, raising the dead, and restoring the blind, lame, and lepers. In fact, when a troubled

John the Baptist wanted proof that Jesus was the expected Messiah, Jesus reminded him that he was doing precisely what Isaiah had predicted: "The blind receive sight, the lame walk, those who have leprosy are cured, the deaf hear, the dead are raised, and the good news is preached to the poor."[26]

This healing ministry lay at the heart of Christ's mission, for it demonstrated that he had come to redeem every last corner of his creation. Not only souls, but bodies too have been wracked by sin, so bodies, not only souls, must be restored. When Christ "took up our infirmities and carried our diseases," he offered a sneak preview of the full and final redemption he would bring to our world.[27]

But though Jesus came to earth to help the poor and "release the oppressed," he disagreed with their rather superficial analysis of their problem. They mistakenly believed that their suffering was entirely someone else's fault. If only they could rid themselves of the Romans or their rigid religious system, life would be good again. While the Romans and the religious leaders were burdensome, Jesus explained that their real problem was not "out there" but "in here." They could live in a prosperous utopia and still be miserable, for their main need was not to be freed from their oppressors but to be liberated from their sin.

So when Jesus announced the arrival of his kingdom—the kingdom that would restore flourishing shalom to his entire creation—he ordered his audience to repent.[28] Only those who repent of their autonomy, saying no to their selfish ambition and yes to the forgiveness of God, are eligible to enter the kingdom. As Jesus often reminded his followers, the path is narrow that leads to life, and only those few who willingly "give up everything" for the kingdom will receive its benefits.[29]

Jesus himself led the way, voluntarily offering his life for the forgiveness and flourishing of the world. Though he cringed to drink the cup of his Father's wrath, he lifted it in somber toast to the world and then drained it, bearing our sin as he hung dying on the cross. Now every person, whether Egyptian or Assyrian, Israeli or Palestinian, who places their trust in Jesus may receive not only the forgiveness of sin, but in time, the flourishing of shalom that comes from sin's complete removal.

Amazing Grace

This free offer of forgiveness and flourishing is a distinctive feature of the Christian faith. Jesus Christ is the only God who claims that our acceptance with God is entirely his gift. We can do nothing to earn God's approval, for even one sin—and we have many—is enough to send us to hell forever. But our Father has graciously intervened, sending his righteous Son to die in our place so that any of us who wish might be forgiven and adopted into the family of God.

No other worldview offers grace in such undiluted form.[30] Some others might suggest that our salvation depends somewhat on the mercy of God, but they invariably add human effort into the mix. Typical is Islam, which encourages its followers to do the best they can in hopes that their good deeds might outperform their sins and tip the scales in their favor. But since no one knows for sure how their deeds are stacking up, those who take their religion seriously must live in fear as they await the last judgment.

There is a simple explanation for this absence of grace in other religions. Most, if not all, false religions are inspired by Satan, and there is doubtless nothing more disturbing to Satan than the idea of grace. He probably considers it extremely unfair that, unlike him and his followers, the human race is offered forgiveness for sin. Satan's failure banished him from God's presence forever, but Adam and Eve—though lower on the scale of being—were given a second chance.

Perhaps this is why Satan finds it impossible to create a false religion that is fueled by grace. Why not plagiarize the Christian redemption story, changing the names and places to really confuse people? Instead of the Jewish Christ it could be a British Charles who came to earth, and instead of a Roman cross it could be a French guillotine that provided atonement for our sin. Satan may be unwilling to concoct such a story precisely because he detests the very idea of forgiveness. He loathes grace so much that he can't even fake it.

In addition to the influence of Satan, there are other reasons why the people involved in these false religions consistently fail to comprehend grace. First, most people don't consider themselves to be all that bad. Sure, they may have made mistakes here and there, but in their hearts they know that they are generally good people. They don't really need grace, for certainly their numerous good thoughts and deeds are sufficient to outweigh the bad.

Second, those few people who truly appreciate their depravity scarcely dare to hope for grace. Those who understand that they have deeply offended a holy God know that their impending punishment is precisely what they deserve. They have no right to ask for or expect leniency. All they can do is brace themselves for the final judgment.

Imagine their surprise when these people hear the gospel's offer of forgiveness. Like Jean Valjean in *Les Misérables*, they tremble before their benefactor. Could it really be true? My crime has been wiped clean? I am free to go? Imagine their surprise when they learn that the gospel that forgives their sin also promises to eliminate it so they can once again flourish in the fullness of their humanity. Specifically, the grace offered in the gospel retraces the path of sin, restoring each of our three created relationships that sin broke. Just as sin alienated us from God, others, and the world, so grace reconciles us to our Father, our neighbors, and the earth itself (Fig. 11.2).[31]

Notice that this redemption is both gift and responsibility. Just as Jean Valjean seized on grace as an opportunity to improve his world, so those who understand that they are reconciled to God, others, and the earth will not rest on these laurels but will actively seek to live out this reconciliation. They will do this by acknowledging God's authority, caring for neighbors, and performing their cultural duties to the glory of God. Since this first relationship with God is rightly

Figure 11.2: How Redemption Repairs Our Image of God

Creation			
Genesis 1:27–28	"God created man in his own image, in the image of God he created him"	"Male and female he created them"	"Be fruitful and increase in number; fill the earth and subdue it. Rule ..."
This means that humans are properly related to	God	Other humans	The world
Because of this humans are	Religious beings	Social beings	Cultural beings
These aspects of human life should produce	Worship of God	Love for others	Joyful work in the world
Fall			
Because of the fall, these image-bearing characteristics produce	Idolatry, self-worship	Greed, selfishness	Laziness, sloth, or self-indulgence
The consequences of sin are	Alienation from God—Wrath	Alienation from others—Hate	Alienation from work—Drudgery
Redemption			
When we become Christians we experience	**Reconciliation with God**	**Reconciliation with our neighbor**	**Joyful resumption of our cultural task**
This involves	**Acknowledging God's lordship**	**Showing love to others**	**Doing our work to the glory of God**
This is suggested in	**1 Peter 2:9**	**Galatians 6:10; 1 John 4:11**	**Colossians 3:23–24**

emphasized in our evangelical churches and the second was examined in our previous discussion of *shalom* (chapter 6) the remainder of this chapter focuses on how redemption applies to our frequently forgotten third relationship—the gift and responsibility to redeem human culture.

Cultural Christianity

Every person is commanded by God to contribute to the development of culture. As we learned in chapter 7, God placed Adam and Eve in the garden to till the soil and manage its resources.[32] He planned that, given enough time to study the creation and learn from past mistakes, our first parents and their children would discover how to harness the earth's potential and generate a vibrant human culture. Judging by the course of human history, this plan has been a smashing success.

For instance, consider the humble grain of sand. Early on, people learned that sand is excellent material for playgrounds, packing, and making weights. Later generations, examining this versatile compound in light of their current needs, found that sand is also useful for mixing cement and marking time. But it was left to twentieth-century scientists to unleash the almost unimaginable potential concealed within a grain of sand. Who would have guessed that such plain and plentiful particles could be used to power computers that dramatically enhance the quality of human life? Who knew that one day our entire civilization would be driven by the abrasive sludge that centuries of cultured people rinsed away after a day at the beach?

This onward and upward push of culture has been the one constant of human existence. We are not a perfect race, but for the most part we have followed God's command to cultivate and improve his creation. Even sin, the dominant destructive force in our world, has not halted our cultural progress.[33] Indeed, it was the evil line of Cain that produced history's first cultural connoisseurs: Jabal, "the father of those who live in tents and raise livestock"; Jubal, "the father of all who play the harp and flute"; and Tubal-Cain, "who forged all kinds of tools out of bronze and iron."[34] Within the shadow cast by Adam's fall, the human race continued to advance its understanding and enjoyment of the earth, diligently honing the skills of music, metallurgy, and animal husbandry. It's almost as if we can't help ourselves. Dogs bark, horses race, and humans—even fallen ones—are wired to cultivate God's creation.

This commitment to cultural progress is perhaps most compelling in our day. Briefly consider just a few of the numerous innovations that have dramatically enriched the quality of our lives. Besides the aforementioned computer, there are the lightbulb, microwave oven, camera, radio, telephone, television, flush toilet, central air conditioning, gas furnace, automobile, airplane, and electricity. What was unimaginable for our grandparents is now routinely ordinary for us, and we can only guess what fantastic inventions our grandchildren will produce.

However, before we get too carried away in our praise for human culture, we should remember that there is a dark side to this cultural achievement. Adam's fall may not have been able to destroy our cultural progress, but it did distort our final products. Thanks to sin, the same innovations that improve our quality of life may also be used for evil.

For example, consider again our humble grain of sand. Fallen people soon discovered that the same sand that provides a heavy counterweight can also whack a foe senseless; the same cement that constructs buildings can also anchor a snitch's body to the bottom of the harbor; the same computers that share helpful information and power our plants can also be used to spread viruses and paralyze our cities.

This ongoing misuse of culture adds another dimension to our cultural responsibility. Because we are human, we will continue to develop culture, but now, because we are Christian, we must also strive to redeem it. It is not enough merely to salvage a few souls from the wreckage of sin. The entire world belongs to God, so it must be the entire world that is redeemed. To paraphrase Abraham Kuyper, we must diligently labor to bring every square inch of human existence beneath the lordship of the Christ who proclaims, "It's mine!"

To do so requires that we carefully distinguish between what belongs to God's good creation and what is a product of sin. In other words, we must discern an object's structural soundness from its use in either an evil or good direction.[35] For example, atomic energy in itself is a structural good of creation. It has potential for enormous good, such as producing clean and cheap energy to light and heat our homes. However, in the wrong hands it can also be used to blackmail peace-loving nations and potentially even blow up the entire world.

Or consider our recent cracking of the genetic code. This achievement represents a high structural good, for it enables us to vastly improve our society. Armed with our genetic information, we can create individualized vaccines and cure birth defects in the womb. However, the same knowledge may be used in an evil direction, for it also enables insurers to unjustly screen high-risk applicants, and doctors to create genetically enhanced designer babies.

With this in mind, Christians must accept a double responsibility for God's world. Because we are human, we gladly unite with other people to develop culture, joining the upward climb from the pristine garden of Genesis 2 to the organized city of Revelation 21.[36] Besides this cultural mandate, our commitment to redemption also inspires us to stay alert for those points where our culture is misused for evil purposes. Whether it be the common abuses of the entertainment industry or the perplexing challenges of medical science, we endeavor to bring the errant piece of culture back to plumb, knowing that only in this way will our developing culture grow straight and true as God intended (Fig. 11.3).

Figure 11.3: Our Twofold Responsibility to Culture

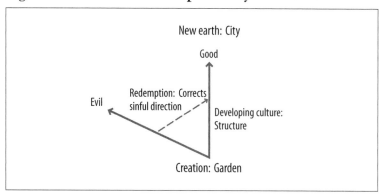

Asking the Right Questions

You may notice here the return of our familiar ontological-ethical distinction. "Structure" refers to what is ontologically good in creation, and "direction" to the ethical use or misuse of these created goods. Just as we found the ontological-ethical distinction indispensable when learning about creation and humanity (chapters 3 and 4), so now we find these categories essential for talking intelligently about the intersection of creation and humanity: the development of human culture.[37]

Indeed, these categories supply the only way through knotty cultural questions. For example, some Christians wonder about the propriety of activities such as dancing, drinking alcoholic beverages, or going to movies. The answer lies in our ability to think biblically, to run each of these issues through the grid of creation, fall, and redemption.

We begin by asking what part of these activities is ontologically sound, or a structural good of creation. Here we may acknowledge that the kinetic movement of dance, the satisfying taste of wine, and the storytelling ability of movies are all structural goods that God has built into his creation. Next, we consider how sin has twisted these structural goods into an evil direction, whether it be the sexual perversion found in some forms of dance, the drunkenness and alcoholism that accompany some instances of drink, or the violence, immorality, foul language, juvenile humor, and inane plots found in some popular movies.

Finally, we inquire into the appropriate response of redemption. Is it possible to cleanse the evil that is present and redirect these cultural goods for God? Or are they too far gone, so shot through with sin, that our only responsible option is to abstain completely? For instance, may Christians reclaim the cultural form of dance, or, given its misuse in our sexually crazed culture, is it best to let this one go rather than risk soiling our souls in a failed redemptive attempt? May Christians redeem a responsible use of alcohol, or does its cultural association with fraternity parties and erratic drivers, not to mention the dangers of drunkenness, persuade us to opt instead for sparkling grape juice? May Christians regularly attend movies, or, considering the presence of immorality and secularism in most popular films, is it wise to find alternative forms of entertainment?

Intelligent Christians may disagree on their final answers, but at least now they won't be talking past each other. When we allow the biblical story of creation, fall, and redemption to set the agenda, not only will we be thinking theologically—correctly sifting through the issues as God intended—but we will also be able to converse with those who disagree with us. We will be able to pinpoint the precise location of our conflict, typically finding that the reasons for our differing responses lie further back, in a more fundamental disagreement over how much of the topic in question belongs to creation and how much has been irreversibly corrupted by the fall.

The End Is Near?

So we may use our grid of creation, fall, and redemption to biblically evaluate culture. But why should we bother? Doesn't the Bible teach that the earth and everything in it will eventually burn up? What does it matter if we redeem the realms of music, literature, or architecture? All recordings, books, and buildings will disappear anyway. Doesn't all this concern for culture amount to polishing the brass on a sinking ship? If so, where is the lasting value in that?

This popular, though misguided notion likely arises from a misunderstanding of 2 Peter 3:10–13.

> But the day of the Lord will come like a thief. The heavens will disappear with a roar; the elements will be destroyed by fire, *and the earth and everything in it will be laid bare*. Since everything will be destroyed in this way, what kind of people ought you to be? You ought to live holy and godly lives as you look forward to the day of God and speed its coming. That day will bring about the destruction of the heavens by fire,

and the elements will melt in the heat. But in keeping with his promise we are looking forward to a new heaven and a new earth, the home of righteousness.

During the sixteenth and seventeenth centuries, the best available Greek manuscripts of 2 Peter 3:10 read that "the earth and all of its works will be *burned up*." This is how every translation of that period, including the King James Version, rendered this verse. It is easy to see how whole generations of Christians learned from their Bibles to expect a future fire that would annihilate the entire world.

However, scholars have since discovered older, more reliable Greek manuscripts, and these texts say that rather than burning up, "the earth and all of its works will be *found*." Instead of being destroyed, this term "found" implies that the quality of our works will be "laid bare," discovered for all to see. Much like gold passing through a smelting furnace, the good that we do will be purified while our less noble efforts will slough off. Read this way, Peter's vision of a coming conflagration seems to be a purging rather than annihilating fire.

Perhaps this is why Peter compares the coming "destruction" by fire with the world's previous "destruction" by water (2 Peter 3:6–7). Just as the Great Flood did not annihilate the world but primarily cleansed it of its numerous sinners, so the impending fire seems to perform an *ethical* cleansing rather than an *ontological* annihilation. In short, if the "destruction" of the flood did not annihilate the world, why should we think that the future "destruction" by fire will do so?[38]

Peter's point is that since the coming conflagration will purge the earth of its impurities, strive to live such good lives that when you and the works of your hands pass through the refining fire, both you and your cultural contributions will survive. Thus, rather than give cause for despair, Peter's admonition actually inspires hope that our highest cultural achievements, such as the *Mona Lisa*, Westminster Abbey, and *Eine Kleine Nachtmusik*, will make it through to the new heaven and new earth.

But even if they do not—even if they are destroyed in the final fire—we may still have confidence that our culture will continue. In some ways, wondering whether a particular piece of culture may survive is a distraction, for what matters most is not the artifact itself but the person who created it. So what if all recordings of *Eine Kleine Nachtmusik* are destroyed with the end of the world? The new earth will be full of talented musicians (perhaps even Mozart himself?) who will have the rest of forever not only to rewrite this serenade but, inspired by the glories around them, to create even sweeter melodies. God may ultimately choose not to preserve this book or that building, but he will spare enough authors and architects to re-create the best of whatever is lost.

Back to the Future

Here is a rule of thumb for figuring what will and will not make it through to our next life: Whatever properly belongs to creation will be restored, while whatever is a product of the fall will be removed. As far as I can tell, there are only three exceptions to this rule.

First, we know from Jesus' response to the Sadducees' question about the widow of seven brothers that our next life will not include the created good of marriage.[39] We are not sure why this is the case, but perhaps it has something to do with the fall. God's original plan was for Adam and Eve to live together forever, but their sin brought the evils of death and divorce into the world. Now separated from their partners, divorced or widowed spouses often marry new mates, sometimes going through several marriages in one lifetime. In this scrambled situation, even redemption can't put one marriage back together without destroying another. Perhaps to prevent this chaos God permits marriage to fall into disuse on the new earth.

But God never takes away any good without giving us something better in its place. In this case, our marriage bond between man and wife is fulfilled in the marriage union between Christ and his church. In other words, the pleasure and purpose of marriage in this life is merely a distant echo, a tangible taste, of the enriching intimacy we will savor when Christ comes to marry his church.[40] As C. S. Lewis explains, just as a child can scarcely believe that sexual love is preferable to chocolate, so we must take it on faith that the joy of union with God far surpasses the deepest satisfaction we will ever experience in this life.[41]

Second, besides this lone good that will apparently be eliminated in the next life, there are two consequences of the fall that won't be fixed: the serpent will remain under its curse,[42] and Jesus will continue to bear the scars of his crucifixion.[43] Perhaps these two consequences of sin will remain to remind us of our redemption: the serpent slithering in the dust as a symbol of our sin, and the pierced hands of Christ as a sign of our salvation.

These three items—marriage, the cursed serpent, and the scars of Christ—are the exceptions that prove our rule: Whatever belongs to creation will be restored, while whatever belongs to the fall will be removed. We still have many questions, for Scripture supplies few details of our next life. For instance, we may wonder whether everyone will be the perfect age (say somewhere around thirty) and whether children who died young will be allowed to mature into this prime age, giving back to them and their parents the childhood they never had.

We may wonder which personal properties are part of creation and which belong to the fall. Will God make short people taller, large people smaller, slow people faster, and average students smarter? To the point, will we have pretty much the same body, IQ, and personality quirks that we presently possess, or may we expect the athleticism of Michael Jordan, the mind of Albert Einstein, and the creativity of Charles Dickens? We may not find clear answers to such whimsical questions, but what Scripture does tell us about our future is enough to make us plenty excited.

Heaven Came Down and Glory Filled My Soul

For starters, Scripture repeatedly reminds us that our next life will be lived on the new earth.[44] The term "new" implies that this final destination will differ somewhat from the planet we currently inhabit, while the term "earth" reassures us that it will still feel very much like home. According to 2 Peter 3:13, the main difference between this world and the next is moral, for the sin and suffering of this present age will be replaced with "a new heaven and a new earth, the home of *righteousness*." This fits well with our general rule of thumb, which says that the *ontological* goods of our present creation will remain while the *ethical* evils of this fallen world will be eliminated. In sum, we may expect planet earth to survive its final purging largely intact, losing only the sinful dross that the fire burns away.

Indeed, our purified earth will be so inviting that even God himself will choose to live here. Our God calls himself "Emmanuel," which means "God with us." Unfortunately, many Christians read this name backwards, as if Emmanuel means "us with God." If we think "us with God," we tend to imagine that the goal of life is to leave this planet and live forever with him in heaven. That is a great thing, but it is just the beginning of what God has planned for us. God isn't content merely to take us to be with him; he wants to return with us to this planet, to live with us in the place where we are most at home.

The story of Scripture is the story of "Emmanuel," for it describes how God progressively comes to live with us on our planet, at each appearance staying longer and in more permanent form. God walked intermittently with Adam and Eve, coming and going as he deemed appropriate. By the time of the Exodus God had established a more permanent presence, leading his people as a pillar of fire by night and a cloud by day, the same cloud that remained to inhabit the Holy of Holies in the tabernacle and temple.

None of these ethereal forms prepared the world for the surprising visit of Jesus Christ, who, according to Matthew 1:23, is the fulfillment of Emmanuel, for God now walked among us in tangible, human flesh. After Jesus' ascension, the Day of Pentecost marks a further revelation of Emmanuel, for henceforth God the Holy Spirit will permanently though invisibly dwell within each of us.[45] Finally, we read John's thrilling conclusion in Revelation 21:1–4. Describing the descent of the New Jerusalem from heaven to the earth, John hears the voice of God saying: "Now the dwelling of God is *with men*, and he will live *with them*. They will be his people, and God himself will be *with them* and be their God" (v. 3).

Notice the thrice-repeated phrase "with them." The biblical story does not conclude with us going to be *with God*, but with just the sort of ending we might expect from Emmanuel: God comes to live *with us*. Could God say any more emphatically that creation is good? This earth is such a pleasant place that when God purifies it from sin, he himself will come to live here with us. Emmanuel indeed.

The Good Life

What will we do with God on this new earth? Certainly we will join the rest of creation's praise to our triune God. Nothing will ever be more fulfilling. As we fall on our faces before our sovereign Lord and gracious Savior, we will truly know, for the first time, why we exist. We were made for this.

But we were also made for more than this. We were made to be human, and on the new earth we will participate in other, human activities. As we mentioned briefly in chapter 1, Isaiah's vision of the future includes a full range of cultural endeavors. In a passage on the "new heavens and a new earth," Isaiah promises that people living there "will build houses and dwell in them; they will plant vineyards and eat their fruit."[46] Elsewhere, Isaiah tells us that the new earth will have enormous wealth, including much silver, gold, and incense.[47] Then, in a statement that John will borrow to describe the New Jerusalem, Isaiah writes: "Your gates will always stand open, they will never be shut, day or night, so that men may bring you the wealth of the nations—their kings led in triumphal procession."[48]

Houses, vineyards, kings, and wealthy nations—these words signal a world of cultural activity on the new earth. Remember that God's first command to Adam and Eve was to develop his creation, to take the raw materials of his good world and make something better.[49] Because this cultural mandate has never been rescinded, we may rightly expect to continue our cultural activity on the new earth, much as we are doing now.

So the new earth will be an exciting, interesting place to be. We will be always growing, always learning more about ourselves, the world, and God. We will never bottom out and become bored, for we will never know as much as God knows. There will always be some new joy to discover, some place to visit or revisit, some new dish to create, a new flower to breed, a new song to sing, a new poem to write, a new golf club to try out, a new lesson to learn and then pass on to someone else, some person to know more deeply, something new in our relationship with God. And this stretching and growing will go on forever.

Consider how high our redeemed culture will eventually climb. Despite being hampered by sin, our few thousand years of human culture have already produced the likes of Plato, Bach, and Michelangelo, plus many recent breakthroughs in science and technology. Imagine what we will accomplish after working a few million years without the limitations of sin! If you enjoy culture, technology, and the triumph of the human spirit, you are really going to feel at home on the new earth.

To summarize, because redemption restores rather than obliterates creation, we will find that its completion in our next life will be the fulfillment of our humanity. Nothing will be more satisfying than dwelling with our Father on the earth we call home, enjoying the well-rounded, flourishing lives he intended for us all along. Our next life will look an awful lot like this one, lacking only the suffering that arises from sin.

12

But What About . . . ?

We take captive every thought to make it obedient to Christ.
***

2 Corinthians 10:5

William was blessed with a golden tongue. Though small, frail, and burdened with weak eyes and a long nose, William's keen mind, indomitable spirit, and above all—that beautiful voice—made him a rising star in British society. Elected to Parliament by the time he was twenty-one, William had an ability to dominate debates and motivate members with his stirring speeches that paved the way for a long career in politics and a probable stint as Britain's prime minister.

But then William gave his heart to Christ. As he wrestled with his new faith, this twenty-five-year-old statesman recognized that his previous life of politicking and partying had been a fairly transparent attempt to advance his own career. If he was serious about taking up his cross and following Christ, William figured he must sacrifice his selfish dreams of being prime minister and instead use his considerable speaking skills as a pastor or itinerant evangelist. This deeply saddened him, for he thoroughly enjoyed his role in Parliament and could hardly imagine giving it up for anything else—even the ministry.

In his distress William sought counsel from John, an older, respected pastor in a nearby parish. To William's surprise, John surmised that while his talent would be put to good use in the church, it might be even more profitable within the halls of government. Given the degenerating condition of British culture, it certainly couldn't hurt to have a clear voice of conviction in the highest reaches of power. Like Esther of old, perhaps the Lord had prepared William for this very purpose.

So with new resolve William returned to Parliament, determined no longer to promote his own career but rather to spend his talent on a cause larger than himself. Within two years he had found it. "God Almighty," he wrote in his journal, "has set before me two great objects: the suppression of the slave trade and the reformation of manners."

Abolishing Britain's slave trade was easier said than done. Most people conceded that it was a messy business, but they also considered it a necessary evil to sustain the nation's prosperity. The shipment of slave labor to the West Indies enabled Britain's colonies there to produce inexpensive imports, such as sugar and cotton, which fueled the economy of the mother country. From the wealthiest investors and their well-funded politicians to the average citizens who appreciated cheap clothes and a strong navy, everyone in Britain benefited from the business of slavery.

Besides, most people assumed that slavery was an inevitable fact of life. Any Africans not stolen by Britain would be snapped up by other countries, such as France and Portugal, who would then use this free labor to surpass Britain in might and affluence. Thus, Britain's very survival as a world power seemed tied to maintaining its competitive edge in the slave trade. Such realism easily overpowered any arguments that questioned the morality of slavery. Stories of severed families and murdered slaves might make legislators shift uncomfortably in their seats, but these moments of conviction were quickly swallowed up in the larger picture of what was best for Britannia.

So for the next twenty years Britain's "responsible" officials defeated William's annual motions to abolish the buying and selling of slaves. Especially considering Napolean's threatened conquest of Europe, most thought this was no time to pass a law that might weaken Britain's ability to defend herself against France. But William never gave up, even when his dogged persistence irritated his colleagues and ruined any chance he once cherished of becoming prime minister. After two decades of defeat and defamation, William finally convinced his peers that ending the slave trade not only was their moral obligation but was also in the best interests of Britain. It took another twenty-six years to convince his fellow legislators to abolish altogether the practice of slavery, but in 1833, just three days before William's death, Parliament succumbed to his relentless pressure and agreed to free all the slaves in the British Empire.

By now you may have guessed that William's full name is William Wilberforce (1759–1833), the legendary dynamo whose legacy altered life not only in Britain but also in the United States, Africa, India, and countless other countries that subsequently abolished slavery. What you may not know is that the pastor who advised William to remain in his civil career was John Newton, a former slave trader himself and celebrated composer of the beloved hymn "Amazing Grace."[1]

As we have emphasized throughout this book, Newton recognized that God's amazing grace reaches us in many forms. It not only saves the soul of "a wretch like me," but also redeems the society in which such wretches live. This multifaceted dimension to grace often raises perplexing questions for serious Christians. Much like a young Wilberforce, we may wonder whether we should invest our lives in professional ministry like Newton or remain in more "worldly" pursuits like politics or business. If Wilberforce's life teaches us anything, it is that such difficult questions belie easy answers. We may certainly agree that nothing is more important than leading "a wretch like me" to Christ, yet not even the most die-hard evangelist among us would second-guess the great good that Wilberforce accomplished in his "secular" work.

It is just this type of question that I address in this final chapter. This book has traced the contours of the biblical worldview by retelling the story of creation, fall, and redemption. I have admittedly focused most on creation, not only because it is foundational to the other two movements, but also because it is too often forgotten in evangelical circles.[2] But perhaps some are wondering if I haven't overplayed this hand, emphasizing the opening movement of creation at the expense of the final two episodes of fall and redemption.

Objections to Our Concern for Creation

From my experience, people typically raise one of the following three objections.[3] First, rather than draw people to God, won't all this talk about the goodness and importance of creation merely give people an excuse to become materialists? Haven't we given them spiritual cover to selfishly accumulate this world's goods, all the while claiming that they are merely celebrating creation?

Second, perhaps this focus on creation fails to seriously consider the plight of the desperately poor. Those who are deeply impoverished don't have the luxury of enjoying creation, for they are fortunate to eke out an existence in this vale of tears. Such people can't wait to get on to the next, and hopefully better, life. Of what benefit is this book to them?

Third, perhaps this concern for creation, while admirable on its own terms, nevertheless amounts to a dangerous distraction in a world that is going to hell. Won't our zeal for creation inevitably sap our energy and divert our resources from the more important task of evangelism? How can we justify writing (and reading) a worldview book when there are millions of souls who still need the Lord?

The following pages address these three questions.

Isn't This Book an Excuse for Materialism?

I suppose someone could use our concern for creation to support an addiction to material things, much as that someone could abuse the savory spread of a home-cooked meal to indulge in the sin of gluttony. However, just as no decent person would blame his wife or mother for that bloated, after-dinner feeling, so we should not criticize the attractiveness of the Christian worldview for those who misuse it. Instead, we must clearly distinguish between the good of creation and its sinful perversion, refusing to allow the wrong that is sometimes done to ruin the right that remains.

We already do this quite well. For instance, most of us recognize that the evils of adultery and rape need not spoil our appropriate enjoyment of sex, drunkenness need not preclude our use of grapes, and robbery and embezzlement need not destroy our appreciation money. In each case we separate the created good—sex, grapes, money—from its unnatural abuse by twisted sinners.[4]

Likewise with materialism, the problem lies with the sinner rather any material item she might covet. Materialists are idolaters, not because they care too much for material things but because they actually care too little about anything except themselves. It's not the money, fine dining, or humongous house that they crave, but rather the personal pleasure that they derive from such possessions. Materialists don't make idols out of money; they make idols out of them-not "too attached to material things" (as if they could e themselves from the physical universe); they are nselves. Money and the finer things of life are ater end—their insatiable desire to provide the g they have persuaded themselves they deserve. ounts to selfishness. This sin occurs whenever heart on riches,[5] not for the wealth per se but for the s it can bring them. If they could only get over themselves, they would quickly conquer materialism, for they would no longer have an incentive to grasp and hoard their possessions. Thus, here again we find that our problem lies not with any created thing, but rather with our selfish abuse of such good things. Our problem is sin, not stuff. Simply put, matter is not the matter.

Contrary to materialists who care only for themselves, we who embrace the Christian worldview are motivated to care properly for the material things of this world. We believe that matter matters, neither for its own sake nor even for ours, but because it belongs to our Father, the Creator of all material things. Our allegiance to God compels us to protect and prosper his creation, seeking to share its resources with those who need it most, both now and for generations to come.

In sum, materialists and Christians alike look after matter, but they differ in their reason why. Materialists run after created goods for their own benefit, hoping to acquire more stuff to consume and perhaps quench their insatiable appetites. Christians care for creation because our Father has commanded us to cultivate the resources of his good world, both for our own enjoyment and to share with those in need.

Unfortunately, Christians too often think like materialists. This is a special temptation in the wealthy Western nations, where our unparalleled affluence and desire to keep step with our neighbors can easily blind us to the truth of our selfishness. Few of us sacrifice anything much to help others. Like any hardened materialist, we labor and plan for our own sake, rarely contemplating the needs of our neighbors or how we might honor God with what he has entrusted to us.

My point here is that such selfishness does not arise from the Christian worldview but rather from the sinful autonomy that Adam bequeathed to us at the fall. Materialism cannot gain traction in the Christian worldview, for it is a perversion of everything this worldview represents. It is our selfish autonomy—not the attractiveness of creation—that compels us to hoard these goods for ourselves. In sum, just as we do not blame the cook for making us fat, neither should we blame creation, nor the Christian worldview that celebrates it, when we sinfully abuse the goods that are here.

Isn't This Book Irrelevant to the Desperately Poor?

Along the lines of the materialism question, some people may wonder whether the content in this book isn't a bit too accommodating to upper-class Christians. It is easy to appreciate creation when we have time and money to spare, but what about the billions in the world who live in poverty? Many of these people have known only hunger and pain during their brief stint on earth. The last thing they want is to be stuck here forever.

Perhaps this is why many Negro spirituals express a longing for heaven. Suffering beneath the injustice and hopelessness of slavery, those with faith sang of life on the other side of the grave, when they would finally be released from their hard lives of forced labor. Aren't these people right to dream of their eventual escape into heaven? Wouldn't they scoff at the goodness of this world, the value of the cultural mandate, and the privilege of being made in the image of God? Isn't the content of the Christian worldview entirely irrelevant to them?

While it may seem so at first blush, a closer look reveals that creation and its enjoyment are more important to the poor and oppressed than we might think. Everyone, no matter how destitute, still yearns to express their humanity and squeeze the most joy from creation that their circumstances will allow. Across the globe, grubby street urchins proudly pluck flowers for their matted hair, street boys knot their shirts together for makeshift soccer balls, and impoverished fathers scrimp and save for a dowry so that, for one very special day, their little girl may become a princess. Ever wonder why some of the world's brightest clothes, spiciest foods, and festive celebrations are found among the most destitute? It is often the poor, not the rich, who party as if there were no tomorrow.

Consider again America's slaves, who, though they often spoke about heaven, set these escapist lyrics to music. In so doing they betrayed their ongoing concern for this world, for the plaintive tunes of their spirituals both expressed their humanity and made their hardships a bit more bearable. Mindless animals may endure beatings and abuse in whimpering silence, but people who are created in the image of God must sing about their pain. Thus, even those unfortunate souls who were born into slavery could not help but respond in human fashion, yearning for a better day while doing what they could to improve their lot here and now.

Considering the importance of creation to the poor and oppressed, they—perhaps even more than the wealthy—need to hear how redemption restores all of life. Remember that Jesus especially targeted the down-and-outers with the good news of the gospel.[6] He wanted them to hear the Word of God that put the lie to their experience. Despite what life had dealt them, they needed to know that creation is better than it seemed, that as the image of God they possessed more dignity than they knew, and that one day soon shalom would come to set the world to rights. Most important, they needed the reassurance that their present predicament mattered to God, to remember that he is Emmanuel, the God who joins them in their sin and misery.

This is precisely the worldview approach that Mother Teresa and her Missionaries of Charity implemented among the impoverished castaways of Calcutta. Alarmed that many sick and elderly were left to expire in the streets, they built shelters where these image bearers could die with the dignity they deserved. Next they built orphanages, schools, and homes for the needy—places where the disabled, blind, elderly, and lepers could live in flourishing community with fellow image bearers on God's good earth. Rather than encourage her charges to let go and long solely for heaven, Mother Teresa and her sisters drew them back from the brink by instilling hope that their lives still mattered and were worth reclaiming.

Perhaps most surprising is how Mother Teresa's Christian ministry resonated within the hearts of India's predominantly Hindu population. The Hindu worldview gives little incentive to help the poor, for it teaches that those born into a lower caste are merely reaping their sins from a previous life. If we interfere with their penance by coming to their aid, we will only create bad karma—for both them and us—in the next life. Instead, we should allow them to complete their penance, hoping that eventually each of us will become so pure that we will no longer be reincarnated back into this world of misery. In this way the Hindu worldview undercuts charity for the needy and is likely a contributing factor to the 300 million Indians who remain stuck in poverty.

Yet, despite their Hindu upbringing, most Indians grew to love the frail nun from Eastern Europe who came to the aid of their wretched poor. Although she broke the foundational rules of Indian society, they had no answer for the tireless energy with which she loved their most helpless people. Could it be that all people, even Hindus, know more about the goodness of creation, the value of human life, and the celebration of this world than they are willing to admit? An entire Hindu nation embraced Mother Teresa's application of her Christian worldview because, despite what they said in their temples, in their hearts they knew she was right. This world and the people in it matter more than we might think, even—especially—to those who are desperately poor.

Isn't This Book a Distraction from Evangelism?

What I have written in this book assigns a full plate of responsibility to believers. Because we are human, we must join other people to develop the good creation that God entrusted to us.[7] Besides this cultural mandate, because we are Christian we must also strive to obey the redemptive mandate of Matthew 28:19–20 and "make disciples of all nations." Making disciples obviously involves sharing the gospel's offer of salvation with lost souls, but it also includes, as we saw in the previous chapter, teaching these disciples to reclaim culture and every last corner of creation for the Lord Jesus to whom it belongs.

And therein lies the rub. Although both the cultural and redemptive mandates belong to believers, shouldn't responsible Christians invest the lion's share of their limited resources in spreading the good news of personal salvation? Millions of people are going to hell for want of the gospel. Isn't our concern for culture, at best, a distraction from the more important matters of missions and evangelism?

C. S. Lewis addresses this important question in his essay "Learning in War-Time." While conceding that winning souls is more significant than developing or redeeming culture, Lewis adds that this question actually amounts to a false choice. It is impossible for anyone, regardless of how spiritual, to suspend his cultural life for the higher concerns of evangelism. Inasmuch as the evangelist is human, he will participate in cultural activities. Comparing the Christian life to military service, Lewis writes:

> Neither conversion nor enlistment in the army is really going to obliterate human life. Christians and soldiers are still men. . . . If you attempted, in either case, to suspend your whole intellectual and aesthetic activity, you would only succeed in substituting a worse cultural life for a better. You are not, in fact, going to read nothing, either in the Church or in the line: if you don't read good books, you will read bad ones. If you don't go on thinking rationally, you will think irrationally. If you reject aesthetic satisfactions, you will fall into sensual satisfactions.[8]

Just as soldiers still make time for eating, sleeping, playing cards, and swapping stories, so Christians on the front lines of evangelism must inevitably participate in other human activities. Their appropriate passion for the priority of the gospel will not prevent them from reading, washing, cooking, and generally caring for what God has entrusted to them. So rather than run from our cultural responsibilities—which is impossible anyway—why not embrace them as a vital concern of the gospel?

Let me explain. Too often well-meaning evangelists reduce the gospel to nothing more than "fire insurance." They assure people that the sinner's prayer will get them out of hell and into heaven, but they say precious little about what following Jesus means for our current life on earth (besides recruiting others to join our journey to heaven). Consequently, many "converts" continue living as they always have, watching the same television shows, running up the same credit-card bills, and suffering the same marital problems that they did before they trusted Jesus.

What might happen if we told these new believers that Christ wants to redeem every facet of their existence? Not content to merely rescue our souls from hell, he intends to transform every nook and cranny of our lives, from how we perform our jobs to how we spend our discretionary time and money. What if we challenged them to deny themselves and serve Christ in every aspect of their cultural lives? What if we diligently studied both the Scriptures and our culture to see how this might go?

Wouldn't such discipleship produce the most attractive form of Christianity? Rather than being insulted by our offers of cheap fire insurance, intelligent unbelievers might actually be impressed by the power of the gospel. They might recognize that we are not so heavenly minded we are no earthly good, but that it is precisely our concern for things above that drives us to excel at life here below.

As C. S. Lewis reminds us, wouldn't it be a great advertisement for the gospel if the best poets, artists, and architects consistently turned out to be Christians? What might unbelievers conclude if, every time they sought an expert, the best in the field was a follower of Jesus Christ? This alone may not lead them to embrace the gospel (there is still the matter of original sin), but they would at least acknowledge the power of it.[9]

So rather than distracting us from more important issues of evangelism, caring for culture may actually contribute to its cause. Before we can reasonably expect unbelievers to accept our faith we must first show them that it works—in our homes, on the job, and on the weekend—not merely when we are at church. Remember that Jesus Christ invested twenty-some years in his father's carpentry shop and that Paul spent whole weeks making tents. Neither of them considered this time wasted or an unfortunate distraction from more important matters, but rather they saw it as an essential component of the gospel itself. If the gospel redeems the entirety of human life, then all of life—from woodworking to tentmaking—must be redirected to the glory of God.

This is precisely what we learned from the life of William Wilberforce. Although he did not intentionally set out to lead people to Christ, his tireless efforts to end slavery impressed millions with the power of the gospel. More than any sermon John Newton ever preached, Wilberforce's life explained why everyone should become a Christian. Why did Wilberforce believe that freedom is an inalienable right, that human life is intrinsically valuable, and that ending slavery was worth sacrificing his own life and career? Because he embraced the Christian worldview, which informed him about the goodness of creation, the dignity of humanity, and the God who gave his own life so that Wilberforce himself could go free.

Thus, in an ironic twist that only God could pull off, Wilberforce's decision to forgo the ministry, far from hindering the advance of the gospel, actually contributed to its glory in the world. Likewise, our participation in the cultivation and redemption of culture, rather than representing an unfortunate drain on the resources of evangelism, may actually serve to reinforce it. The Christian worldview is not a distraction from the gospel. It is the gospel in all its fullness, a gospel that not only saves our souls but also restores the rest of us—and the rest of our world—to their original goodness. This is a compelling gospel to share—and live.

The Normal Christian Life

It is tempting to close this book with an inspiring story about some contemporary figure, such as Chuck Colson, who has caught the biblical vision espoused in these pages and is using it to dramatically change our world.[10] But let's be honest. Most of us will never be a Chuck Colson or a William Wilberforce. We probably won't do anything so grand as ending slavery or alleviating prison conditions around the globe. We're just normal Christians—but that's okay. Indeed, it is better than okay, for it is precisely what God expects from us.

Paul concludes his first letter to the Thessalonians by giving his readers something to shoot for in their Christian life. He tells them to "make it your ambition to. . . ." Can you guess how he finishes that sentence? Does he urge them on to new heights of devotion, encourage them to spend more time in worship and evangelism or give more money to the church? Surprisingly, no. Instead, Paul commands these new believers "to lead a quiet life, to mind your own business and to work with your hands, just as we told you, so that your daily life may win the respect of outsiders and so that you will not be dependent on anybody."[11]

Make it your ambition to lead a quiet life, earning a decent wage while tending to your vocations? How utterly ordinary! Paul, is that really all you expect from Spirit-filled believers? Pretty much. Paul confides to Titus that "our people must learn to devote themselves to doing what is good, in order that they may provide for daily necessities and not live unproductive lives."[12]

Why were such ordinary duties important to Paul? Because they alone made the gospel seem credible. Paul could preach all day long about the life-changing power of Christ, but he would convince few people without firsthand evidence that it really works.[13] So he encouraged his followers to become good neighbors, responsible citizens who faithfully serve society by minding their callings and caring for the needs of others. No one and no job was too insignificant, for even slaves—the least influential people in Roman society—could still "make the teaching about God our Savior attractive" when they quietly and swiftly carried out their master's orders.[14] These common Christians apparently impressed their friends and family, for their new faith spread so swiftly through the empire that in just a couple of centuries it had conquered the entire Roman world.

Come to think of it, maybe a community of normal Christians doing ordinary things for Christ can change the world. It happened once. It just might happen again.

Notes

Chapter 1. What You See Is What You Get

1. Mark Twain, *The Adventures of Huckleberry Finn* (New York: Random House, 1988), 5–6.
2. 2 Corinthians 5:6–9; Philippians 1:21–24; 1 Thessalonians 4:14, 17.
3. It is not impossible for bodies to live in heaven, as Jesus' presence there now proves, but it is not where bodies are meant to live. Even Jesus will return bodily to live forever with his saints on a newly restored earth (Revelation 21:1–4).
4. First Corinthians 15:44 states our new bodies will be "spiritual," and 2 Peter 3:13 declares that the new earth will lack the presence of sin.
5. Luke 24:36–43. The King James Version adds that Jesus ate honey, though this statement is not found in the best Greek manuscripts.
6. 1 Corinthians 15:20.
7. Isaiah 60:3–11; 65:17–25.
8. Isaiah 60:9; 65:21.
9. For a provocative look at Isaiah's vision of the new earth, see Richard Mouw, *When the Kings Come Marching In* (Grand Rapids: Eerdmans, 1983; rev. 2002).
10. These definitions come from Brian J. Walsh and J. Richard Middleton, *The Transforming Vision* (Downers Grove, IL: InterVarsity Press, 1984), 17; James W. Sire, *The Universe Next Door* (Downers Grove, IL: InterVarsity Press, 1988), 17; and Albert M. Wolters, *Creation Regained* (Grand Rapids: Eerdmans, 1985), 2.
11. Walsh and Middleton list variations of these four questions: "who am I?" "where am I?" "what's wrong?" and "what is the remedy?" (*The Transforming Vision*, 35).

12. You can find my answers in two bonus chapters at www.heavenisaplaceonearth.com, but for now resist the urge to look there.

13. See James H. Olthuis, "On Worldviews," *Christian Scholars Review* 14, no. 2 (1985): 153–64, for a stimulating discussion of a worldview's relation to prior faith commitments and experience.

14. Job 21:34.

15. Job 42:5–6. I am indebted to Eleonore Stump for her insights on the role of God's presence in resolving the problem of evil in the book of Job. See Stump, "Second-Person Accounts and the Problem of Evil," in *Seeking Understanding: The Stob Lectures, 1986–1998* (Grand Rapids: Eerdmans, 2001), 497–529.

Chapter 2. Creation: Where Lies the Great Divide?

1. Anselm, *Proslogion*, chaps. 2–5. This work is published in many places, one of which is *A Scholastic Miscellany: Anselm to Ockham*, Library of Christian Classics, ed. and trans. Eugene R. Fairweather (Philadelphia: Westminster Press, 1956), 69–93.

2. For a powerful restatement of Anselm's argument for God's existence, see Alvin Plantinga, *God, Freedom, and Evil* (Grand Rapids: Eerdmans, 1974), 85–112.

3. This new view of God, called "open theism," claims that God does not know the future, for if he did, our future acts would be fixed and we would not be free when we did them. Open theists maintain that despite this lack of foreknowledge, God sovereignly governs the universe, for he is resourceful enough to cope with any contingency. Books that support open theism include Greg Boyd, *The God of the Possible* (Grand Rapids: Baker, 2000); Clark Pinnock, *Most Moved Mover* (Grand Rapids: Baker, 2001); and John Sanders, *The God Who Risks* (Downers Grove, IL: InterVarsity Press, 1998). Opponents who argue for a more classical understanding of God include Bruce Ware, *God's Lesser Glory* (Wheaton, IL: Crossway Books, 2000); John Frame, *No Other God* (Phillipsburg, NJ: Presbyterian and Reformed Publishing Co., 2001); and Millard Erickson, *What Did He Know and When Did He Know It?* (Grand Rapids: Zondervan, 2003).

4. For example, Galatians 5:16; Ephesians 2:3; Colossians 2:11 KJV.

5. John 4:24.

6. Hebrews 2:7 is quoting Psalm 8:5, which in its original Hebrew form states that humans are made a little lower than *Elohim*, an ambiguous term that could refer either to angels or to God. Thus it is not clear whether Psalm 8:5 means that humans are created lower than angels or merely lower than God. However, the author of Hebrews 2:7 is not citing the Hebrew text of Psalm 8:5 but the Septuagint, the ancient Greek version of the Old

Testament, which translates *Elohim* here as "angels." Since I believe that the author of Hebrews was inspired by God to write his infallible word, I must take seriously his statement that people are lower than angels, whether or not that was David's original intent when he wrote Psalm 8.

7. Comments concerning whether or not angels bear the image of God can be found in Thomas Aquinas, *Summa Theologiae* 1a 93.3; John Calvin, *Institutes of the Christian Religion* I.15.3; and Herman Bavinck, *In the Beginning*, trans. John Vriend, ed. John Bolt (Grand Rapids: Baker, 1999), 80–83, 189.

8. Matthew 24:36.

9. Luke 2:52.

Chapter 3. Where Are We?

1. The best resource for a theology of creation remains Langdon Gilkey, *Maker of Heaven and Earth* (Garden City, NY: Doubleday, 1959). For more accessible, inspiring accounts of a biblical view of creation, see Scott Hoezee, *Remember Creation* (Grand Rapids: Eerdmans, 1998), and Paul Marshall, *Heaven Is Not My Home* (Nashville: Word, 1998).

2. The magical formula of the Gnostic Jesus can be found in Carol Zaleski and Philip Zaleski, eds., *The Book of Heaven* (New York: Oxford University Press, 2000), 69–70.

3. 1 Timothy 4:1–5.

4. 1 Timothy 4:6.

5. Colossians 2:20–23.

6. Colossians 1:16.

7. An early story supports our contention that John 1:14 was specifically written against the likes of Cerinthus. Irenaeus, in his work *Against Heresies* III.3.4, says that he knew people who had heard from Polycarp, who as a youth had known the apostle John. Polycarp told a story how once John entered a bathhouse in Ephesus only to find that Cerinthus was there. John immediately came rushing out, saying to his disciples: "Let us fly, lest even the bath-house fall down, because Cerinthus, the enemy of the truth, is within."

In the same passage, Irenaeus emphasizes the early church's hatred toward heretical views of creation when he recounts Polycarp's chance meeting with Marcion (a man with sympathies similar to Gnosticism). When asked by Marcion whether he knew who he was, Polycarp replied, "I do recognize you, the first-born of Satan."

8. I owe this insight on the Apostles' Creed to Richard Muller.

9. Genesis 1:31.

10. Colossians 3:5–10.

11. Colossians 3:12–17.
12. I thank Ginger Rohwer for bringing this to my attention.

Chapter 4. Creation: Who Are We?

1. Mariah Carey, "Hero." Copyright © 1993 Columbia Records.
2. John Calvin, *Institutes of the Christian Religion* I.14.2.
3. Genesis 1:26–28.
4. Genesis 3:17.
5. Genesis 4:10–11.
6. Genesis 6:7.
7. Genesis 9:8–11.
8. Philippians 3:20; 1 Peter 2:11.
9. To better understand what Paul means by "our citizenship is in heaven," consider his phrase "heavenly realms." In Ephesians 6:12 Paul warns that "our struggle is not against flesh and blood, but against the rulers, . . . authorities, . . . powers of this dark world and against the spiritual forces of evil in the heavenly realms." But Christ has triumphed over these heavenly powers (Ephesians 1:19–21) and thereby has full authority in heaven and the guarantee of eventual victory over the entire world (Ephesians 1:10; Colossians 1:20). In the meantime, we on earth should consider ourselves already seated with the triumphant Christ in these heavenly realms (Ephesians 2:6; Colossians 1:5; 3:1–4). In other words, not only should we consider ourselves to have already received the "spiritual blessings" Christ has won for us there (such as election, adoption, sanctification, redemption, and forgiveness—Ephesians 1:3–14), but we also should resist the sin that is present in our world and obediently live as if we belonged to heaven, the one place where God's will is unwaveringly followed (Ephesians 4:1ff.). Thus, being citizens of heaven does not imply that we are meant to dream about ethereal, celestial things, but rather that we should seek to do the will of our Father on earth "as it is in heaven."
10. Genesis 1:27.
11. The best resource for understanding what it means for humans to bear the image of God is Anthony A. Hoekema, *Created in God's Image* (Grand Rapids: Eerdmans, 1986).
12. See bonus chapter 1 at www.heavenisaplaceonearth.com.
13. While my analysis of the *imago Dei* is generally accurate, not everything related to our divine image breaks neatly along ontological and ethical lines. For instance, although in general our ontological capacities remain unaffected by sin, yet we know that certain skills, such as our ability to think clearly, have been damaged by sin. (Theologians call this sin's "noetic effects," from the Greek term, *nous*, which means "mind.") Furthermore,

people whose minds have been severely damaged by the ravages of the fall, such as those plagued by mental retardation or Alzheimer's disease, remain in the image of God despite lacking certain basic human skills. This fact suggests that the essence of the image of God lies deep within the human being. The core of the *imago Dei* lies well beneath the surface of our ontological capacities, so far down that we can't get a clear enough look to explain entirely what it is.

Besides oversimplifying the ontological side, I also inevitably spoke too broadly concerning the ethical. While it is generally true that sin spoiled our relationship with God, others, and the world, it did not entirely eliminate these relationships. Thanks to the common grace of God, even unregenerate people may still enjoy some basic knowledge of God, deep intimacy with others, and even productive care for God's earth. Although nothing they do will ever be righteous enough to merit everlasting life, they are still able to accomplish some good.

Thus, although my generalization about the image of God is largely true, it is too easy on the ontological side and too hard on the ethical element. Sinners lose more of the image ontologically and lose less of the image ethically than my general description allows. Nevertheless, despite these specific reservations, my general description remains a useful starting point for speaking about the *imago Dei*.

14. Used with the permission of Douglas A. Felch, associate professor of theology at Reformed Bible College in Grand Rapids, Michigan, who created this chart for his class entitled "Christian Doctrine."
15. The other powerful metaphor for the Trinity is the church, which, according to John 17:20–23, tangibly portrays the community of the Godhead when its individual members unite in love and fellowship.
16. Galatians 3:28.

Chapter 5. To Love God

1. Matthew 16:24–26.
2. Matthew 13:45–46.
3. Matthew 10:39.
4. Augustine, *Confessions*, Book 1.1.
5. Peter Berger, *A Rumor of Angels* (Garden City, NY: Doubleday, 1969), 65–94. Philip Yancey writes provocatively on this subject in *Rumors of Another World* (Grand Rapids: Zondervan, 2003).
6. Philippians 3:8.
7. Colossians 3:17, 23.
8. *What Luther Says*, comp. Ewald M. Plass (St. Louis: Concordia Publishing House, 1959), III:1512.

9. Matthew 13:44–46.
10. Matthew 13:33.
11. See Herman Bavinck, "The Catholicity of Christianity and the Church," *Calvin Theological Journal* 27 (November 1992): 223–24, 236, 248.

Chapter 6. To Serve Others

1. Matthew 22:37–38.
2. Matthew 22:39–40.
3. Augustine, "Sermon 350: On Charity," in *The Works of Saint Augustine: A Translation for the 21ˢᵗ Century III*, vol. 3, no. 10, ed. John E. Rotelle, trans. Edmund Hill (New York: New City Press, 1995), 108: "Charity is in secure possession of the whole length and breadth of the divine utterances, the charity with which we love God and neighbor."
4. Martin Luther, "The Freedom of a Christian," in *Luther's Works* 31, ed. Harold J. Grimm and Helmut T. Lehmann (Philadelphia: Muhlenberg Press, 1957), 365: "Therefore he should be guided in all his works by this thought and contemplate this one thing alone, that he may serve and benefit others in all that he does, considering nothing except the need and the advantage of his neighbor."
5. 1 John 3:14.
6. For a provocative account of our Christian obligation to care for our larger society, see Nicholas Wolterstorff, *Until Justice and Peace Embrace* (Grand Rapids: Eerdmans, 1983). To learn more about the subtle dangers of our technological world, read Quentin J. Schultz, *Habits of the High-Tech Heart* (Grand Rapids: Baker, 2002).
7. Numbers 6:24–26.
8. Cornelius Plantinga Jr., *Not the Way It's Supposed to Be: A Breviary of Sin* (Grand Rapids: Eerdmans, 1995), 9–12.
9. 1 Chronicles 22:9.
10. 1 Kings 5:4.
11. 1 Kings 10:23. The wealth that accompanies the absence of war is what financial analysts call "the peace dividend."
12. 1 Kings 10:7–8.
13. Psalm 72:1–3.
14. Psalm 72:4–7. The phrase "abundance of peace [shalom]" comes from the New King James Version.
15. Genesis 1:28–31.
16. Isaiah 1:10–15.
17. Isaiah 1:17, 23; 10:1–2.
18. Isaiah 3:15.
19. Isaiah 3:11.

20. Isaiah 2:12–21.
21. Isaiah 5:13; 39:6.
22. Isaiah 9:6.
23. Isaiah 53:5.
24. Luke 2:14.
25. Isaiah 2:2–3.
26. Isaiah 2:4.
27. Isaiah 61:1–2. Jesus applies this passage to himself in Luke 4:18–19.
28. Isaiah 32:16–18.
29. Isaiah 32:15.
30. Isaiah 11:1–5.
31. Isaiah 11:6–9.
32. Matthew 25:31–46.
33. See Matthew 23:4, 15, 27. "Devour widows' houses" occurs in verse 14, which some English Bibles, including the NIV, omit as inauthentic, but the expression also appears in Mark 12:40 and Luke 20:47.
34. Philippians 4:7.
35. Jeremiah 29:7.
36. John 17:21.
37. Ephesians 2:14–18.
38. Galatians 3:28.
39. Although many English versions translate Romans 12:1 as "living sacrifices," the Greek text is actually singular, or "living sacrifice."
40. Romans 15:6.
41. Helpful commentary on the corporate aspects of Romans 12 is found in Marva Dawn, *Truly the Community* (Grand Rapids: Eerdmans, 1992).
42. Ephesians 4:16.
43. 1 Corintians 12:12–31. I am indebted to John Lillis, whose course "Spiritual Formation" first alerted me to the corporate emphasis of New Testament piety. This course is available from the Institute of Theological Studies, a division of Outreach, Inc., in Grand Rapids, Michigan.

Chapter 7. To Responsibly Cultivate the Earth

1. Luke 38–42.
2. Matthew 6:19.
3. The most helpful books on the value of culture and its role in the Christian life are Cornelius Plantinga Jr., *Engaging God's World* (Grand Rapids: Eerdmans, 2002); Albert M. Wolters, *Creation Regained* (Grand Rapids: Eerdmans, 1985); Paul Marshall, *Heaven Is Not My Home* (Nashville: Word, 1998); Brian J. Walsh and J. Richard Middleton, *The Transforming*

Vision (Downers Grove, IL: InterVarsity, 1984); Michael S. Horton, *Where in the World Is the Church?* (Chicago: Moody, 1995); and David Bruce Hegeman, *Plowing in Hope* (Moscow, ID: Canon Press, 1999).

4. Martin Luther, "Lectures on Genesis," in *Luther's Works*, ed. Jaroslav Pelikan (St. Louis: Concordia, 1970), 6:10.

5. Indeed, since ʿābad is the verb form of the Hebrew term for slave, Genesis 2:15 may be translated as a command to "serve" the garden. This important point should protect the church from those errant theologies that take God's command "to have dominion" (Genesis 1:26, 28 KJV) as an excuse to dominate and even abuse his creation.

6. Roland H. Bainton, *Here I Stand: A Life of Martin Luther* (New York: Abingdon-Cokesbury Press, 1950), 288.

7. To read more about the "Reformation of the natural," see Bavinck, "The Catholicity of Christianity and the Church," *Calvin Theological Journal* 27 (November 1992): 220–51, and "Common Grace," *Calvin Theological Journal* 24 (April 1989): 35–65.

8. Os Guinness, *The Call* (Nashville: Word, 1998), 29. For excellent summaries of the Reformers' views on vocation, consult Gustaf Wingren, *The Christian's Calling: Luther on Vocation*, trans. Carl C. Rasmussen (London: Oliver and Boyd, 1957), and Ronald S. Wallace, *Calvin's Doctrine of the Christian Life* (Tyler, TX: Geneva Divinity School Press, 1982).

9. Luther's Large Catechism can be read in many places, but one particularly authoritative source is *The Book of Concord: The Confessions of the Evangelical Lutheran Church*, trans. and ed. Theodore G. Tappert (Philadelphia: Fortress Press, 1959), 368.

10. For examples of Luther's statements that our vocations are the mask of God, see Wingren, *The Christian's Calling*, 137–40. In his "Exposition of Psalm 147," Luther states, "What else is all our work to God—whether in the fields, in the garden, in the city, in the house, in war, or in government—but just such a child's performance, by which He wants to give His gifts in the fields, at home, and everywhere else? These are the masks of God, behind which He wants to remain concealed and do all things" (*Luther's Works* 14:114). In his "Lectures on Galatians (2:6)," Luther adds, "Thus the magistrate, the emperor, the king, the prince, the consul, the teacher, the preacher, the pupil, the father, the mother, the children, the master, the servant—all these are social positions or external masks" (*Luther's Works* 26:95).

11. John Calvin, *Institutes of the Christian Religion*, I.17.4 (my translation of the following: *providentiam Dei, non semper nudam occurrere, sed prout adhibitis mediis eam Deus quodammodo vestit*).

12. *What Luther Says*, comp. Ewald M. Plass (St. Louis: Concordia, 1959), II:560.
13. Plantinga, *Engaging God's World*, 115–17.
14. I am indebted to Michael S. Horton, "How to Discover Your Calling," *Modern Reformation* 8 (May/June 1999): 8–13, for his helpful distinction between vocation and avocation.

Chapter 8. To Savor the Works of Our Hands

1. The story about Ridgewood, New Jersey, was filed by the Associated Press on Monday and Wednesday, March 25 and 27, 2002.
2. Genesis 2:1–3.
3. Helpful works on Sabbath-keeping include D. A. Carson, ed., *From Sabbath to Lord's Day* (Grand Rapids: Zondervan, 1982); Marva Dawn, *Keeping the Sabbath Wholly* (Grand Rapids: Eerdmans, 1989); and Abraham Heschel, *The Sabbath: Its Meaning for Modern Man* (New York: Farrar, Straus, & Giroux, 1951).
4. The Hebrew term is *nāpash*, the verb form of the Hebrew word for "breath."
5. Isaiah 40:28.
6. Genesis 1:22, 28.
7. Exodus 20:8–11.
8. The same word is used in Genesis 2:15 for the cultural mandate (see chapter 7), where Adam was to ʿābad, or serve the garden.
9. Deuteronomy 5:12–15.
10. Genesis 2:15; Exodus 20:9.
11. Exodus 31:12–17.
12. Isaiah 58:13–14. The words "delight" and "joy" come from the same Hebrew term, ʿōneg.
13. Ezekiel 20:12–24.
14. Jeremiah 17:19–27; see Leviticus 26:34–35 and 2 Chronicles 36:21, where Judah's survival also depends on observing the Sabbath rest for its land.
15. Nehemiah 13:15–22.
16. Matthew 5:21–30.
17. Romans 14:5–6.
18. Colossians 2:16–17.
19. Hebrews 4:1–11.
20. Insightful discussions of Hebrews 4 can be found in the following commentaries: William L. Lane, *Hebrews 1–8* (Dallas: Word, 1991), 91–105; and David A. DeSilva, *Perseverance in Gratitude* (Grand Rapids: Eerdmans, 2000), 151–69.
21. John Calvin, *Institutes of the Christian Religion*, II.8.28–34.

22. John Calvin, *The Sermons of M. John Calvin Upon the Fifth Booke of Moses Called Deuteronomie,* trans. Arthur Golding (London: 1583; reprint, Carlisle, PA: Banner of Truth Trust, 1987), 204. This particular sermon expounds Deuteronomy 5:12–14, the thirty-fourth in Calvin's sermon series on Deuteronomy.

Chapter 9. The Original Sin

1. James Burtchaell, *The Giving and Taking of Life: Essays Ethical* (Notre Dame, IN: Notre Dame University Press, 1989), 219.
2. Adam and Eve did not wear clothes, so unless they were members of the Polar Bear Club, I stand by my admittedly wishful, and ultimate, point.
3. Genesis 2:9.
4. Richard A. Muller, *Dictionary of Latin and Greek Theological Terms* (Grand Rapids: Baker, 1985), 183.
5. Genesis 3:22.
6. Genesis 3:1.
7. Genesis 3:2–3.
8. Leviticus 11:8; compare Deuteronomy 14:8.
9. I don't mean to imply that Eve was Jewish, but only that her initial response would have been readily understood by the original Jewish readers of Gensis. For more on the Jewish context of Genesis 3, see Wayne Townsend, "Eve's Answer to the Serpent," *Calvin Theological Journal* 33 (November 1998): 399–420. Townsend observes that the rules governing unclean things are the likely reason that God waited to confront Adam and Eve until the "cool of the day" (Genesis 3:8). According to Leviticus 11:25ff., an unclean person remained that way until evening. Thus any Jew would understand why the holy God must wait until the cool of the evening to make contact with Adam and Eve, for they had made themselves ceremonially unclean when they touched and ate from the unclean tree.
10. Genesis 3:4–5. My translation of Genesis 3:4 differs slightly from the NIV. Whereas the NIV reads, "You will not surely die," which implies that it is still an open question, I believe that the Hebrew text *(lō' môt tᵉmûtûn)* is better translated, "You will surely not die," a phrase that better captures the serpent's emphatic denial of God's word.
11. Genesis 3:22.
12. The word "autonomy" comes from two Greek terms: *nomos,* which means "law," and *auto,* which means "self." Autonomous people are those who sinfully reject God's perspective on the truth and become a law unto themselves, doing what they want when they want just because they want.
13. Genesis 3:6.

Chapter 10. The Fallout from the Fall

1. Genesis 3:14.
2. Revelation 21:5.
3. Genesis 4:9.
4. Genesis 4:10, my paraphrase.
5. Genesis 4:25.
6. Genesis 4:23–24.
7. Genesis 34:7; 1 Samuel 20:34; 2 Samuel 19:1–4.
8. Genesis 6:7.
9. Genesis 1:30; 2:7.
10. Genesis 6:17.
11. Genesis 6:11–13.
12. Romans 8:20–22.
13. Genesis 6:9.
14. Used with permission from Douglas A. Felch, associate professor of theology at Reformed Bible College in Grand Rapids, Michigan, who created this chart for his class entitled "Christian Doctrine."
15. Genesis 3:21.
16. Leviticus 16.
17. 1 John 2:2.
18. Genesis 3:19.
19. Albert M. Wolters, *Creation Regained* (Grand Rapids: Eerdmans, 1985), 42.

Chapter 11. The Cosmic Reach of the Gospel

1. Victor Hugo, *Les Misérables*, Wordsworth Classics (Great Britain: Mackays of Chatham, 1994), 1:73.
2. Acts 3:21.
3. Colossians 1:19–20; Ephesians 1:9–10.
4. Abraham Kuyper, "Souvereiniteit in Eigen Kring," in *Abraham Kuyper: A Centennial Reader,* trans. and ed. James D. Bratt (Grand Rapids: Eerdmans, 1998), 488 (emphasis Kuyper's).
5. Genesis 1:22, 28.
6. Genesis 3:14, 17; 4:11; 9:25; 6:7.
7. Genesis 18:18; 22:18; 26:4; 28:14.
8. Exodus 19:4–6.
9. Admonitions concerning these practices are found in Leviticus 11, 18, and 13–14 respectively.
10. Exodus 20:3.
11. Leviticus 19:35–36.
12. Deuteronomy 23:19.

13. Leviticus 19:9–10.
14. Leviticus 25:8–17.
15. Deuteronomy 15:7–11.
16. Exodus 20:10; Leviticus 25:1–7.
17. Isaiah 44:9–20; Amos 2:7; 8:4–6; 2 Chronicles 36:21.
18. Deuteronomy 28.
19. Isaiah 2:3, Micah 4:2; see Zechariah 8:20–23.
20. Isaiah 19:23–25.
21. Isaiah 11:1.
22. Isaiah 11:3, 4, 6.
23. Isaiah 11:9.
24. Luke 4:18–19, quoting Isaiah 61:1–2.
25. Luke 4:20–21.
26. Luke 7:22.
27. Matthew 8:17, quoting Isaiah 53:4.
28. Matthew 4:17; Mark 1:15.
29. Matthew 7:13–14; Luke 14:33.
30. The religions that come closest to teaching grace are Amida Buddhism and the Ramanuja and Madhva forms of Hinduism. The former grants escape into the "pure land" to anyone who trusts in the Buddha, while the latter sometimes suggests that believers are saved by God just as kittens are passively carried in the mouth of their mother. However, since neither of these religions teaches our need for atonement—a substitute to die in our place—they seem to lack a full appreciation for the severity of sin. This shallow understanding of sin, or our need for deliverance, must also produce a corresponding superficial appreciation for the grace that saves us. Thus, although these religions may speak of grace, it is not the robust Christian view of the God who endured our punishment for sin.

    Furthermore, since salvation in both Buddhism and Hinduism amounts to the termination of individual existence, it turns out that its offer of grace is not so free after all. Whereas Jesus Christ graciously restores our humanity, these religions promise to extinguish our personal existence, dissolving our individuality into the oneness of the universe. In sum, their free offer of personal extinction sounds more like death than anything that might count as grace.
31. Used with permission from Douglas A. Felch, associate professor of theology at Reformed Bible College in Grand Rapids, Michigan, who created this chart for his class entitled "Christian Doctrine."
32. Genesis 2:15.
33. Al Wolters insightfully compares the cultural development of sinful humans to the maturation of an ill child. He observes that much like a sick

youth may still grow into adulthood, so human culture continues to mature despite the presence of sin (Albert M. Wolters, *Creation Regained* [Grand Rapids: Eerdmans, 1985], 39).

34. Genesis 4:20–22.

35. Wolters, *Creation Regained*, 49, 72–95, and Brian J. Walsh and J. Richard Middleton, *The Transforming Vision* (Downers Grove, IL: InterVarsity Press, 1984), 88–90.

36. Some readers may be dismayed to learn that the story of Scripture begins in a garden and ends in a city, for nowadays most people prefer the clean air of the country to the asphalt, noise, and crime of urban life. However, according to Revelation 21–22, the beauty of the New Jerusalem, with its streets of gold and gates of pearl, far surpasses the blight of our modern cities. In fact, considering that the center of this final city will feature both the river of life and the tree of life, it appears that our future home also boasts the very best that nature can offer (Revelation 22:1–2). Regardless, the theological point behind this progression from garden to city is to remind us that God will preserve the works of our hands. The difference between a garden and city is people, for they are the ones who develop the raw materials of nature into an organized community. Thus, the New Jerusalem reassures us that, rather than obliterate our efforts, God will incorporate our cultural accomplishments into his final redemption.

37. Culture is essentially the combination of humanity and creation, for it is the product of our participation with nature. A stream by itself is nature. Add people, and it becomes a canal, which is now a part of culture. A piece of rock is nature, but in the hands of people it may become a diamond, which now belongs to culture. Gorillas in the wild belong to nature, but the photographers who snap their pictures are creating culture. Indeed, it seems impossible for people to contact nature "in the raw," for our very presence inevitably inserts a human element into the scene, the consequence of which will always be a form of culture.

38. For a helpful analysis of this passage, see Al Wolters, "Worldview and Textual Criticism in 2 Peter 3:10," *Westminster Theological Journal* 49 (1987): 405–13. Wolters observes that the same Greek root for "to be found" in 2 Peter 3:10 appears in 1 Peter 1:7 in connection with a refining fire: ". . . that your faith—of greater worth than gold, which perishes even though refined by fire—may be proved genuine and may result [or be found] in praise, glory and honor when Jesus Christ is revealed."

39. Matthew 22:30.

40. Matthew 22:2–14; Ephesians 5:21–32; Revelation 19:7.

41. C. S. Lewis, *Miracles* (1947; San Francisco: HarperSanFrancisco, 2000), 260–61.

42. Isaiah 65:25.
43. John 20:27.
44. Isaiah 65:17; 2 Peter 3:13; Revelation 21:1.
45. John 14:15–27; 16:5–16; Acts 2.
46. Isaiah 65:17, 21. Many Christians believe that Isaiah's vision of building houses and planting vineyards describes the millennium, a future period of one thousand years that immediately precedes the final judgment and the new heaven and new earth. Without delving into the merits of this view, it is worth noting that there is nothing in this position that precludes houses and vineyards from also reappearing on the new earth. Indeed, the new earth is precisely what Isaiah seems to have in mind. Besides, inasmuch as the new earth is superior to any future millennium state, we may safely surmise that most goods (except marriage) present in the millennium's penultimate silver age will also be enjoyed during the final, golden era of the new earth.
47. Isaiah 60:5, 6, 9.
48. Isaiah 60:11; see Revelation 21:24–26.
49. Genesis 1:26–28; 2:15.

Chapter 12. But What About . . . ?

1. The best biographies of Wilberforce's life include John Pollock, *William Wilberforce* (New York: St. Martin's Press, 1978), and Garth Lean, *God's Politician* (Colorado Springs: Helmers & Howard, 1987).
2. For example, Rick Warren's popular book *The Purpose Driven Life* (Grand Rapids: Zondervan, 2002), 306, reduces the meaning of life to worship, ministry, evangelism, fellowship, and discipleship. In an otherwise fine book that has inspired many, it is unfortunate that Warren neglects to mention our responsibility for creation as one of the five central purposes of life. He does mention in passing that caring for creation is "a part of our purpose" (p. 44), but in the next chapter he blunts this insight by stating that this world is temporary anyhow so we should not be overly concerned with it (pp. 47–52). My point is not to disparage Warren's helpful book, but to demonstrate how often evangelical piety overlooks our link to this world.
3. Besides these theological questions, I also want to briefly address the biblical passages that some may offer against my argument.

    a. Matthew 6:19–21 instructs us to lay up our treasure in heaven rather than on earth. Doesn't this mean that only our "spiritual" pursuits last forever? Not exactly. We lay up treasure in heaven whenever we obey God. While this certainly involves worship, evangelism, and other ministry activity, it also includes such obedient acts as changing diapers, fixing dinner, and walking the dog. Whenever we faithfully discharge our vocations, not merely for our own sake but primarily from obedience to the God who has called us, we are storing up treasure in heaven.

b. John 14:1–3 reports that Jesus has gone to prepare a place for us in heaven, a city that Hebrews 11:9–16 says Abraham continually longed to inhabit during his sojourn on earth. Don't these passages imply that we will eventually leave this planet forever? No. Fast forward to Revelation 21:1–4, where we learn that the New Jerusalem—the heaven where Jesus is preparing a place and the city for which Abraham yearned—ultimately will descend to our planet, apparently becoming the capital of a newly restored earth.

c. Several passages suggest that our present earth will eventually disappear. Typical is Isaiah 51:6, which asserts that "the heavens will vanish like smoke" and "the earth will wear out like a garment" (see Psalm 102:26–27; Hebrews 1:10–12; 2 Peter 3:10; and Matthew 24:35). Doesn't this imply that the earth as we know it will end? Not exactly. We know that our final destination is the new earth, a planet that is both similar (earth) and different (new) from the home we currently enjoy. The path God takes to this final end is up to him. He may choose merely to cleanse the earth, or he may decide to annihilate it and start over. While I favor the former (for reasons given in this book), I find comfort in knowing that ultimately our end is the same. Either way, whether through renovation or wholesale recreation, the new earth will be ontologically similar and ethically superior to our present home.

d. Second Corinthians 4:18 encourages us to "fix our eyes not on what is seen, but on what is unseen. For what is seen is temporary, but what is unseen is eternal." Doesn't this imply that we should avoid the fleeting affairs of this life and focus solely on the spiritual realities that last forever? No. In context, Paul is bemoaning his persecution, which was so intense that at one point he even wished he were dead (2 Corinthians 1:3–11; 4:7–12). He found solace in knowing that although his suffering was taking its toll on his outer man, it nevertheless was forging a depth of character he never could have reached without it. So he chose to focus on his internal progress rather than on the "light and momentary troubles" that had caused his growth (2 Corinthians 4:16–18). There is nothing in this passage about the dangers of becoming distracted by the good things of this world. Rather, it is a reminder not to focus on the fruits of the fall—with its intense persecution and deterioration of the physical life—but instead to contemplate the prospects of redemption, which ultimately will reward our renewed character by supplying us with new, resurrected bodies to match our flourishing souls.

e. But doesn't the ensuing passage (2 Corinthians 5:1–10) indicate that Paul desires to leave this earth behind and live forever in heaven? No. There are two things Paul longs for in this passage: to be with the Lord and to remain in his body. Paul is looking forward to seeing Christ (5:6–8; the only reason Paul wants to go to heaven is that Jesus is there) but dislikes the fact that, unless the Lord returns and spares him from death, he will be a disembodied soul when this meeting finally occurs. (Unlike the incipient Gnostics prevalent in Corinth, who hoped to slough off their physical prisons and return as disembodied souls to their heavenly home, Paul doesn't seem too pleased with the bodiless, intermediate state he will experience between death and the resurrection.) So he laments the perishable nature of his present body and longs to receive his immortal, heavenly body, which will clothe his "naked" soul and make him fully human—body and soul—once more (5:1–4).

But why does Paul call his resurrection body a "heavenly dwelling" and "an eternal house in heaven" (5:1–2)? Regarding "heavenly dwelling," Paul uses the same idea in 1 Corinthians 15:45–49 to indicate the *source* of our resurrection body. There he states that just as our mortal bodies came from Adam, the first earthling, so our resurrection bodies are given by the Second Adam, Jesus Christ, who comes from heaven. Therefore Paul uses "heavenly dwelling," not to designate its everlasting location, but to signal its source in the perfect human, Jesus Christ.

Regarding "an eternal house in heaven," Paul seems to use this phrase to indicate the invisible quality of the Christian hope. Unlike his opponents in Corinth who gloried in their visible demonstrations of power (5:12; 10:1–12; 11:5–6, 12, 18–23; 12:11), Paul emphasizes the need for faith to grasp God's work in the world (5:7). So rather than assume that Paul's persecutions and physical demise mean that he is on the losing side, the Corinthians should recognize that God is reserving a heavenly dwelling for Paul, no less real because it lay beyond their present perception. Finally, as we saw above in Revelation 21:1–4, Paul's "eternal house in heaven" does not remain forever "up there," but ultimately descends with Christ to the new earth.

4. As Luther warned his congregation, we must never condemn anything simply because it is misused. Just as the idolatrous worship of the heavens does not lead us to "pull the sun and stars from the skies," and the abuse of wine and women does not prompt us to "kill all the women and pour out all the wine," so the perversion of any part of creation should rouse us to protect rather than vilify it. If we insist on destroying every created thing that might possibly tempt us to sin, Luther said, we must ultimately kill ourselves, for how often have our sinful desires been fanned by the evil

in our own perverse hearts? See Martin Luther, "Fourth Sermon at Wittenberg," in *Luther's Works* 51:85.

5. Psalm 62:10.

6. Luke 4:18–19; 7:22.

7. Genesis 1:26–28; 2:15.

8. C. S. Lewis, "Learning in War-Time," in *The Weight of Glory and Other Addresses* (San Francisco: HarperSanFrancisco, 1980), 52.

9. C. S. Lewis, *God in the Dock*, ed. Walter Hooper (Grand Rapids: Eerdmans, 1970; reprint 1990), 93. A stimulating discussion of this point occurs in Paul Marshall, *Heaven Is Not My Home* (Nashville: Word, 1998), 210–20. Marshall observes that besides contributing to the cause of evangelism, our redemption of culture has value in its own right. Indeed, it is only this intrinsic value that empowers it to aid evangelism, for Christians who engage culture not for its own sake but merely for its evangelistic potential, signal loudly to their targeted unbelievers that they care little about culture or even about them. If we wish our cultural efforts to be taken seriously, we must respect our tasks enough to pour our entire selves into them, whether or not there is an unbeliever present to observe our effort.

10. See Charles Colson and Nancy Pearcey, *How Now Shall We Live?* (Wheaton, IL: Tyndale, 1999) for insightful applications of the Christian worldview to real life.

11. 1 Thessalonians 4:11–12.

12. Titus 3:14.

13. Paul's ministry seems to possess a division of labor. On the one hand, he takes responsibility for preaching the gospel, pointedly asking the churches to pray for his evangelistic efforts, that he might boldly and clearly proclaim the good news of salvation (Ephesians 6:19–20; Colossians 4:3–4). On the other hand, Paul never prays for or even commands ordinary laypeople to share their faith. He obviously would not oppose such endeavors, but he is apparently more concerned that new believers practice rather than preach the gospel. He repeatedly instructs them to love each other (Romans 12:10; 13:8–10; Galatians 5:13; Colossians 3:14) and live worthy of the gospel (Ephesians 4:1; Philippians 1:27; Colossians 1:10), knowing that when they do so, they inadvertently provide a compelling advertisement for the power of Christ. In business terms, Paul is the marketer and the laypeople are the product. So long as they are sacrificially loving one another and maintaining a pure life worthy of Christ, Paul figures he will have little trouble attracting new converts to the church.

14. Titus 2:9–10.

Expanding Your Worldview

Chapter 1: What You See Is What You Get

1. What lasts forever? Consider things that, like our bodies, may temporarily go out of existence but will reappear on the new earth. Read Isaiah 60; 65:17–25; 1 Corinthians 15; 2 Peter 3:3–13; Revelation 21 and 22.

2. Attempt the exercise on pages 26, following your beliefs backward until you can state your ultimate beliefs.

3. Are you pleased with these ultimate beliefs? Do they seem sturdy enough to bear your weight, or do they buckle your knees with the terrifying feeling that your life is built on a house of cards? If you were free to choose any set of ultimate beliefs, which ones would you prefer to believe?

4. Describe an experience that has challenged your worldview. How deeply did it penetrate: halfway in, or all the way to your ultimate beliefs? Explain how your worldview changed to accommodate this new experience. Were only minor adjustments necessary, or a major overhaul?

5. Pretend, if you can, that some great evil has befallen you or someone you love. With a specific evil in mind, imagine how this terrible event would challenge the core of your worldview. What sort of questions would it raise, and how might you go about answering them? In what way would this experience become a trial of faith?

6. What should we think when a member of another religion claims that God has miraculously answered her prayer? Would you conclude that she is worshiping the true God, or is there another plausible explanation?

7. What are the implications of worldview formation for Christian evangelism? Does it mean inviting unbelievers to add Jesus to their worldview, or is more required? In what ways might evangelism be considered an inherently violent activity?

Chapter 2: Where Lies the Great Divide?

1. Do you accept Anselm's argument for the existence of God? If so, how useful would it be when talking with unbelievers? Should we only use this argument to confirm our faith, or is there something valuable in it that we might also share with others?

2. Why do you think God chose to create the world? Did he create to fill a need?

3. Besides the Trinity and the incarnation, what other difficult questions might best be solved by remembering the ontological distinction between God and creation? How does this distinction inform the debate over divine sovereignty and human freedom?

4. If eternity means to live outside of time with no beginning and no end, then humans will never be eternal, because we had a beginning and will always live within the parameters of time. Is it appropriate, then, to say that Christians possess eternal life, and if not, what term should we use? Can you suggest other examples where we may incorrectly assign divine attributes to ourselves? Do any of these cause serious theological misunderstandings?

5. Which do you think are higher beings, humans or angels? Are angels also made in the image of God?

Chapter 3: Where Are We?

1. Remembering the important distinction between ontological and ethical categories, evaluate the following (fictional) devotional.

   During the summer of 1982 Americans fell in love with Steven Spielberg's huggable alien, "E.T.," who, mistakenly left behind by his departing spaceship, was befriended by a young boy named Elliott. Although Elliott and E.T. became fast friends, they both recognized that E.T. belonged on his home planet. So in a daring escape from the authorities, Elliott pedaled E.T. across the sky to a secret rendezvous with his waiting spaceship, where the bosom buddies said their tearful good-byes.

   According to 1 Peter 1:1 and 2:11, Christians have much in common with the misplaced E.T. Like him, we may become so enamored with our friends and the pleasures of this world that we forget that we are just "aliens and strangers" on this planet. We also have come from heaven and, after our temporary stay on this temporary planet, will return to our true home in the skies. May God help us to remember that this earth is but a rest stop on the way to our true home and that, like E.T., the more we become attached to the transient things of this earth, the harder it will be when we finally say good-bye.

   Application: To gauge whether you are living as God's alien on planet earth, make a list of any three possessions, hobbies, or activities that you enjoy. Would their loss throw you into turmoil, or would you continue to love God as much as ever?

   Thought for the day: This world isn't real. Only heaven lasts forever. Live for what matters most.

2. Consider the vast diversity of Christian merchandise available to the evangelical public. Cite specific items that fill a useful niche and others that seem to devalue both creation and the gospel. How can you tell which items belong in each category?

3. Think of some hymns or choruses that celebrate creation. Can you think of others that, perhaps in the interest of elevating God, disparage creation as relatively inferior? Is there a way to reconcile these motifs?

4. Reflect on what the goodness of creation means in your life. How does this truth impact different areas of your life, such as worship, work, rest, play, family, time, and money? Write down one way that you will live differently today in light of this truth.

5. Contemplate the difficult quest for balance in the Christian life. On the one hand, we must not focus so much on spiritual things that we adopt a Gnostic, disdainful attitude toward the things of this world. On the other hand, might not all this concern for the earth distract us from more important, "eternal" matters? What principles or safeguards may we implement to ensure that creation will lead us toward rather than away from its Creator?

Chapter 4: Who Are We?

1. What does our culture say it means to be human? Consider our movies, music, magazines, and advertisements. What messages are they sending? How much and for what reason does our culture value its people? Contrast our culture's estimation of people with the biblical view. How would our lives change if we fully embraced our culture's view? The biblical view?

2. Discuss the idea that the more we focus on ourselves, the less meaning we find, while the more value we place on God, the more value we discover for ourselves. If you agree, how might this affect your life?

3. Reflect on our physical and theological connectedness to this creation. How does this influence your understanding of the meaning of life? How might it change the way we view our bodies, other creatures, the environment, or our jobs? Write down one or two specific applications for your life.

4. Think through at least one of the perplexing problems of medical ethics presented in this chapter. For instance, consider genetic engineering. Is it ever permissible to change one of our genes? In the case of dangerous genetic problems, such as the gene for breast cancer, is it ever permissible not to? What criteria determine when we should and shouldn't alter our genetic code?

5. How do you define what it means to be created in the image of God? What element(s) do we always retain by virtue of being human and what element(s) do we forfeit to sin and recover in Christ? How does this chapter's ontological-ethical distinction help your thinking?

Chapter 5: To Love God

1. Which experiences in today's world serve as signals of transcendence for you? Are there some that regularly seem to work? Are there others you may have been overlooking? What might be an appropriate response the next time you encounter a pointer to God?

2. Evaluate the common evangelical claim that only those things that last forever (the Word of God and our souls) have lasting value. What criteria determine ultimate value, and what role, if any, does longevity play?

3. This chapter examines two opposite errors concerning our love for God. We must avoid modernity's tendency to eliminate God altogether while steering clear of the idea prevalent among some Christians that love for God calls us to forsake the world. Is one error worse than the other? How might Christians avoid these extremes and place the correct value on both God and the world?

4. Consider how the gospel metaphors of pearl and leaven inform various facets of daily life. That is, how do we demonstrate the pearl and leaven qualities in our families, churches, jobs, and friendships? How might this dual nature of the gospel shape our response to a strong-willed child, an unfair employer, or a two-faced friend?

5. Many worship songs and hymns emphasize the pearl aspect of the gospel, such as "Turn your eyes upon Jesus, / look full in his wonderful face, / and the things of earth will grow strangely dim." What are some songs that emphasize the leaven aspect of the gospel, making "the things of earth grow strangely significant"?

Chapter 6: To Serve Others

1. Do you think this chapter gives a fair assessment of community in the modern world? Are you content with the quality of your friendships? Why or why not? What positive steps have you taken or can you take to foster community at church, on the job, or in your neighborhood?

2. Does modern communication technology (such as television, computers, and the Internet) tend to help or hinder genuine community? How can we use modern technology to enhance our quest for community?

3. Evaluate this statement: It is impossible to live as a Christian in a world without neighbors. Discuss how the structures of the modern world affect our Christian witness. How might we change the way we build neighborhoods, conduct our jobs, and do church in order to enlarge our witness?

4. Explore the link between peace and prosperity that we see in the biblical hope for shalom. Why and how does this link exist? Can you think of exceptions to this rule? For instance, does peace guarantee prosperity? Conversely, do some people prosper apart from peace?

5. As God's primary model for shalom, does the church also bear any responsibility to promote shalom outside its borders? Should the church be involved with social issues, such as racism, sexism, or the right to life of the unborn? If so, what guidelines might help the church combine its social activism with its commitment to proclaim the gospel?

Chapter 7: To Responsibly Cultivate the Earth

1. Reflect on our responsibility to select wholesome career paths that honor God and contribute to society. What particular jobs might these criteria eliminate? Likewise, in light of the cultural mandate, what professions might we consider to be more valuable than we had previously thought?

2. If it's true that all believers are "full-time Christians," how might churches recognize and affirm their various vocations? Should churches "ordain" those called by God into secular vocations the way they ordain those called into pastoral ministry? Why or why not?

3. Is there a sense in which those in vocational Christian ministry possess a higher calling? If so, why? How should we regard pastors, missionaries, and others in vocational Christian ministry?

4. Discuss whether this chapter's talk about culture and creation risks leading us into secularism. Might our concern for this present world lead us to forget God? Why go to church if we already serve God by going to work?

5. List the many vocations that God has entrusted to you. Which ones are you doing well? Select one that needs attention, and write down three ways you will develop it in the coming week.

Chapter 8: To Savor the Works of Our Hands

1. Like most areas pertaining to Christian liberty, it is difficult to discuss the Sabbath rest without falling into the error of legalism on one side or licentiousness/lawlessness on the other. How well does this chapter navigate between these two extremes? Is there a better way to say it?

2. Describe your personal approach to the Sabbath-day rest. If you believe you have a balanced approach, what suggestions can you offer others toward that end?

3. What activities, if any, should all Christians avoid on their day of Sabbath rest? Are some activities appropriate for some Christians and not for others? How might one's occupation affect the appropriateness of Sabbath activity?

4. Describe how you understand the relationship between labor (previous chapter) and rest (this chapter). Do we work in order to rest and enjoy the fruit of our labor, or do we rest in order to replenish our energies so we can work some more? Are work and rest equally important, or does one take precedence over the other?

5. If rest is the goal of life, embedded in both creation (Genesis 2) and redemption (Hebrews 4), what practical implications may we draw for our lives? How might this truth alter how we work, play, and relate to others? Cite specific ways that our culture both encourages and discourages our enjoyment of rest.

Chapter 9: The Original Sin

1. Examine your life for the telltale signs of autonomy. Where does this self-centered pattern regularly appear, and what do you plan to do about it?

2. Explore how the story of the fall adds a complex twist to the Christian life. How might we rightly celebrate the goodness of creation (chapters 3–8) without misusing it or transforming God's good gifts into idols (this chapter)? How can we tell when our enjoyment of creation has become idolatry?

3. Does God ever lead his children to perform undesirable roles or tasks? If so, how does this fit with his concern for our flourishing?

4. If God is all-good and all-powerful, how can we explain the existence of evil?

Chapter 10: The Fallout from the Fall

1. Examine your own life and culture for examples where you celebrate the fall, choosing to be entertained by sin rather than resisting it. How can we account for this fatal attraction to the fall? Given the consequences of sin, why do we eat forbidden fruit?

2. What experiences of life have awakened you to the destructive nature of the fall? To what extent have these experiences empowered you to resist temptation?

3. As this chapter shows, it is crucial to distinguish between creation and fall when we tell the story of the Christian worldview. What theological questions might this pose to the theory of evolution?

4. What should we make of what theologians call "natural evil"—the destruction caused by such natural disturbances as tornadoes, floods, and earthquakes? Do these natural events properly belong to creation or the fall?

5. Is biological death inherent in creation, or is it a consequence of the fall? Do you think that before the fall Adam would have eaten carrots and potatoes and cut fresh flowers for Eve? Might lions attack and eat gazelles before the fall? How might our reading of nature (the fossil record, the razor sharp teeth of carnivores) and Scripture (Genesis 1:30; Isaiah 65:25) help us answer this question?

6. Is death always our enemy? In the case of a terminally ill patient suffering from intense pain, how might we account for the desirability of death without detracting from its dreadfulness?

Chapter 11: The Cosmic Reach of the Gospel

1. What does Noah's Ark tell us about God's concern for all of creation? Why did God rescue more animals than people from the flood? Consider the closing lines of the book of Jonah: What effect did the presence of many cattle have on God's decision to spare Nineveh, and why?

2. In light of Isaiah's vision of the future in Isaiah 60:1–11, discuss whether some animals live forever.

3. If redemption restores all things, what should we make of hell, whose presence signals that not all people will be saved? Furthermore, how does the redemption "of all things" apply to specific plants and animals—this tree and that squirrel—that likely will not make it to the new earth?

4. God is not content to merely redeem creation, restoring it to its original condition. He also intends to consummate it, or bring this world to that higher state it would have eventually reached if it had not fallen into sin. Can you name any elements of this consummation— ways the end of the world is better than its beginning? Consider such passages as Revelation 21:1–4; 1 Corinthians 15:35–58; 1 Peter 1:10–12; and Jude 24.

5. Is it only Christians who participate in the redemption of culture? What should we make of nonbelievers who, though unaware of their responsibility to God, seek to correct cultural evils? In what sense are we on the same team, and how are we different?

6. Practice using the biblical model of creation, fall, and redemption by evaluating a contemporary issue through the lens of structure and direction (for example, human cloning, divorce and remarriage, the role of women in ministry). List your comments beneath the headings of Creation (what is good here?), Fall (what is wrong here?), and Redemption (what should we do about it?). Invite a friend with different views to do the same. Notice how this grid enables you and your friend to understand each other and perhaps even find some common ground for consensus.

7. It is a true saying that "you can't take it with you when you're gone." However, in light of the purging fire of 2 Peter 3:10, what things might you come back to? Make a list of items that may still be here when you return with Jesus to our restored planet.

Chapter 12: But What About . . . ?

1. How can we tell if we are materialists? For help, read Matthew 19:16–30; 1 Timothy 6:6–10; and Psalm 62.

2. Consider the competition and compatibility between the cultural and redemptive mandates. On the one hand there is competition, for that evening you spent weeding your garden is one less evening for evangelism and that $300 you just spent on new wallpaper is $300 you won't be giving to missionaries. Yet, as we saw in this chapter, a compatibility exists between these two commands, for the gospel that inspires us to perform our cultural tasks to the glory of God (Colossians 3:23) is made more attractive when we do so (Titus 2:10). How might we keep this competition and compatibility in perspective, avoiding paralysis while leading productive lives for God? (Does the role of vocations help here? See chapter 7.)

3. Which is more important: to be a good soul-winner or a good parent, to go on church visitation or mow your lawn, to support a missionary family or buy fresh vegetables for dinner? How do these questions illustrate the competition and compatibility of the cultural and redemptive mandates? In what sense are these genuine questions or false choices?

4. Evaluate Abraham Kuyper's model for implementing our cultural and redemptive responsibilities. A pioneer with regard to Christian worldview, Kuyper (1837–1920) said we must distinguish between the organized church and individual Christians, remembering that the gospel of personal salvation is the focus of the former and cultural duties are the emphasis of the latter. In other words, when Christians gather for worship we must celebrate our salvation in Christ. If we become distracted by cultural issues we may easily succumb to a social gospel, commenting on current events rather than preaching the eternal truths of God's Word. Conversely, individual Christians during the week must concentrate on doing their jobs. Those who seek to use their vocations primarily as platforms for evangelism will not only fail at their jobs but in so doing will also bring disrepute upon the gospel.

But despite their differing focus, these two spheres also complement one another. Individual Christians who do their jobs well may expect opportunities to point others to Christ and the organized church, while not focused on cultural duties, should nevertheless instruct believers on the basics of the Christian worldview.

How helpful is Kuyper's model? Can you suggest any improvements to his view?

Case Studies

Chapter 1: What You See Is What You Get

1. You are sharing your faith with a Muslim coworker, attempting to express to her the joy and satisfaction that you have found in Christ. She responds that she already knows God. In fact, she says, over the past year God has answered her prayers for her ailing mother and unemployed husband. So thanks for sharing, but she is quite happy with her current religion. What do you say now?

2. The telephone startles you awake one Saturday morning. It's Jim, a nearby friend who six months ago lost his wife and three children in a tragic car accident. He tells you that he didn't get much sleep last night, for his early grief is slowly boiling over into rage at God. "Why?!" he nearly shouts into the phone. "Why would God take my family away from me?" Now fully awake, how do you respond?

Chapter 2: Where Lies the Great Divide?

1. You run into an old friend in the supermarket, and as you catch up on your families and recent history, you are surprised to learn that he has converted to Islam. When you ask why, he answers that the Muslim view of God just makes better sense than the Christian Trinity. It's easier to believe that God is one than to believe the absurdity that he is somehow both one and three. Then he turns the tables, asking why a rational person like you would believe in such a God. How do you reply?

2. The fellow sitting next to you during your three-hour flight is reading a book entitled *God, Satan, and Other Myths*. When you inquire about the book, he cheerfully tells you that he has examined all the arguments for and against God's existence and found them all inconclusive. And since he can't know for sure, he has decided to be honest and say that he just doesn't know whether or not God exists. What would you say next?

Chapter 3: Where Are We?

1. Over the past year you have scrimped and saved an extra $2,000 to surprise your family with a Florida vacation over spring break. But the weakened economy has crippled your church's finances, and your pastor announced last month that the board is considering removing several missionary families from its payroll. A special offering will be taken this Sunday to determine whether the church can sustain their support. You realize that your $2,000 would be a significant contribution to the offering, but you've been planning this vacation for a long time. What do you decide, and why?

2. One of your closest friends has been absent from church for several weeks. When you call to check on him, he thanks you profusely for lending him the book *Heaven Is a Place on Earth*. "Chapter 3 changed my life," he said. "Once I realized that this world is good, I figured that I could worship God from the lake just as much as I could from a pew. So I've decided to get back to my bass fishing—and I do believe that I've never felt closer to God than during the stillness of the dawn these past Sunday mornings."

   "Herb," you begin, "I think you may have missed the point of that chapter. It's really about...." How do you finish this thought?

Chapter 4: Who Are We?

1. While sharing lunch with a casual friend, she confides in you that she sometimes has thoughts about ending her life. When you ask why, she says, "Well, look at me. I can't find a job in my field, I'm still living at home with my parents, and I spend most of my free time either reading or watching television—alone. I honestly doubt that very many people would miss me when I'm gone. Besides, we're all going to die eventually, so in the big

scheme of things, what does it really matter if my life ends this week or in another fifty years? What's the point anyway?" What would you say to your friend?

2.   Unable to become pregnant during their first ten years of marriage, Tom and Sheila followed their doctor's recommendation and tried in vitro fertilization. Of the seven eggs that were fertilized, two were implanted in Sheila and five were put on ice. The pregnancy was successful, and they are now the proud parents of twin sons. Everything would be fine, except that Tom and Sheila are wondering what they should do with their five frozen embryos. Now approaching forty, it seems a bit risky to attempt another pregnancy. Their Christian beliefs do not allow them to destroy the embryos, but it also seems wrong to let them continue in limbo. What should they do?

Chapter 5: To Love God

1.   You have invited a visitor in church over for Sunday dinner, and during the course of your conversation you learn that he is a new Christian. When you ask him how he came to Christ, he excitedly tells you that he first became interested in God when he realized how utterly empty this life is without him. "I used to spend a lot of time in my woodshop," he relates, "making finely crafted furniture to fill my house and give away to friends. But now that I've found the meaning of life, I'm considering selling my tools and entering the ministry. After all, no one on his deathbed ever said he wished he had spent more time sanding wood, but many have wished they had done more to save the lost." How would you respond to this testimony?

2.   Your new job pays you a 5 percent commission for every lawnmower you are able to sell. By the third month your diligence and creativity are selling more lawnmowers than the owner ever thought possible. While he is thankful for the business, he realizes that if he pays you the promised commission, you will be earning more than he earns, which doesn't seem quite right. So he revokes your commission and pays you a flat salary, less than half of what you should be earning. Remembering that the gospel is both "pearl" and "leaven" (worth more than the world, yet meant to cleanse its corruption), how do you respond? How might this response be similar to and different from your natural reaction?

Chapter 6: To Serve Others

1. A letter comes in the mail asking you to sponsor a poor child in South America. The letter informs you that for just $1 per day you can provide food, housing, health care, and education for a child who otherwise might do without. Do you send in your pledge card? Why or why not?

2. The evening news carries a story about protesters picketing your local department store because it allegedly purchases its blue jeans and sneakers from Third World sweatshops. This story is followed by an interview with a college professor who, though appreciative of the picketers' compassion, suggests that they are mistakenly protesting a valuable source of income for these Third World countries. He explains, "No one is forcing Third World people to work against their will. Instead, there is often a waiting list to get into one of these Western factories, for the pay and working conditions there far exceed what they can find elsewhere." What's a shopper to do, and on what will you base your decision?

Chapter 7: To Responsibly Cultivate the Earth

1. Your pastor is on the phone, asking if you're available to help put a new roof on the church building this Saturday. You check with your wife, who reminds you that you had promised to take your two sons camping this weekend and that they are really looking forward to it. When you mention this to your pastor, he encourages you to consider helping with the roof, for this "is the Lord's work" after all and you'll be blessed for serving him. What do you say next?

2. Emily is a twenty-two-year-old senior biology major. A recent missionary conference convicted her to forsake the easy life of her affluent culture and devote herself to "full-time Christian service." She has already been accepted into the prestigious medical program at the University of Michigan and is now wondering whether she should give this up to serve the Lord. She has come to you, a trusted family friend, for advice. What do you say to her?

Chapter 8: To Savor the Works of Our Hands

1. As a single mother of two young children, Cindy depends on the steady income she receives from her cashier's job at the local grocery store. The store has recently decided to open its doors from noon until 8:00 p.m. on Sundays. When Cindy asked to be excused from these Sunday hours, she was told that the company could not grant exceptions and that any employee unwilling to work at least one Sunday out of three would be fired. What should she do?

2. Your favorite team has made the playoffs, and the opening game is Sunday at one o'clock. Tickets are more than you can afford, but one of your suppliers at work has offered to share his company's luxury box with your entire family. You won't have time to attend morning church and still make it to the game on time, and your teenage sons—ecstatic over this unexpected opportunity—implore you to go to the game. What do you decide, and why?

Chapter 9: The Original Sin

1. Your peaceful evening is interrupted by angry shouts coming from the family room. You arrive just in time to see your two children fighting over the same action hero toy.

   "It's mine!" says one.
   "I had it first!" says the other.
   "No, I did!"
   You're too late to know who took it from whom, but you'd like to instill godly character in your little ones even as you restore peace and quiet. What are your options?

2. In his book *The Sunflower*, Jewish author Simon Wiesenthal recounts his ordeal in a Nazi concentration camp. On one occasion he was called to the bed of a dying Nazi, a young man who wanted to confess to a Jew for shooting a defenseless Jewish family. Obviously distraught over the crime he had committed, the Nazi soldier begs Wiesenthal to forgive him so that he can die in peace. Wiesenthal writes that he was unable to forgive the man and, without saying a word, turned and left the room. Should we view Wiesenthal's failure to forgive as a sinful act of autonomy? Should he have forgiven this man? Would a quick assurance of forgiveness further cheapen the lives of the deceased family? Are some sins so heinous that they can't be forgiven on the spot?

Chapter 10: The Fallout from the Fall

1. George's memorial service was a "celebration of his life." Various friends shared poignant and humorous anecdotes, the congregation sang several hymns about the glories of heaven, and the preacher reassured the grieving family that George is in a better place and that it would be cruel "to wish him back into this vale of tears." Is this a fully Christian funeral, or is something important missing here?

2. One consequence of the fall is the failure of America's black community to achieve the same level of success as its white counterpart. Affirmative action attempts to remedy this by giving black applicants bonus points when competing with white candidates for openings in public schools or jobs. Is affirmative action a sinful policy, or is it a necessary "evil" to correct a greater injustice? Explain.

Chapter 11: The Cosmic Reach of the Gospel

1. How would you comfort your ten-year-old daughter, who is saddened by the death of Princess, the family dog? What truths can you share that might encourage her? How would you answer if she asks whether or not she'll ever see her doggy again? What if she asks whether all things must die, including you and her?

2. You are telling a new friend about the gospel of Christ, and he interrupts, saying, "Let me get this straight. You're telling me that anyone who does not repent of their sin and believe in Jesus goes to hell. I know that neither of my parents wanted anything to do with Jesus or the church. So then, if I believe you and trust Jesus, I also have to believe that my parents are in hell?" How do you reply?

Chapter 12: But What About . . . ?

1. As the president of a Christian relief agency, you have been invited by the United States government to participate in the rebuilding of Afghanistan. Specifically, the Afghanis will take all the medicine, blankets, and food you can supply, as long as you do not seek to evangelize them in the process. Do you agree to these terms, or do you pretend to agree but secretly plan to break them as soon as you gain a foothold in the country, or do you decide to withhold humanitarian aid until your agency is permitted to openly share the Christian faith?

2. The text is the story of the rich young ruler, and the sermon is on the danger of wealth. The preacher explains that America is one of the most affluent nations in the history of the world and it is only getting more prosperous with each passing year. "Just look at the expanding size of our houses, cars, and waistlines—it is obvious that we are increasingly addicted to the things of this world." The preacher warns the congregation to repent of their materialism and give to those who have little, just as Jesus commanded the rich young ruler. Is this sermon on the mark, or does it miss something important? Is having wealth the same thing as being a materialist? How can we possess things without becoming possessed by them?

Scripture Index

Subject Index

ʿâbad, 124, 143, 145, 231
Anselm, 37–40
Apostles' Creed, 58–59
Aquinas, Thomas, 45
Autonomy, 120, 146–47, 157–59,
   167–70, 176, 180–82, 191, 193,
   212–13, 232
Augustine, 48, 87, 91, 102, 127

Bavinck, Herman, 45, 99–100,
   128–29

Calvin, John, 45, 72, 131, 150–52
Church community, 83, 118–21
Common grace, 114
Consummation, 249
Creation
   blessed, 142, 189
   foundation for the gospel, 53,
      57–58
   goodness of, 12, 55–68, 74,
      106–8, 162, 165–66, 170,
      177–78, 212–14, 236, 238–39
   responsibility for, 12, 81–82,
      124–26, 180–81
Cultural analysis, 198–201, 212–14,
   250

Cultural mandate
   description, 82, 108, 124–26, 141,
      197–99, 206–7, 215, 234–35
   relation to redemption, 131–33,
      197–201, 216–21, 239, 250

Death
   cause of, 171–72, 181
   effects of, 16, 181–82

Earth
   "earthly things" in Scripture,
      63–65
   new earth, 18–19, 205–7, 235–37
   our true home, 12, 15–19, 73–75,
      201–7, 237–38
   target of redemption, 111, 201–4,
      237
Evil, 159–60, 168–69, 172–73,
   248–49

Flesh, 43–45

Gnosticism
   description, 54–55, 126, 238

4 important questions Ps 24

We want to hear from you. Please send your comments about this book to us in care of zreview@zondervan.com. Thank you.

GRAND RAPIDS, MICHIGAN 49530 USA

ZONDERVAN.COM/
AUTHOR**TRACKER**